Women Who Wrestled with God
Biblical Stories of Israel's Beginnings

Irmtraud Fischer

Translated from
the second German edition
into English
by Linda M. Maloney

A Michael Glazier Book

LITURGICAL PRESS
Collegeville, Minnesota

www.litpress.org

A Michael Glazier Book published by the Liturgical Press

Cover design by David Manahan, O.S.B. Woodcut illustration: *Hagar and Ishmael* by Jakob Steinhardt (early 20th century). Arca Artium.

Originally published by Verlag W. Kohlhammer, Stuttgart, as *Gottesstreiterinnen. Biblische Erzählungen über die Anfänge Israels.* © 1995 W. Kohlhammer GmbH, Stuttgart, 2nd revised edition 2000. Translated from the 2nd revised edition.

Translations of biblical passages are adapted from the author's German translations.

1	2	3	4	5	6	7	8

Library of Congress Cataloging-in-Publication Data

Fischer, Irmtraud, 1957–
    [Gottesstreiterinnen. English]
    Women who wrestled with God : biblical stories of Israel's beginnings / Irmtraud Fischer ; translated from the second German edition into English by Linda M. Maloney.
       p. cm.
    "A Michael Glazier book."
    Includes bibliographical references and index.
    ISBN 13: 978-0-8146-5160-5 (alk. paper)
    ISBN 10: 0-8146-5160-7 (alk. paper)
    1. Women in the Bible. 2. Women—Biblical teaching. I. Title.

BS680.W7F56813 2004
221.9'22'082—dc22   2004018297

Contents

Foreword to the First German Edition

In the pages that follow I want to give a voice to the stories about the beginnings of the history of the relationship between YHWH, the God of Sarah, Hagar, and Abraham, the God of Rebecca and Isaac, the God of Leah, Rachel, Zilpah, Bilhah, and Jacob, with God's people Israel. In contrast to previous efforts along this line, I see the stories of the women as the basic framework. This approach is not intended merely to sharpen our sense of the context and connections from another point of view; it is also legitimate in literary-critical terms because many of the stories of the women are among the oldest texts in Genesis. Nevertheless, the object of my reading is the canonical final text. I will examine the literary layers within the individual texts only to the extent that their embedding in a larger context has shifted or changed their intention.

The Hebrew text is quoted whenever an understanding of structure or style demands it. In every case a translation follows immediately. The biblical texts that are quoted are given a translation that adheres as closely as possible to the Hebrew original. To keep the character of the original language vivid, I have not made accommodations to achieve a fluid modern translation. The notes primarily refer to publications by women, in order to make evident what a great number of women exegetes are already engaged in biblical scholarship. Those who are primarily interested in the topic and not in the state of scholarship, however, can easily read the book without referring to the notes.

This book is a further development of my Habilitationsschrift, *Die Erzeltern Israels*. BZAW 222 (Berlin: Walter de Gruyter, 1994) and is related to my preparations for writing the volume on Genesis 12–36 for Herder's *Theologischer Kommentar zum Alten Testament*.

I am grateful to my colleagues, Dr. Josef Schmuck (who unfortunately died before publication of the book) and Dr. Michael Unger, for assistance in reading the proofs of the book.

Graz, January 1995   Irmtraud Fischer

Foreword to the Second German Edition

Some years have passed since the first publication of this book, and during that time important works on Genesis and Ruth have appeared in both German and English. Since this book was conceived primarily as a monograph for people interested in theology, for students, and for people engaged in practical theological work, and thus is not much concerned with the history of research, I have decided, apart from some small stylistic corrections, to revise only those passages about which I myself have in the meantime formed different ideas, especially as regards a literary-critical view of their development. Hence newer literature is only incorporated where it is actually cited. For the history of scholarship let me refer readers to my commentary on Ruth (*Rut: übersetzt und ausgelegt* [Freiburg: Herder, 2001]). It will be a few years yet before my Genesis commentary on the patriarchal narratives appears in the Herder commentary series.

This time I thank my colleague Claudia Rakel, as well as Alexandra Nau, Carmen Gierschner, and Kristiane Sleegers for reading proofs of the book.

Bonn, March 2000   Irmtraud Fischer

Chapter One

The "Fathers" and the Beginnings of the People:
An Introduction to Israel's Ancestors

When the Bible speaks of the beginnings of the people of God it refers to the "Fathers." According to the common conviction, Israel traces its origins to the patriarchs, that is, to those men who stand at the beginnings of the people's story as their primeval ancestors. The God who called them and gave them the promises is the "God of Abraham, Isaac, and Jacob." The story of Israel: is it a "his-story"? The beginnings of the people of God: is it purely a "men's story"?

In OT scholarship the collection of stories in Genesis 12–36 is called the stories of the fathers, the primitive fathers, the patriarchs. The technical term "patriarchal narratives" produces an impression that these narratives are *exclusively about male protagonists*. The stories of the fathers, or the stories of the patriarchs—these are stories about men; there can be no doubt about it. Scholarly publications, through their very choice of language, induce the notion that in these stories the "God of the fathers" deals only with representatives of the male sex and is exclusively *their* God. Such a choice of language, which suggests that the stories of Israel's beginnings are exclusively about men, is not arbitrary or accidental. It is the lens through which the texts are read. It is the expression of the theologians' understanding of this part of Genesis.

But it is striking how many texts in Genesis, and even at the beginning of the book of Exodus, as well as the prehistory of the Davidic royal dynasty that is told in the book of Ruth, are about women. Biblical exegesis, whether for scholarly or pastoral purposes, has never been able to do very much with all these "women texts." This appears in a number of ways at various levels of engagement with the Bible:

1. The texts about women are assigned a special place in exegesis and theological reflection:

- Only texts about men are theologically relevant. This is obvious not only in the major works on OT theology, but also in scholarly monographs and in the lectures of a good many professors, where as a matter of course the texts about the so-called election of Abraham (Gen 12:1-9), the counting of his faith as righteousness (Genesis 15), the covenant with him (Genesis 17), Abraham's sacrifice (Genesis 22), and for the Jacob cycle the appearance of God in Beth-el (Genesis 28) and Jacob's struggle at the Jabbok (Genesis 32) are introduced as those most fruitful for theological exegesis. All these are stories in which women are at best silently included in the context of the story.
- Studies of the textual complex Genesis 12–36 for the most part show interest in the "women texts," when at all, only because they are double or even triple traditions in which (or in their oral predecessors) one can demonstrate the postulated sources of the Pentateuch. Scarcely any attention is paid to what it means that women are at the center of these stories; all too often the focus of attention is the theoretical question of the literary-historical origins of the Pentateuch.
- Still less is there any reflection on the significance of these multiple traditions for the theological evaluation of the texts. What is considered a matter of course in the double tradition of the Decalogue or the double narrative of God's covenant with Abraham (Genesis 15 and 17) is dismissed in the case of the women's texts in Genesis as due to an enthusiasm for telling tales.

2. The limitation of scholarly discussion has far-reaching consequences in *practice:*

- The selection of pericopes for scriptural reading in the *liturgy* is in large part made in such a way that the women's texts do not appear at all, or only in marginal positions, as for example in the weekday readings in the Roman Catholic lectionary. *Preaching* on these texts is accordingly even rarer.
- Aids to biblical-pastoral work and so-called *spiritual reading* primarily present the men as great figures of the faith.[1]
- Religion texts that are required reading in the *schools,* when they have to present a selection of biblical texts, as a matter of course choose stories about male believers.

---

1. We can note with pleasure the initiatives that some biblical societies have undertaken in recent time. In Germany, for example, we may cite the new series FrauenBibelArbeit (Stuttgart: Katholisches Bibelwerk, 1999ff.), edited by Bettina Eltrop and Anneliese Hecht. (In the United States such initiatives have come from publishing houses.—Tr.)

- I am always made drastically aware of how few female biblical figures appear in traditional parish Bible study courses when, in the course of giving a lecture on the Bible, I ask about women in the Bible. Knowledge of the OT, which in any case is narrow and usually loaded with prejudices, reaches a height of ignorance in the case of women. It may be, however, that this biblical-pastoral deficiency is primarily a Catholic problem.

3. Another revealing finding transcends confessional boundaries: The freely chosen *section and chapter titles offered by translators of the Bible,* placed over individual pericopes for the purpose of summarizing the story in a few words for those less well-versed in the Bible, show that the restriction of terminology is no accident, but is an expression consistent with their understanding of the texts. The titles intended as aids to reading thus become systems of guidance that channel the interest of the readers from the outset toward the male actors, and permit the biblical women to appear only as marginal figures.[2]

When the Bible speaks of the "fathers," does it really mean only the men? A saying from Second Isaiah teaches us how we ought to understand biblical language:

> Listen to me,
> you who pursue righteousness
> and seek YHWH!
> Look to the rock from which you were hewn,
> to the cave of the fountain
> from which you were dug!
> Look to Abraham, your father,
> and to Sarah, who bore you!
> For as an individual I called him,
> blessed him and made him increase. (Isa 51:2)

Abraham and Sarah, rock and cave of the spring, the fathers and mothers of Israel are the underlying foundations and sources of Israelite-Jewish identity in a time that knew salvation not from what was present, but from hearing the story. The call to attentiveness: "Listen to me!" addresses

---

2. To give only a few examples from the most commonly used German translations: The *Einheitsübersetzung* has only the patriarchs (!) present in both stories of the abandonment of the wives (Genesis 20; 26: "Abraham/Isaac in Gerar" [Genesis 20, NIV: "Abraham and Abimelech," but NRSV: "Abraham and Sarah at Gerar"; Genesis 26, both: "Isaac and Abimelech"—Tr.]). Genesis 16 is headed "The Birth of Ishmael" (so also the NRSV, whereas the NIV has "Hagar and Ishmael"—Tr.). The revised Luther translation heads the stories of Leah, Rachel, and their maidservants' giving birth with "Jacob's Children" (so also NIV), and Exod 2:1-10, "Birth of Moses and his Miraculous Rescue" (NIV: "The Birth of Moses"; NRSV: "Birth and Youth of Moses"—Tr.).

hearers who seek and do not find God. It tells them: Take Abraham and Sarah as figures who guarantee that *he* calls, that *he* blesses even today, and will still give increase! When the divine speech continues its call to look to the ancestral father and mother in grammatically masculine singular language, the call to attentiveness has to apply to the exegetes: Listen to me! The father who was called, who bears the promises of blessing and increase, is not the patriarch alone! The "fathers" are Israel's parents! It is not eisegesis and wishful thinking on the part of women exegetes today that understands the "fathers" of Israel as parents, but the biblical texts themselves: Deutero-Isaiah as an irreproachable and early exegete of the Genesis texts and the stories of the people's origins, which are able to tell us so much about women.

Exegesis must correspond to this situation within the text. I can no longer use gender as the decisive exegetical category for evaluating individual narratives or whole complexes of text, thus making heroic stories out of those with male protagonists and trivializing those with major female figures. My plea is for gender fairness in research, but one that will have to have a feminist, pro-women option as long as women do not have equal opportunity and power to participate in shaping culture, religion, the economy, and scholarship. The fact that even at the beginning of the third millennium, and even in Western societies, we are still far from that state of things is evident from women's lack of participation at the leadership levels of all the socially relevant institutions that have any power. A gender-fair initiative in research creates the preconditions for seeing the stories of women and men in Genesis as a unity and abandoning the dichotomizing tradition of interpretation based on a largely unconscious, but no less effective category of gender that is evident in traditional scholarship.[3]

The narratives of the primeval ancestors, with their focused interest in women's life-contexts, should be set alongside the first chapters of the book of Exodus and the book of Ruth. In both these text complexes women, by their active engagement, bring about a crucial turning in the people's history. Both are, in addition, linked to the narratives of the earliest ancestors through genealogical ties and narrative coloration, and therefore are to be read as a logical continuation of the earlier stories. The subversive women associated with the people's beginnings in Egypt (Exodus 1–2), as well as Ruth and Naomi, are therefore presented in this book as part of the "genealogy" of Israel. The story of these women should be

---

3. For the question of a gender-fair initiative in research see my article appearing in the documentation volume of the Colloquium Biblicum Lovaniensis for 1999: Irmtraud Fischer, "Das Geschlecht als exegetisches Kriterium. Zu einer gender-fairen Interpretation der Erzeltern-Erzählungen," in André Wenin, ed., *Studies in the Book of Genesis: Literature, Redaction and History.* BEThL 155 (Leuven: Leuven University Press, 2001).

distinguished from the leading female political figures of the early period, such as Miriam and Deborah, but also from the numerous women told of in the Deuteronomistic history. The women of the ancestral narratives, the prehistory in Exodus, and the book of Ruth are the mothers, the ancestresses of the nation, those who "built up the house of Israel" (cf. Ruth 4:11). Israel's self-understanding and the foundations of its identity are viewed, with these women, in terms of the female line—in contrast to an androcentric narrowing of the view to include only the fathers.

In a patriarchal society like the one that must be presumed to have existed in ancient Israel, such an emphasis on women's share in history, in society, and in the genealogy is unusual and worth noticing. In the texts that are addressed in the following chapters, not only is a lot said *about* women; they are also allowed to speak. In these stories women interpret their own life-situations and actions. Some of the texts are explicitly partisan on behalf of the women, especially where they are abandoned, oppressed, or disadvantaged. The question of female authorship and female participation in the literary development of women's experiences therefore presents itself unavoidably. As regards the book of Ruth, scholars have already, with good reason, proposed that the story could have been written by a woman.[4] Harold Bloom has ventured this proposition as regards the so-called "Yahwist" strand.[5] Since the Hebrew Bible itself attributes the composition of texts to women, such considerations are legitimate. I consider it appropriate, for the Torah, to presume male authors, especially since the texts were reworked and revised through many stages of redaction that clearly reflect the male point of view. Hence as regards the Torah I will speak of a male *"narrator"* when I attempt to examine the point of view of the narrative passages, but in the book of Ruth I will talk of a *"woman narrator,"* since there the plausibility of composition by a woman seems to me much greater. As Fokkelien van Dijk-Hemmes and Athalya Brenner have shown,[6] however, what is relevant is not so much the question of female or male authorship as the point of view from which the texts are written. Do they reflect an exclusively male perspective, even when they tell about women, or is the female voice authentically present in the texts, perhaps even audible through the formulations of a male author? I will attempt to show, by concrete examples, that this is largely the case in the narratives I will discuss.

4. Thus Edward F. Campbell, *Ruth*. AB 7 (Garden City, NY: Doubleday, 1975) 21–23. See the summary of the arguments in Fokkelien van Dijk-Hemmes, "Traces of Women's Texts in the Hebrew Bible," in Athalya Brenner and Fokkelien van Dijk-Hemmes, eds., *On Gendering Texts*. BIS 1 (Leiden: Brill, 1993) 17–109, at 106–107.

5. Harold Bloom, *The Book of J* (New York: Grove Weidenfeld, 1990).

6. See especially Brenner's introduction to *On Gendering Texts*, 5–10.

If we are to understand these texts, something else must be made clear: They are not intended to be biographies of individual historical persons. We are not dealing with family histories in the sense that the national history of Israel can be traced from an individual through family, clan, and tribe to the nation. The ancestral narratives were from the outset stories about the beginnings of the people Israel.[7] The narration of those beginnings in terms of colorful life stories of women, men, and their children is a method of expression and a literary technique. Since the family group was at all times in ancient Israel the basic social unit, this narrative technique could be used both to tell the history of the nation, with Israel's ancestors standing for the social entity of the whole group of people, and as a way for the addressees to identify the message that was repeatedly realized in the various phases of Israel's history.[8]

This literary technique of telling national history as family history has far-reaching consequences for our understanding of the narratives about women: The women in the ancestral narratives are not simply the mothers of nuclear families. Hence they do not, as patriarchal clichés presuppose, act solely within the narrow, private sphere of the home, where they are fully occupied with cooking and bearing children. Anyone who wants to fix the women in the history of Israel's origins within a stereotypical woman's role will have to suppose that their husbands, too, act only within the family, interact with father, mother, wives, brothers, and relatives, and never appear in a broader public, political sphere. For the men, too, the primary concern is the maintenance of the family. It is just as important for them to have children as it is for the women. It is thus not appropriate to interpret these narratives, as they apply to women, as idyllic "family stories," and to see them as they apply to men as ultra-political "national history." A gender-fair approach to scholarship shows us that the acts of both women and men in the family narratives are *political actions,* because the family *is,* in the form in which the national history is presented here, the *public, political sphere!* What both men and women experience with their God at the beginnings of the people is not to be restricted to individual, private experience of God; it is the narrated and highly-analyzed theology of Israel.

---

7. For this see the discussion in Erhard Blum, *Die Komposition der Vätergeschichte.* WMANT 57 (Neukirchen-Vluyn: Neukirchener Verlag, 1984) 501–506.

8. For this approach cf. Matthias Köckert, *Vätergott und Väterverheißungen.* FRLANT 142 (Göttingen: Vandenhoeck & Ruprecht, 1988) 304–10.

❧ Chapter Two ❧

Sarah, Hagar, and Abraham:
Scenes From a Marriage Under the Promise

1. Diagnosis: "Barren!"—Yhwh promises many descendants

Abraham and his extended family are depicted as the last branch of the Semite family tree (Gen 11:26-32).[1] The father, Terah, takes his son Abram, Abram's wife Sarai, and Abram's nephew Lot and sets out with them from Ur in Chaldea to go to the land of Canaan, but they only travel as far as Haran (11:31-32).[2]

The first thing the Bible has to say about Sarai is that her marriage is childless (Gen 11:30). The first thing Yhwh says to the couple is a promise of land and a great nation (12:1-2). What a contrast at the beginning of that great nation that Yhwh will choose for his own! A man with a barren wife who has stopped moving and settled down is called out of his land, his

---

1. The notes for this chapter cover only what is most necessary. The scholarly discussion of the topic can be found in my Habilitationsschrift, *Die Erzeltern Israels.* BZAW 22 (Berlin: Walter de Gruyter, 1994), which focuses on the Sarah-Abraham cycle.

2. The relationships stated in the canonical final text of Gen 11:26-32 are complicated: Terah is at the end of the Semite family tree. He begets three sons: Abram, Nahor, and Haran (11:26-27). Haran in turn begets Lot, and dies before his father Terah (vv. 27b-28). Finally, Terah leaves Ur in Chaldea with Abram, Sarai, and his grandson Lot, to go to the land of Canaan, but he travels only as far as Haran and settles there (vv. 31-32). This narrowing of the family to Terah is traceable to the Priestly writing. The second and probably older genealogical location of Abram is found in 11:29-30. There it is reported that Abram and Nahor took wives. It is said of Sarai, Abram's wife, that she was barren, and of Milcah, Nahor's wife, that she was the daughter of Haran and the sister of Iscah. Thus in the final text Haran is the father of three children: Milcah, Iscah, and Lot (vv. 27, 29). The older layer knows Haran only as the father of two daughters. In order to incorporate Lot, who in this layer has no relationship to Abram and is described as accompanying him, into the genealogy of Terah, he is presented as the son of Haran, although there is no explicit conclusion drawn that Milcah and Iscah thus become his sisters.

family, and his paternal house to travel to a land yet to be shown him, in order to become a great nation!

Abram (Isa 51:2 tells us who he is) responds to the call, relying on the promise. In hope, Abram and Sarai set forth. They have, as yet, none of the goods promised them. The only token of the future is YHWH's word, and following that word is one of the great blessings (12:2-3). But YHWH's solid word of promise in Gen 12:1-3 was not originally set within the Abraham-Sarah cycle. It was composed in the exilic period as an overture, a message to make the ancestral narratives current for those stricken by the loss of their nation and their land. Even in this situation that seems so accursed, YHWH can establish the people and the land anew. The blessing for the ancestors continues, for Israel living in the time of exile and even, through Israel, for all the tribes of the earth (מִשְׁפְּחֹת, 12:3b; cf. 10:32), out of which Abram was called by YHWH.

When the Priestly writing (P) dates this event of departure as if it were an entry in a chronicle (12:4b, 5), it sets the first milestone in the life of the patriarch. It locates notices of departure at God's call to Abram like a frame. The incomplete move by Terah (11:31) is now completed by his son, together with his son's wife Sarai and nephew Lot.[3]

The oldest account of Abraham's entry into the land of Canaan is in Gen 12:6-9. The couple travels through *the* land (הָאָרֶץ, 12:6) from north to south. In Shechem YHWH shows himself and makes an implicit promise of offspring and possession of *this* land:

> To your offspring will I give this land! (Gen 12:7)

Read in the context of 12:1-9, this makes concrete the land of promise, which is left indefinite in the speech itself. Abram responds to this promise by building an altar, then continues moving southward through the land. Between Bethel and Ai he again builds an altar to YHWH and calls upon his name (12:8). Only then does he move onward into the Negev, where he will settle. The ancestors have thus traveled through what will later become the land of Israel. The altars Abram builds make *this* land, in which the Canaanites dwell, to be a YHWH-land.

All the places he takes possession of on behalf of his God lie within the later Northern Kingdom of Israel and were originally associated with traditions from the Jacob cycle (cf. Genesis 28; 34). No other stories in the Abraham cycle are linked with these cities. The passage thus weaves in a strand of narrative that will be taken up again in the Jacob cycle. It belongs

---

3. The formulations in 11:31 and 12:5 correspond in their wording: (. . . ויבאו כנען ארצה ללכת ויצאו: "and they set out to go to the land of Canaan, and they came . . ."). The departure from Ur Chasdim now corresponds to the departure from Haran. The people are the same, except that Abram has now replaced his deceased father Terah.

to the layer of Genesis that sets the northern ancestors in a single genealogical line with those of the south. The linking thread of the promises
of land and offspring binds the ancestors, now fashioned into a succession
of generations, to YHWH, the real owner of the land.

The narrator deliberately leaves the function of these altars obscure. Ordinarily one builds an altar in order to offer a sacrifice. But Abram prays
in these places. This is understandable if the text comes from a time when
the Northern Kingdom had been lost, with the conquest of Samaria in 722
B.C.E., and YHWH could no longer be given cultic worship there. Even so,
his land remains the possession of Israel, even though no sacrificial cult
could be exercised there any longer.[4]

2. Sarah's abandonment and rescue

Over the land YHWH has designated as a gift of promise (12:6) falls a
famine (12:10). Abram moves to Egypt, the classic land of refuge for
people from the Syro-Palestinian land bridge fleeing famine (cf. the
Joseph story in Gen 42:1-5; 43:1; 47:4). Egypt's fertility is assured by the
Nile, whereas the Negev in particular is heavily dependent on precipita-
tion. But what appeared to be a solution to the problem of hunger proves
to be burdened, even before their arrival in Egypt, with still greater problems: Abram fears for his life because of his wife's beauty. As they approach Egypt the patriarch begins to speak of his fear:[5]

> See, I know that you are a woman beautiful to look at! Thus it will come to
> pass, when the Egyptians see you, they will say: "She is his wife!" And they
> will kill me, but you they will allow to live. Therefore say you are my sis-
> ter, that it may go well with me because of you and for your sake I may live!
> (Gen 12:11-13)

Abram first pays Sarai a compliment. But the introduction is already
pleading for understanding of what the man has at heart. He puts a fictive
scene before Sarai's eyes, painting in strong colors the threat that his
wife's beauty represents for him. To get at the wife, the Egyptians will kill

4. On this see Fischer, *Erzeltern,* 345–46.

5. J. Cheryl Exum, "Who's Afraid of 'The Endangered Ancestress'?" in eadem and David
J. A. Clines, eds., *The New Literary Criticism and the Hebrew Bible.* JSOTSup 143 (Sheffield:
JSOT Press, 1993) 91–113, attempts to interpret the three stories of the abandonment of the ancestral mother in Gen 12:10-20; Genesis 20, and Gen 26:1-11, from her reader-oriented herme-
neutical stance, in terms of depth psychology. Central in each case was fear of female sexuality
and male fantasies about women's sexual contacts. The three versions of the story represented a
successive conquering of the neurosis, until at last sexuality could be lived and the moral code
internalized (Genesis 26). Exum's stimulating article, however, omits one thing: in each case God
intervenes on behalf of the abandoned woman, with the result that the story of the two men who
control female sexuality becomes a story about the rescue of the woman.

the husband. Abram's speech culminates in his fear that he will be killed while she will remain alive. In the language itself this conclusion is emphasized by a chiasm between Abram's fate and that of his wife. What Abram here presents as the alternative is not, as he pretends, threat or preservation, but the threat to his own person and the preservation of Sarai. He suggests as a solution to the dilemma that the woman should deny the marital tie and present herself as his sister. What this means in plain language is that Sarai is to be made available to other men.[6] Abram is afraid; he wants to survive—even at his wife's expense![7] She, however, remains silent. There is not a single word of assent from Sarai, and no dialogue between the couple. The narrator thus clearly places her in the role of victim. Abram controls her. Even the lie he wants to put on her lips is formulated by him: "*my* sister."

What actually happens in Egypt is then reported in the next scene (12:14-16). The Egyptians see the woman and decide that she is very beautiful. The husband's "compliment" is elevated still more. But the Egyptians do not seek Abram's life; they do not prove to be, as he had feared, sexually unbridled men. As faithful subjects, they praise the woman to Pharaoh. In accordance with the hierarchical order of power and prestige, the best is reserved for the Pharaoh—including the most beautiful women.

> And the woman was taken into Pharaoh's house. He was gracious to Abram for her sake. (Gen 12:15b, 16a)

The passive formulation shows that this was not a violent seizure of the woman. Sarai is brought into the master's house with full honor. The Pharaoh gives her "brother" rich gifts (v. 16), which in this situation should be regarded as a bride-price for his "sister." The tension created by the man's mortal fear is deflated. Abram experienced good things, as he had imagined he would (v. 13). Sarai, *his* wife (vv. 11-12) becomes, in the course of the story, *the* woman/wife (vv. 14-15), and with her entrance into the master's house she becomes *Pharaoh's* wife. Her husband has abandoned her, exposed her to adultery. The problem is solved for Abram, but not for Sarai!

YHWH does not agree with this solution. He goes into action immediately:

6. Fokkelien van Dijk-Hemmes, "Sarai's Exile: A Gender-Motivated Reading of Genesis 12.10–13.2," in Athalya Brenner, ed., *A Feminist Companion to Genesis*. FCB 1/2 (Sheffield: Sheffield Academic Press, 1993) 222–34, also sees a reworking of the theme of sexual violence against women in this narrative.

7. Thus Frank Crüsemann's translation in ". . . er aber soll dein Herr sein' (Genesis 3,16)," in idem and Hartwig Thyen, *Als Mann und Frau geschaffen*. Kennzeichen 2 (Gelnhausen: Burckhardthaus-Verlag, 1978) 15–106, at 74–75.

> But YHWH sent great plagues on Pharaoh and his whole house because of
> Sarai, the wife of Abram. (Gen 12:17)

Now, for the first time since Sarai's abandonment, the whole truth is spoken. Sarai is Abram's wife. YHWH takes the side of the abandoned spouse—
not to give Abram back his wife,[8] but to rescue the woman at whose
expense he has made himself comfortable; that is why YHWH strikes
Pharaoh. God intervenes with the strongest on behalf of the weakest. It is
not said which plagues strike the Egyptian ruler, and how he could connect
them with the woman in his harem.[9] What is decisive is that Pharaoh acts.
He has Abram summoned and calls him to account:

> "What have you done to me? Why did you not tell me that she is your wife?
> Why did you say: 'She is my sister!' so that I took her as my wife? But
> now—see, here is your wife. Take her and go!" (12:18-19)

In a threefold set of questions, Pharaoh calls the patriarch to take responsibility. After the accusation that introduces the complaint he first asks
about Abram's suppression of the truth, then about the lie. The words of
Abram that the Pharaoh quotes speak volumes: It was not the wife who
told the lie (as he had imagined in 12:13), but the husband. The questions
the foreign ruler poses are rhetorical. He does not even wait for an answer,
but gives the woman back without asking the return of a single one of his
gifts. Nor does he impose any punishment. He does not want to have anything more to do with such a man. He simply orders his men to kick these
two out of the country (12:20).

The Egyptian ruler shows himself to be a nobler, and even a more god-
fearing man. He reacts immediately to YHWH's intervention and takes no
more thought for the bride-price he had needlessly paid. The Egyptians are
not what Abram had so fearfully imagined.[10] The fact that the Pharaoh
took Sarai as his wife was ultimately due to her husband's lie. And people
had to praise the woman to him before that. It is simply out of the question to say that "the Egyptians" killed men in order to get access to their
beautiful wives. Abram's mortal fear has proved groundless. He betrayed
his wife when there was no real danger of death at all. The husband's
motive for abandoning his wife is thus shown to have been not prudent

8. Thus, for example, Hermann Gunkel, *Genesis* (8th ed. Göttingen: Vandenhoeck &
Ruprecht, 1969) 171: "Thus YHWH intervenes and helps Abraham to recover his wife."

9. Extra-biblical versions of this narrative elaborate this missing detail to the maximum in
order to illuminate YHWH's deed of rescue still more clearly (on this see Fischer, *Erzeltern*,
244–58).

10. In contrast, the first king to rule all Israel fulfills all these prejudices: David knows that
Bathsheba is someone else's wife, yet he has her brought to him. Uriah is in David's army and
cannot protect his wife against the encroachments of the ruler. For the common features of the
narrative about Sarai's abandonment and 2 Samuel 11 see Fischer, *Erzeltern*, 236–40.

anticipation, but cowardice based on prejudice-laden fear. Abram has to admit it. When called to account, he has to remain silent.

Sarai was her husband's silent victim. She was disposed of without her own consent. The apparent rescue of her husband was oppression for her. Pharaoh, too, became a victim. He, the mightiest of these actors, was betrayed, and then was punished for taking a woman into his harem. Believing he was taking a single woman, and having paid a princely bride-price, the holder of power is brought by a still more powerful One to return what he has taken. Can it be that YHWH, by striking Pharaoh, has not only rescued Sarai, but has raised an objection also against the claims of powerful men always to have access to the most beautiful women?

This story was probably conceived originally as an individual narrative. Although Sarai has no voice, it is *her* story that is told here. All Abram's actions are at her expense. But this oppression comes to an end when YHWH acts on her behalf. Genesis 12:10-20 is thus a rescue narrative preceded by a description of the woman's distress.

When this story is read in the context of Gen 12:6-9 the original intention is altered, if not entirely lost: It is the bearer of the promise who leaves the land promised to him when the first difficulties, serious though they be, arise. It was promised that this land would be lush and fruitful, but now it is a life-threatening place. Without seeking a word from YHWH about leaving *the* land, he departs. In the foreign land he feels threatened and, in consequence, abandons the wife on whom the fulfillment of the promise of offspring depends.[11] Genesis 12:10-20 thus acquires an additional dimension of meaning: the betrayal of YHWH's promises.

With the insertion of Gen 12:1-4a the story is given still another context. The man of blessing who is to be a blessing for all the tribes of the earth becomes, through his lie, a threat to the ruler of a foreign land. He is not true to his calling. But Pharaoh's deed also acquires a different value. The one who touches YHWH's blessed vessel of promise falls under a curse (cf. 12:3).

In the final, canonical text of the Torah the story's meaning is displaced still one more time. The nameless Pharaoh becomes, in the book of Exodus, the image of Israel's oppression. He gives the command to kill all the male offspring of the people, while allowing the daughters to live (Exod 1:16, 22). Abram's feared alternative, that they would kill him and allow Sarai to live (Gen 12:12) is thus fulfilled. The blows, the plagues that YHWH sends upon Pharaoh (12:17, נגע) liberate Sarai from the harem. The last and greatest of the Egyptian plagues, the death of the firstborn, will ultimately liberate the nation (which, like the ancestral couple, had emi-

---

11. This aspect is emphasized by Klara Butting, "Die Gefährdung der Ahnfrau oder: Wer erzählt wohl dreimal eine ähnliche Geschichte?" *Texte und Kontexte* 30 (1986) 11–25.

grated because of a famine) from the land of Egypt (Exod 11:1, נגע).[12]
Sarai thus embodies in anticipation the people of Israel bound in slavery.
Her liberation prefigures the liberation of the people from Egypt!

3. A life between promise and fulfillment

Once back in the Land, Abram returns along the way he had traveled, as
far as Bethel and Ai, to the altar he had set up (12:8). There he calls on the
name of YHWH (13:4). In the wake of his self-willed digression, Abram again
seeks his God. He must begin again at the place where he had stood before.

The patriarch has become rich in a not altogether honorable way,
through the abandonment of his wife (12:16).[13] But his wealth in flocks
produces the next set of difficulties. Abram's and Lot's shepherds quarrel
over the resources of the land. Abram suggests separation as a solution to
the conflict and allows his relative to choose the part of the land in which
he wants to settle. Lot chooses the Jordan plain, which is as magnificent
as the garden of YHWH (13:10).

When this is read in the context of Genesis 12, then, Abram comes by
accident to reside in the land of Canaan, the land promised to him! In giving his nephew the choice, the patriarch has once again put the promised
land at risk. Hence the divine speech in 13:14-18 reads like a renewal of
the twice-abandoned promise of land and offspring. Abram is ordered to
traverse the land in its length and breadth: The Land must be experienced!

Genesis 13 skillfully ties in strands of narrative that will be developed
in what follows:

- With the departure of Lot, the barren couple remains alone in the land
  of promise. They have separated from Lot, who might have been an
  heir from their own family circle. Now either the promise of offspring
  must be fulfilled or they will have to look for another heir (Gen 15:16).
- Lot dwells in the blooming region of the Jordan, near Sodom. But the
  men of Sodom do not match the Eden-like landscape. They are altogether wicked and sinful before YHWH (13:13). The visit in Genesis
  19,[14] which will test this behavior, is already anticipated.

---

12. On this see Fischer, *Erzeltern,* 368, and van Dijk-Hemmes, "Sarai's Exile," 228–31.

13. The contrast presented in Butting, "Ahnfrau," 16, is delightful: The great famine (12:10)
matches the great wealth of the patriarch (13:2). "Just let anybody say that the liberation of
women would not be a blessing to men as well!"

14. The stories about Lot's daughters (like Genesis 36), which also belong among the
women's stories in Genesis, are omitted in this book because it is conceived as a women's history of *Israel's* beginnings.

- In Gen 13:18 Abram is tenting at the oaks of Mamre, near Hebron. There he builds an altar for YHWH. In 18:1-15 he will host three men in that place, in front of his tent.

The promises have been confirmed (13:14-18), but Abram and Sarai continue to be childless. The canonical sequence of narratives creates the impression that half a life lies between the speeches of God in Gen 13:14-17 and Gen 15:1-21.[15] Abram meets YHWH's renewed assurances with a resigned skepticism. He has given up hope of an heir of his body. Eliezer of Damascus, who dwells in his house, will inherit from him. YHWH had promised the couple offspring, but did not give it (זרע, 15:3; cf. 12:7; 13:15-16). How, now, is the promise of the land to be fulfilled? Then YHWH's word comes to him:

> "This man shall not be your heir, but rather the one who comes from your own body; he will be your heir!" (15:4)

Then he leads Abram outside, to open his eyes. As numerous as the stars of heaven, that is how countless his offspring will be. Against all experience Abram believes YHWH, who makes a covenant with him and assures him with an oath that his offspring will inherit the land.

The childless man who is already thinking about who will inherit from him allows himself to be comforted because he believes his God. The attempt to make a member of his household his heir has been rejected by YHWH. The promise is not only given anew, but confirmed through covenant and oath.

4. A human attempt to fulfill the promise

While Genesis 15 views the problem of childlessness from Abram's point of view, Genesis 16 looks at it from Sarai's side. She does not resign herself to her fate; she takes the initiative. The exposition in 16:1 already anticipates what will happen: Sarai, Abram's wife, does not bear for her husband, but she has an Egyptian slave named Hagar. The two women are presented as polar opposites.[16] The verse begins with "Sarai" and ends with "Hagar." Between the two stands the problem of childlessness, the husband Abram, and the fact that Hagar is in the socially weaker position of slave.

The unfree woman is described as an Egyptian, which inevitably flings one back to Gen 12:16. Sarai's bride-price included slaves, men and women.

---

15. The literary-historical origins of Genesis 15 have, in my opinion, not yet been satisfactorily explained. For the discussion see Fischer, *Erzeltern,* 349–50.

16. This stylistic peculiarity has been described by Phyllis Trible in her foundational work on the Hagar narratives in *Texts of Terror* (Philadelphia: Fortress, 1984).

The next verse also returns our thoughts to the narrative of Sarai's abandonment: Her speech to Abram in 16:2 begins similarly to his in 12:11. With "see!" the partner in each case presents her or his problem, which the other is to solve for him or her. Abram's problem was his mortal fear because of his beautiful wife. Sarai was supposed to solve it by agreeing to deny the fact of their marriage. Sarai's problem is her barrenness, which she attributes to YHWH. Abram is to solve it by going to her slave and begetting a child with her. What Sarai suggests here is not some kind of surrogate motherhood that would have been morally repugnant in the ancient Near East, but a socially legitimated institution, a slave's bearing children for the primary wife.[17] When the husband who begets a child with his wife's slave gives it a name (the act by which the child is adopted as his), it is regarded as the legitimate child of the wife and her husband.

Sarai's language is just as revealing as that of her husband in Genesis 12. She has only herself in mind, not her partner. Her primary concern is not for the child they will have together, but for her own descendants:

> "See, YHWH has closed up my womb! Go, then, to my slave; perhaps from *her* I will get a child!" And Abram listened to the voice of Sarai. And Abram went to Hagar and she became pregnant. (Gen 16:2, 4a)

In Genesis 12, Sarai's agreement was omitted. But Abram obeys his wife's word. The third person involved in Egypt had been the most powerful man, the Pharaoh; here it is the weakest woman, Hagar. Apparently obtaining her agreement is superfluous. She, in her bottom social status, belongs to her mistress in everything, including her sexuality.

But Hagar is not an automaton, the pure object of the ancestors. When she becomes pregnant, she also becomes a subject (v. 4b). The knowledge that she is fertile makes her mistress lower in her eyes. We do not hear how she expresses this, but Sarai senses it. Instead of confronting her slave and managing the conflict between themselves as women, she turns to her husband:

> "May the wrong done to me be upon you! I, I gave you my slave to have sex with. As soon as she sees she is pregnant, I am nothing in her eyes! May YHWH judge between me and you!" (Gen 16:5)

Sarai shifts the conflict to the level of her equals. So as not to continue placing herself on the same level as her slave, she calls her husband to account,[18] even though he had obeyed her command. The husband to whom

---

17. For a slave's representative bearing on behalf of the primary wife see Fischer, *Erzeltern,* 97–101.

18. On this see also Mieke Bal, Fokkelien van Dijk-Hemmes, and Grietje van Ginneken, *Und Sara lachte . . .* (Münster: Morgana-Frauenbuchverlag, 1988) 41.

she had given the woman dependent on her for sexual congress (and only that) is responsible for her status as mistress. With the typical phrase used to put pressure on someone, "May the wrong done to me be upon you!" she appeals to YHWH. YHWH alone counts for her as judge, not, for example, Abram as the head of the patriarchal family.

The reaction of the man between two women is cold-blooded. He shoves the conflict back to the level of the women and thus shrugs off any responsibility: "'See, your slave is in your hand. Do with her what seems good in your eyes!'" (Gen 16:6). Abram wants to remain neutral and not be bothered. He supports neither woman, but points Sarai to the power that is hers. Patriarchy is not simply the rule of men over women.[19] Patriarchy means a hierarchically ordered society in which women of the upper class share in power over those who are socially lower. Sarai is not powerless. Her slave is subject to her, not to Abram. When Abram refuses responsibility for the conflict by pointing to her rights, he withdraws all support from the woman who is bearing his child.

What is told here is, viewed from our present standpoint, the sexual exploitation of a dependent woman. However, it is not appropriate for Christians to impose moral judgment on the socially legitimated opportunity to use a slave as a surrogate mother, since it was precisely in the name of Christianity that the most insupportable abuses of slavery were propagated. But how does the narrator evaluate the behavior of his characters? In the narrative passages the unfree Egyptian is always called by her own name. But on Sarai's and Abram's lips Hagar has no name. She is referred to according to her social status as slave, which places her in the lowest social position. Hagar is exploited exclusively as a problem-solver. When she does not function as planned, and new problems arise from the triangular relationship they themselves have initiated, they are not human enough to acknowledge that the slave, made pregnant for the benefit of the married couple, is owed a place within the family circle. Thus discord is created among all three participants.

Sarai takes her husband's disengagement as giving her carte blanche to oppress her slave. Thereupon the self-assured Hagar solves the problem in her own way: she flees from her harsh mistress. Slaves who ran away[20] in the ancient Near East were threatened with the most drastic punishment possible. At all costs the escaped unfree persons had to be brought back into their owners' house. That was the only way to maintain an institution that denied human beings their self-determined humanity. The Hebrew

---

19. Here I am following the definition of patriarchy in Elisabeth Schüssler Fiorenza, *In Memory of Her* (New York: Crossroad, 1983) 29: "While androcentrism characterizes a mind-set, patriarchy represents a socio-cultural system in which a few men have power over other men, women, children, slaves, and colonialized people."

20. On this see Fischer, *Erzeltern,* 102–103.

Bible knows no such codified law. Deuteronomy 23:16-17, for example, forbids giving up escaped slaves and instructs the local community to receive and integrate them. In Exod 21:7-11 the Book of the Covenant, in cases of conflict over liberation, gives preference to (Israelite) slave women who have had sexual contact with free male persons in the family. It is hard to imagine that under such legal conditions slavery could have been maintained. Instead, these texts reflect Israel's ethics of liberation, culminating in the fundamental principle that their own origins, in slavery in Egypt, demanded that they act in solidarity with oppressed persons. Under what legal conditions Hagar's flight is to be evaluated, then, must remain open. Genesis 16, as we will show, offers us two different concepts.

5. Hagar: From oppression to liberation—and back again

Hagar flees into the wilderness and rests at a spring. There YHWH's messenger finds her and says to her: "'Hagar, slave of Sarai, where are you coming from and where are you going?' and she answers: 'I have fled from Sarai, my mistress'" (Gen 16:8). In her flight the slave woman meets a man who knows her and asks her why he finds her in this place. According to ancient Near Eastern slave law (cf., for example, the Codex Hammurabi §15-19) he would have to bring the slave back to her mistress or be threatened with death himself. However, he is the first person who not only addresses her in terms of her status but also calls her by name. The questions he asks her are about her past and her future. The first, Hagar herself can answer. She speaks the truth by deliberately confessing her flight.[21] Sarai, too, has a name on Hagar's lips, and is not simply referred to by her social status as mistress. The conflict that has blazed up over social rank is thus present to the text.

The question about the future is something Hagar cannot answer. It is true that this Egyptian woman is fleeing toward Egypt (cf. v. 7b), but without any particular goal. Her primary purpose in running away is to escape from oppression. The angel of YHWH responds to this by speaking a saving word about Hagar's future: "'See, you are pregnant and will bear a son. You shall call his name Ishmael, for YHWH has listened to your oppression!'" (Gen 16:11). The saying resembles the announcement of a birth,[22] although Hagar already knows that she is pregnant. The angel explains the name he announces to the mother in terms of rescue from oppression. But Hagar fled on her own initiative. In what sense, then, will she be rescued? The

21. Phyllis Trible, *Texts of Terror*, 15, pointed out that the additional personal pronouns in vv. 5 and 8 correspond to each other. Both women state the case from their own point of view.

22. Matitiahu Tsevat, "Hagar and the Birth of Ishmael," in eadem, *The Meaning of the Book of Job and Other Biblical Studies* (New York: Ktav, 1980) 53–76, includes 16:7-14 among the "proclamation narratives."

oracle for the child's life story, which the angel adds (16:12), leaves no doubt that Y<small>HWH</small> refers to rescue from Sarai's oppression (vv. 6b, 11b, ענה, oppress). For even the son will be free as a wild ass and will maintain himself against his brothers. The image of the unbridled wild animal also indicates that he will be born far from civilization, in the wilderness. In the oldest version of the story Hagar did not have to return to her mistress. Y<small>HWH</small>'s messenger approves of the slave's flight and puts an end to the woman's humiliation and unfreedom.

In response to the liberating word Hagar names the God who has appeared to her with a saving and freeing message. By naming the place she constitutes it as holy. The spring Beer-Lahai-Roi is not simply a watering-place in the wilderness, but that memorable place where God made God-self visible and gave a blessing for liberation.[23]

When we look at Hagar's reaction to the encounter with God, however, the question arises whether the narrator of Genesis 16 has not made use of older, perhaps orally transmitted material.[24] The God who speaks to her is Y<small>HWH</small>, who conveys his word through a messenger. The child's name should, correspondingly, be Ishmaya (ישמעיה; cf. 1 Chr. 12:4). Ishmael is a name containing "El," like the name El-roi by which Hagar calls the God who appears to her. If this tension reveals the existence of an earlier layer of tradition, one thing is certain: The experiences reflected here are in any case a woman's experiences of God. The narrator of Genesis 16 embeds them in his story in such a way that they form the conclusion of the rescue story of an oppressed slave.

In the ongoing narrative of the Bible, Hagar is the first person who is favored with an encounter with God through an angel, the first who names the God who has been revealed to her, and the first to found a place in which she has received the word of God as a shrine to Y<small>HWH</small> by giving it a name. None of the mothers of Israel is her equal in this regard.

The basic narrative of Genesis 16 thus far described is probably among the oldest traditions in the Abraham-Sarah cycle, which as a whole consisted of individual, self-contained traditions. Through one of the successive expansions of this text complex, the parallel narrative of Gen 21:8-19 was likewise inserted. For the thread of the narrative to continue and so

23. Trible, *Texts of Terror,* 13, 21, points both for Genesis 16 and for Genesis 21 to the choice of words for oppression and liberation, so close to the Exodus tradition. Hagar thus prefigures the oppression of the people in Egypt. Trible considers only the final text and thus does not recognize here a narrative of liberation. Marie-Theres Wacker, "1. Mose 16 und 21: Hagar—die Befreite," in Eva Renate Schmidt et al., eds., *Feministisch gelesen 1* (2nd ed. Stuttgart: Kreuz-Verlag, 1989) 25–32, at 28, who also sees that some editing has been done at vv. 9-10, emphasizes "that *God* is also present to help *at the Exodus of an Egyptian woman from Israel.*"

24. For the difficulty of the text and the question of previous oral layers see Fischer, *Erzeltern,* 266–70.

that Hagar could be expelled (again), the slave had to be sent back to the house of oppression. The traces of this redaction are visible in Gen 16:9: "And YHWH's messenger said to her: 'Go back to your mistress and submit yourself beneath her hands!'" Verses 9, 10, and 11 each begin with the same introductory words, even though Hagar never interrupts the messenger's speech. In the final text, as a result, the passage in Gen 16:7-11 is awkward. If we are not to suppose that redactional work was nothing but a stupid insertion of bits of text, there must be a reason why this passage was not smoothed out.

Verse 9 contains a message from God that transforms the narrative of rescue in the basic layer into a "text of terror."[25] The statement about Hagar's future consists in an order to return to her harsh mistress. While Abram had given Hagar into Sarai's *hand,* now YHWH gives her into both *hands* of her oppressor. The command shatters Hagar's attempt to flee. The messenger acts according to the ancient Near Eastern slave laws according to which anyone who found an escaped unfree person had to bring her or him back into the house of slavery. The command to allow herself to be oppressed, and even more than before, gives legitimation after the fact to Sarai's harshness as something justified. Since it is contained in the speech of a messenger, YHWH is presented as the guarantor of a hierarchical social order that approves of repression. The image of God that is thus drawn is diametrically opposite to that of YHWH, the God of the Exodus from slavery. The redactor was apparently aware of that. By inserting the newer introduction to the speech into the text without smoothing, he signals the break in the narrative and thus makes the original story of liberation more visible. His primary interest was not to legitimate oppressive slavery. Therefore he does not intervene in the rest of the story, even though it is hard to reconcile with the command to return to slavery. The redactor has to make it understandable that Hagar appears again in the ancestors' house if he wants to insert the narrative of her expulsion (Gen 21:8-19) into this context.

Another seam, this time pointing to a much later expansion of the text, is visible in v. 10.[26] The great promise here made to Hagar, again with a fully developed introduction to the speech, corresponds to the promise made to the fathers. None of the mothers of Israel is the addressee of such a promise:

---

25. The title of Phyllis Trible's book containing her essay on the Hagar narratives.

26. In the first edition of this book I supported the thesis that vv. 9-10 belonged to a single redactional layer. As a result of further work with the Genesis texts, however, I am now persuaded that v. 9 is connected to Gen 21:8-19 and is therefore exilic, while v. 10 is part of the layer that was worked into the text last of all and construes the image of the ancestors as a model of faith. In what follows I will include 16:10 when speaking of this post-exilic layer, without referring to the changes I have made since the first edition.

> And YHWH's messenger said to her: "Indeed, indeed, your offspring will so increase that their numbers will be beyond counting!"

With this promise Hagar, the tribal mother of the Ishmaelites, is given a share in community with the God of her ancestral house (cf. 22:17; 26:4, 24). Certainly, in this context the gracious speech sounds like the carrot offered with the stick. If the promise had been placed elsewhere, after v. 11 for example, it would have been revolutionary. Placed here, it softens the harshness of the command to return by augmenting that return to oppression with a promise. Verse 10 therefore belongs to the layer that will also redact the parallel narrative in Gen 21:11-13 in order to shape the figures in the action into models of faith.

6. The story of a climber

The narrative in Genesis 16 does not remain in the final text as a story of oppression. Before the insertion of v. 10 established the text as we now have it, it was worked over once more, with the result that the sense was again shifted.

The Priestly variant of the narrative is unaware of oppression and flight, and knows nothing of Hagar's encounter with God. **P** tells Hagar's story through genealogical notes:

> And Sarai, Abram's wife, took her slave Hagar, the Egyptian, after the ten years that Abram dwelt in the land of Canaan, and gave her to Abram, her husband, as wife. And Hagar bore Abram a son. And Abram called the name of his son, whom Hagar had borne, "Ishmael." Abram was eighty-six years old when Hagar bore Ishmael to Abram. (Gen 16:3, 15-16)

The Priestly passages in Genesis 16 constitute a homogeneous unit. All the persons involved are presented anew, with name and status. Here again the sexual congress between Abram and Hagar is initiated by his wife, Sarai. But she does not give him Hagar to bear for her; she gives her as wife (אשה). The word used here, אשה, ordinarily refers to a free woman.[27] Sarai gives her slave to her husband as his wife. As such, Hagar bears him a son. Ishmael is not born for Sarai, nor does she undertake the naming of the child, as Rachel and Leah do later (cf. Gen 30:3-13). The son is named by the patriarch. Although he gives him a name that is connected with the mother's experience of rescue, the narrator allows him to do the naming and, by stating the age of the father, inserts the time of the son's birth into the continuing story of Abram's life.

---

27. Cf. N. P. Bratsiotis, art. איש, *TDOT* 1:222–35, at 224–25 (it is significant that "woman" is treated under the word "man"!).

P's sole interest is in the genealogical line of Abram; it reports marriage and birth without any narrative context. When the marriage is dated by the length of time Abram had dwelt in the land it is clear, in this layer also, that the fulfillment of the promise has been delayed and that the couple are trying to help themselves. However, Ishmael is born under the care of his father, without any previous conflict. Hagar's story thus becomes the story of a social climber.[28] A slave, she becomes the wife of her master and thus a free woman. She bears him a son and achieves the position of mother of Abram's firstborn.

Previous redaction had made this a story of oppression, but its embedding in the Priestly narrative weakens it. The messenger orders the slave to return to her mistress and permit herself to be oppressed. There is no account of her having carried out the command. In the final text **P**'s notice of the birth (vv. 15-16) serves this function by its placement. However, contrary to the messenger's statement, after her return Hagar is not confronted by her harsh mistress, but only with the child's father. She bears for *him,* not for her mistress as v. 2 had predicted. Abram takes Ishmael as his son by giving him a name.

The ruptures caused by the literary-historical genesis of the text are not smoothed out. Hence the sense of the original narrative of liberation is still present in the final text, even though the interest of the three redactions of v. 9, the **P** insertion, and v. 10 is evident. By closing with the notice of Hagar's bearing for Abram, Genesis 16 ends with a family idyll. The escaped slave bears her son in the house of the child's father; the jealous wife and mistress is no longer present. The shift of the name-giving from the mother (v. 11) to the father results in the absurdity that Abram gives his son the memorial name that calls to mind the liberation of the mother from slavery, a slavery in which he was essentially involved (v. 6). Female experience is usurped and conveyed to the man—a phenomenon that can be demonstrated in the two subsequent chapters, Genesis 17 and 18.

7. *"Where is Sarah, your wife?"*

"Where is your brother Abel?" This question in Gen 4:9 introduces Y̲HWH's calling of Cain to account after he had attempted to make his brother disappear. "Where is Sarah, Abraham's wife?" is a question we could pose in the same sense to many exegeses of Genesis 17–18. Sarah's share in the announcement of the birth of her son is minimized in such a way that it almost disappears. Sarah is only relevant as Abraham's wife, with whom he will beget the son of the promise. A first beginning of this

---

28. On this see Irmtraud Fischer, "'Geh, und laß dich unterdrücken!' sprach der Gottesbote zu Hagar," *Conc* 30 (1994) 155–60.

tradition of interpretation is already visible in the biblical text itself, as a result of the insertion of Genesis 17 before Genesis 18.[29] Therefore in what follows I will first discuss Genesis 18, and only then address the canonical sequence of Genesis 17–18.

Genesis 18:1, by locating the action at the oaks of Mamre, links to the narrative thread at Gen 13:18. YHWH appears while Abraham is sitting at the entrance of his tent, in the midday heat. The subsequent visit of the three men is introduced in the manner of a divine appearance. Until the end of the narrative of 18:1-16 it is left unclear how the three men relate to the one out of whom YHWH speaks. It is possible that in a pre-literary stage two narrative traditions were molded together here, one of them about a visit by three men and the other about an appearance of YHWH. The attempts to disentangle these narrative threads are legion.[30] I will consider the narrative as a harmonious whole into which these ruptures were deliberately inserted in order to indicate the simultaneous immediacy and distance of an encounter with God.

Abraham receives these three men with exceptional hospitality. He runs to meet them and bows down before them (v. 2): "And he said: 'Adonai, if I have found favor in your eyes, do not pass by your servant!'" (Gen 18:3). Abraham's address to the men is, according to the Masoretic punctuation, an address to God. Without vocalization it can also be read as "my lord."[31] However, such a respectful greeting is also possible between human beings; Jacob, for example, bows to the ground seven times before Esau and addresses him in very similar words (Gen 33:3, 8, 10). Our text has thus from the very beginning been kept deliberately enigmatic.

The hospitality Abraham offers is excited and swift, and is intended to include every comfort: The guests are given opportunity to wash their dusty feet; they are invited to sit in the shade of a tree, out of the noonday heat; they are offered a meal. The three men are sparing in their words. No extensive greeting, no thanks for the invitation—all they do is assent: "Do as you have said!" (18:5b).

Abraham rushes into the tent and gives instructions to Sarah to bake bread. He himself runs to the herd, chooses a nice, tender calf, and gives it to his servant to be quickly prepared. Then he fetches curds and milk and presents both to the guests along with the roast veal. He, however, remains standing under the tree while they eat. Abraham behaves like a servant, not a host who eats together with his guests. Then the men speak:

---

29. Sharon Pace Jeansonne, *The Women of Genesis* (Minneapolis: Fortress, 1990) 22, works consistently from the final text and regards the double birth notice as necessary because in Genesis 17 Abraham does not inform Sarah.

30. For the discussion see Fischer, *Erzeltern,* 14–17.

31. For the rabbinic interpretation see Benno Jacob, *Das Erste Buch der Tora. Genesis* (Berlin: Schocken, 1934) 438.

"Where is Sarah, your wife?" And he said: "See, she is in the tent!" And he said: "Return, yes, I will return in the cycle of life. And see, there will be a son for Sarah, your wife!" (18:9-10a)

The men evidently have no interest in Abraham. They treat him like a servant. He is to go and serve them, but they leave him standing and do not ask him to sit with them. When they speak to him again, their attention is on his wife. This is indecent behavior on the part of these taciturn male guests, to ask about the host's wife! Abraham answers curtly. Sarah is in the tent, because apparently this visit is men's business. She has not even greeted the gentlemen.

Then, suddenly, only one person speaks, without any indication which of the three men it is or what his relationship to them is. Erhard Blum has characterized this shift of persons very well: "The practical reason for this shift is evident: Such a promise can no longer be part of the incidental 'small talk' of anonymous 'men.' It belongs in a divine speech."[32] This is a visit between men, and the conversation is a conversation between men. Nevertheless, Sarah moves, step by step, to the center. *For her* a child is promised in the course of a year, not for Abraham, who is addressed.

> But Sarah was listening at the entrance to the tent, behind him. Abraham and Sarah were old, advanced in age. It had ceased to be with Sarah after the manner of women. And Sarah laughed to herself: "Now that I have grown old, shall I enjoy the pleasures of love? My lord is old, too!" Then YHWH spoke to Abraham: "Why is Sarah laughing, and saying: 'Indeed, truly, shall I bear now that I have grown old?' Is anything impossible with YHWH? Around this time I will return to you, in the cycle of life, and Sarah will have a son!" (18:10b-14)

The narrator fades out the men's conversation and shifts attention to Sarah. She is standing at the entrance to the tent in front of which the speaker is sitting. Even before her reaction to what she hears is told, we receive information about the age of the ancestors. Both are old and used up; Sarah is already beyond her fertile years. She gives an accurate estimate of her situation and laughs at the guest's announcement, because apparently, so it seems to her, he does not know how old she really is. Sarah's laughter at this point should not be misinterpreted as flagrant disbelief. She does not know who is giving the message.

The narrator dissolves back to the men's conversation and clarifies the mystery of the speaker's identity, which he had already announced to the readers in v. 1. It is YHWH, who not only hears Sarah's laughter, but repeats what she is thinking. The question is posed to Abraham, her husband,

---

32. Erhard Blum, *Die Komposition der Vätergeschichte*. WMANT 57 (Neukirchen-Vluyn: Neukirchener Verlag, 1984) 278.

maintaining the construction of the conversation with the visitors. But the message is not for him; *Sarah* is meant to hear what YHWH says. To the renewed promise of a birth in a year's time he adds the explanation that opens the woman's eyes: for YHWH, nothing is impossible. Now for the first time it is clear to Sarah who is the speaker, and that he is not speaking in ignorance of her situation.

> Then Sarah denied it, saying: "I did not laugh!" For she was afraid. But he answered her: "No, but you did laugh!" (18:15)

The conversation that was conceived from the beginning as taking place between men ends in a conversation between YHWH and Sarah. YHWH emerges from the group of visitors at the moment when *she* enters the conversation. This structuring makes it clear that Sarah's listening at the entrance to the tent (v. 10b) was not impertinent eavesdropping on men's important conversation, but that the story places Sarah there precisely so that she may hear the message, which is intended for her. With each successive speech she is drawn further into the conversation, until finally YHWH addresses her directly. Sarah does not deny her laughter because she feels she has been detected in an improper action, but because she did not know who was speaking. At the moment when she realizes this, it is clear to her that laughter is an inadequate reaction. A realistic estimate based on the state of the couple gives way to faith. And now she really stops laughing. That YHWH insists so strongly that she did laugh is not to be misunderstood as a reproach against the woman. Her laughter (צחקה) is a premonition of the name of the son announced to her. She will call him Isaac (יצחק), an interpretation of her experience of God.

The couple has waited all its life long for the fulfillment of the promise of a son. With advancing age Sarah had impatiently tried to help the process. The attempt succeeded; her slave became pregnant, but the couple was unable to cope with the tensions that resulted. Hagar and Abraham's son was not born for Sarah. When Sarah entered menopause all her hopes died, so that she could only laugh at the announcement of a birth in a year's time. Only when she recognizes the authority of the one who proclaims the message is the woman's realism exploded; then her fear of God comes to the fore. Her husband, Abraham, plays a subordinate role in this story. While he is present on the surface of the text, in the crucial scene between YHWH and Sarah he disappears completely. The son is promised *to her;* the visit is *for her;* the conversation is directed toward *her;* it is *her* experience that will give the child his name!

8. The alienation of female experience

The narrative of the announcement to Sarah of the birth of a son, which is one of the oldest texts in the Abraham-Sarah cycle, is placed in the canonical final text *after* Genesis 17, the only major "narrative" from the Priestly writing in Genesis 12ff. At the center of that chapter are covenant and circumcision, but it also contains an assurance of the immediate fulfillment of the promise of a son. Consequently, in the arrangement of the text of Genesis the older text, Genesis 18, is read as if it were a doublet of Genesis 17. First the fulfillment is promised to the man, and only afterward to the woman.

Although **P** chooses "Elohim," God, as divine title, and contains the divine name "El Shaddai" in God's self-presentation, in 17:1 the dialogue is introduced by an appearance of YHWH, creating a deliberate parallel with 18:1.[33] Abram is given a covenant. He is to be greatly numerous (v. 2b).[34] As he bows down before God, the divine discourse makes the pre-announcement more precise:

> "I, behold, my covenant with you! You shall be the father of a multitude (אב המון) of nations! Your name will no longer be called 'Abram' (אברם), but your name shall be 'Abraham' (אברהם)! For I give you as father to a multitude of nations. And I will make you very fruitful and make you nations. And kings will come forth from you!" (Gen 17:4-6)

The covenant God concludes with Abram makes him a different person: He receives a new name corresponding to his new way of being. Joined in him are the promise at creation (cf. Gen 1:28) and that of multiplying to become a great nation (cf. 12:2): Abram is to become a great multitude of nations, and so he is called Abraham. God's covenant with Abraham consists in this: that God will be the God of the ancestors (v. 7). But this self-obligation is not merely for that generation; it is for their whole offspring and for all time (vv. 7, 8). This is an everlasting covenant to which God obligates Godself: to give the land in which Abraham and his wives are still living as strangers to them and their descendants as an eternal possession (v. 8).

God establishes a sign as a covenantal obligation, something that the members of this house (only the males, however) and their successors are to carry out: the circumcision that must already be done to newborn males is to be borne by them as a sign of the covenant, whether they are free or unfree (vv. 10-14). This is clearly a central point of significance for males.[35]

---

33. Both texts begin with וירא יהוה אל-. In Genesis 18 it continues homogeneously as to this name, while in Genesis 17 this introduction conflicts with the divine name in the rest of the chapter. Therefore we may presume that here we can see the hand of the redactor who assembled the two chapters into a single narrative sequence.

34. The word-field of increase unites the primeval history up to the Exodus (cf. the tables in Gordon F. Davies, *Israel in Egypt.* JSOTSup 135 [Sheffield: JSOT Press, 1992] 182).

35. For the problem of the sign of the covenant being carried out exclusively in males and the marginalization of women it implies see Judith Plaskow, *Standing Again At Sinai. Judaism from a Feminist Perspective* (San Francisco: Harper & Row, 1990) 82.

Women do not bear this covenantal sign in their bodies. But in the very next verse the ancestral mother is brought to the fore. She is thus included in the covenant just as Abraham is.

> And God said to Abraham: "You are no longer to call Sarai, your wife, by the name 'Sarai,' but 'Sarah' is her name! I will bless her and I will give you a son from her as well! And I will bless her and she shall become nations. Kings of peoples shall come forth from her!" (Gen 17:15-16)

The divine promise about Sarah is in no way less than that about Abraham; in fact, its chiastic form makes it still more prominent. She, too, is incorporated in the eternal community of God through her renaming. Her new name, which means "lady" or "mistress," is explained by the twofold blessing: Not only a multitude of nations, as with Abraham, is promised to her, but also that her tribe will govern. She will be the tribal ancestor of the kings of nations!

In the **P** context Abraham already has a son. Hagar has borne him Ishmael. According to the chronology (16:15; 17:1) he is now thirteen years old. If Abraham is to be the ancestor of many nations there must be at least one other son, since otherwise the only offspring, Ishmael, will be the tribal ancestor after whom the genealogy will branch. That son is now promised to Abraham, from Sarah. As in Genesis 18, the promise of fulfillment is given to the man, because God speaks with him. And here also the reaction is laughter:

> Then Abraham fell on his face and laughed. And he said in his heart: "Shall a hundred-year-old man have a child born to him? And Sarah is ninety; shall she yet bear?" (17:17)

Reacting to the announcement of a late birth with laughter is reported of Sarah in Genesis 18. Now Abraham laughs. While Sarah, when she laughed, did not know who was the speaker of such a message, and while she laughed because she had a realistic view of her own age, Abraham knows who he is speaking with. He falls on his face (vv. 3, 17), but he seems to have very little faith and respect. While Sarah withdrew her laughter the moment she knew that the word came from YHWH, Abraham laughs in his face![36] Abraham is a doubter, as the subsequent objection shows:

> "If only Ishmael may live in your sight!" Then God said: "No, Sarah, your wife, will bear a son for you and you shall call his name 'Isaac'! I will establish my everlasting covenant with him, and with his offspring after him!" (17:18-19)

36. For the different evaluation of the laughter of Abraham and Sarah in the history of scholarship, which can only be called misogynistic, see Melanie A. May, "1. Mose 18,1-15: Saras Lachen," *Feministisch gelesen* 1:33–38; 33–35.

The patriarch no longer hopes that the promise will be fulfilled. If only the one son he has begotten with Hagar may live, that will be enough for him. But God insists that the promise is not given to Abraham alone, so that he can realize it with just any woman; it is given to the couple. The son of the promise is therefore Sarah's son, not Abraham's firstborn! Isaac will be the heir of the covenant, not Ishmael, even though a great promise is made to this son as well (v. 20). There is dead silence about Hagar, Ishmael's mother, throughout this chapter. Ishmael is exclusively Abraham's son, not hers. In contrast, there is insistence about the mother of the son of the promise (v. 21): Sarah, the bearer of the promise, must give birth to him; her firstborn will enter into the covenant, not the patriarch's firstborn! And this son Sarah will bear at the same time in the following year: "'I will make my covenant with Isaac, whom Sarah will bear for you at this time next year!'" (17:21). After the announcement of the birth in a year's time, also known to us from Genesis 18, the divine appearance ends. Abraham, as commanded, circumcises himself and Ishmael, and all the male members of his household (17:23-27).

The Priestly version of the announcement of Isaac's birth concentrates on Abraham. Women's experience is deprived of its character and transferred to the man. Within **P** this point of view is consistent, since the ancestral narratives are presented over long stretches as agnatic (male-identified) genealogies. The new thing in Genesis 17 is the everlasting covenant with the genealogical line of the promise, as well as the covenantal sign of circumcision borne only by the male members of the nation. Nevertheless, it is surprising that despite such an androcentric perspective the text does not speak of the begetting of the son by the man, but exclusively of the woman's giving birth. Both the introduction of the proclamation as an appearance of God and the conclusion with a statement of the time when the child will be born, in the next year, as well as the etiology of the name "Isaac" in terms of laughter at the late birth, give visible evidence that Genesis 17 and Genesis 18 have been accommodated to each other. The points of the older narrative of the visitors in Genesis 18 are incorporated like citations within Genesis 17. The direction of the give and take between the texts can be clearly established, since the weight of the older tradition can no longer be suppressed or denied. Nevertheless, the prior placement of chapter 17 displaces the narrative of the announcement of the birth to Sarah into second place.

With regard to Abraham's firstborn, the same tendency is evident. The promise for Ishmael is originally given to Hagar (cf. 16:11-12). In Genesis 17, however, God also gives the promise of this son's becoming a nation to the father and so anticipates the divine speech in Gen 21:18. Genesis 17 thus concentrates every expression of divine promises on Abraham. Since the older narratives set the women at the center of interest, the dominance of the patriarch must be created. The canonical final text achieves this by means of sequence: First God speaks to Abraham, the primal father. Only then does he give the message to the women as well, the mothers of the two children of Abraham. The weight of the ancient women's traditions was apparently so great, at the time when this arrangement was created, that they could no longer be suppressed. They remain in place, but now we read them *after* Genesis 17. By adopting citations from the women's texts, and through the sequencing of Genesis 17 and 18, the biblical text causes us to read the old narrative from Mamre in light of the primary gift of the promise to the patriarch.

9. *The abandonment of the old bearer of the promise*

The visit of the two men ends, in Gen 18:16, when they journey onward to Sodom. The fulfillment of the promise of a son is now almost within reach. In the course of the next year Sarah will become pregnant and give birth. The fulfillment of the divine message is reported in Gen 21:1-7. But another narrative has been inserted between these events, one that is totally out of place here. Genesis 20 tells of a second abandonment of Sarah by her husband, who once again presents her in foreign territory as his sister and so exposes her to adultery. Scholars, if they take any notice at all of the ordering of the texts, usually see Genesis 18, 19, 20, 21 as clumsy redactional interweaving of strands from different sources.[37] The new direction in research, which sees the final text as the result of a literary process, makes it clear how unsustainable such an evaluation is. Genesis 20 is not accidentally placed between the the announcement and the occurrence of the pregnancy and birth. Genesis 20 has a well-founded place there!

In the year during which Sarah is to become pregnant the couple leaves its established place of settlement and, after a few stages of travel, settles again in Gerar. There they live as foreigners.

> And Abraham said of Sarah, his wife: "She is my sister!" Then Abimelech, the king of Gerar, sent and took Sarah. (20:2)

Genesis 20:1-2 presents an unexplained situation. It is neither said why Abraham and his wife leave the land nor is any motivation given for the husband's denial of his wife so that Abimelech takes her. Genesis 12:10-20 gave motives for all these things. It spoke of a famine, of the woman's beauty, and of the husband's fear that he would be killed because of it. The denial of the marital tie was presented as a means of protection for the husband. In Genesis 20 there is no explanation at all. The readers of Genesis, of course, know all this by the time they arrive at Genesis 20. The narrator can omit the information *if* he is writing for a context in which Gen

---

37. Cf., for example, Hermann Gunkel, *Genesis,* 220.

12:10-20 is already fixed. But in this narrative context it is no beautiful young woman who enters the harem of the foreign potentate; it is Sarah, the old woman who in the near future is to become pregnant. Now she is in danger, in Abimelech's harem, of being integrated into a foreign genealogical line. With his lie about their brother-sister relationship, Abraham has abandoned her. But God will not let the divine plan be frustrated:

> Then God came to Abimelech in a dream by night and said to him: "See, you are condemned to death because of the woman you have taken, because she is the wife of a husband!" Then Abimelech said: "Did he not tell me: 'She is my sister!'"? And God answered: "So now give the woman back to her husband and you will live. But if you do not give her back, know this: You will certainly die! you and all who are with you!" (20:3-7*)

Genesis 20 is not a literary unit. A basic narrative that I will first describe was redacted at a later time.[38]

God appears in a dream to Abimelech, who has just taken Sarah into his house, and threatens him with death because he has taken a wife from her husband. Abimelech defends himself by saying he acted in good faith, quoting as evidence what Abraham had said. God, however, makes it clear to him that he was lied to and therefore changes the proclamation of death into a conditional threat. Abimelech must give the woman back; then he will live. If he does not do it, he will die. Stylistically, the conditional promise of life and threat of death are emphasized by the fact that the individual parts of the statement are chiastically arranged. Verse 7 thus appears as the center of the narrative. Abimelech's future fate is made dependent on his behavior. In this narrative version, then, the arc of tension is not initiated with the abandonment of the woman, but with God's intervention.

> And Abimelech got up in the morning and called Abraham. And he said to him: "What have you done to us? And how have I sinned against you, that you have caused so great a sin to come upon me and my kingdom? You have done unthinkable things to me!" (20:8*-9)

The foreign king reacts immediately. On the morning after the dream he calls Abraham and confronts him. Abraham, in pretending that his wife was his sister, has deceived the ruler. By his lie Abraham has created the conditions for a great sin in Abimelech's house. God's threat of death (v. 7) included all the people round about. Therefore Abimelech also formulates his accusation to show that Abraham's dangerous behavior affects his whole kingdom. He has offended against morality and decency as well as against law. Abraham's defense, in contrast, sounds like a pious excuse:

---

38. For the literary-critical distinction of the two layers see Fischer, *Erzeltern*, 137–56.

> Then Abraham answered him: "I thought that there could be no fear of God in this place, and that you would kill me because of my wife!" (20:11)

The patriarch grounds his behavior primarily on anxiety: he thought there could be no fear of God in Gerar. The argument is vitiated by the very fact that Abimelech took the initiative immediately after the dream. What is significant in this context is the explanation of his mortal fear: It is not the wife's beauty that is dangerous for the husband—Sarah is already an aged woman—but the very fact that he has a wife. In contrast to the sharpness of the accusation, the defense seems amazingly thin!

> And Abimelech took sheep and oxen, and male and female slaves, and gave them to Abraham. And he gave Sarah, his wife, back to him. And Abimelech said: "See, my land lies before you. Settle wherever it seems good in your eyes!" (20:14-15)

Abimelech acts as God had demanded of him. He gives Abraham back his wife, Sarah, and pays princely reparations to the husband. The wealth of the ancestral father, which originated in Gen 12:16 with the bride-price, is here founded on reparation gifts. It appears that the idea that the prosperity of the ancestors was connected with the abandonment of the wife was an integral part of the narrative material. Last of all Abimelech offers Abraham his land as a place to dwell. He does not put him out of the country, as Pharaoh had done, but tries to make things right on every level.

God's demands have been fulfilled. Abimelech has given the woman back. But to resolve the tension it must also be reported that God has fulfilled the conditional promise of life:

> And God healed Abimelech and his wife and his maidservants, and they were able to bear again. For YHWH had closed, yes, closed every womb in Abimelech's house because of Sarah, the wife of Abraham. (20:17b-18)

At the very end of the story the readers learn of a healing, even though they had not been previously informed that there was any sickness. The threat of death leveled at Abimelech was thus not the first divine sign. God had brought infertility upon the king's house, and now that Sarah is back with her husband he removes it. He intervened on her behalf because her husband had abandoned her.

The final sentence seizes our attention. The divine title changes suddenly; YHWH is called by name. *He* has brought infertility on Abimelech and his house for Sarah's sake. The immediately following verse (21:1) continues the theme of fertility preserved or refused: YHWH takes Sarah's part; she becomes pregnant and bears a son. Genesis 21:1-7 never tires of emphasizing that Abraham is the father of this son.[39] Now it is clear why

39. Cf. Jeansonne, *Women,* 24–27.

the note about the healing appears so late in Genesis 20, and why the reasons for it are named even later. YHWH closed every womb in Abimelech's house and struck him with impotence because Sarah was living in his harem during the year in which it was promised that she would be pregnant and give birth. The placement of the notice in 20:17b, 18 is not, then, the result of a narrative style that provides information at a late point or of clumsy insertion by a redactor; it was deliberately chosen. The information has to be immediately present to the mind when one is reading about Isaac's conception. Abraham had abandoned his wife, again, at a point when the fulfillment of the promise of a son was imminent. *Sarah* had been promised that she would be pregnant within the year. There is the highest degree of danger that Abimelech could be the father of this child. Both the change in the divine title and the placement of 20:18 allow us to conclude that the narrator has formulated it for an already existing context and inserted his story between 18:1-15 and 21:1-7. YHWH had promised the birth of the son in the coming year, but Abraham, the bearer of the promise, did not shelter his wife from adultery, and so endangered the promise. Therefore YHWH intervenes and blocks the foreign man's opportunity for encroachment. After her rescue, YHWH takes Sarah's part and does for her what he had said he would.

10. The immunity of the prophet Abraham

The basic narrative in Genesis 20, which tells of the abandonment of the mother—and thus of the promise—immediately after the concretely expressed promise of the birth of a son within the year, does not remain unchallenged in the canonical final text. A post-exilic layer of redaction, which hones the picture of the ancestors as models of faith, has left its traces in the story of Sarah's abandonment and rescue. This editing was done after the insertion of the Priestly writing and thus after the concentration of the whole narrative context on the ancestral father. This layer is interested in softening and, by clarification, adjusting the meaning of the scandalous features of the stories that the older texts had deliberately inserted as prophetic critique of their own ranks (cf. 16:10).

It is likely that the information inserted in v. 1 about the stages of the journey to Gerar belongs to this redaction. But it is blatantly clear in v. 4:

> But Abimelech did not approach her. *And he said:* "My lord, will you destroy a nation even if it is just? *Did he not say to me: 'She is my sister!'?* And she, she too said: 'He is my brother!' I have done this with a pure heart and clean hands!" (20:4-5; the basic text is in italics)

With the insistence that the king did not come near Sarah the scandalous possibility of adultery is written out of the story. Abimelech locates the problem on a general level: He inquires about God's justice, which must, after all, distinguish between the righteous and the guilty! This theme was treated by the same layer in Gen 18:23-33 with reference to the inhabitants of Sodom. God's answer there was clear: God would not destroy a single righteous person. If there should be one in the city, that person was removed before the judgment (Genesis 19). Abimelech is guiltless. He acted in good conscience and according to his best knowledge. Not only the husband, but also the wife had lied to him, telling him a falsehood about their supposed sibling relationship. Both are quoted directly. The foreign ruler has been deceived; God must take that into account.

To protect God from the suspicion of not being able to know what had happened in Abimelech's house, v. 6 emphasizes that God not only knows there was no adultery, but it was God who protected Abimelech from it. In v. 7 God's demand is expanded to the extent that now it is not simply giving back the wife that will protect against death, but Abraham, who in God's speech has now been advanced to the rank of prophet, must pray for Abimelech. This very insertion in v. 7, placed between the demand for restitution of the woman and the conditional promise of life connected with it, makes the seam obvious. The older narrative has been altered, but it does not lose its value!

The inclusion of the people in the fate of their king (v. 4) provokes the expansion of v. 8 into a scene of morning awakening. Abimelech summons everyone in his capital city and tells them of the night's events. The men's reaction is like that of the ship's crew in the book of Jonah: They are very much afraid (cf. Jon 1:6-16).

The king's demand for an explanation is also expanded with a second speech that, all the same, does not introduce any new line of thought. Verse 10 (much like 16:9, 10) contains a complete introduction to the speech, even though Abimelech has not been interrupted. The question allows the king to inquire whether the guilt lies with himself. Correspondingly, Abraham's explanation is also expanded (vv. 12-13). He says that the brother-sister relationship the couple had claimed is in fact the truth, since Sarah is his half-sister. In this way not only the scandal of adultery, but the further scandal of lying is done away with. Moreover, the personal declaration, now become a half truth, is presented as a general survival strategy on the part of the couple. Everywhere they travel, Sarah is supposed to say, as a kindness to her husband, "He is my brother!" In line with the direct quotation in v. 5, the lie is now also placed on the lips of the woman. The sibling relationship is formulated by her, not by her husband (cf. Gen 12:13, 19; 20:5). Sarah has thus moved from the role of victim to that of an active participant. The edited version of Genesis 20 is thus no longer a narrative of abandonment. It has become a narrative of preservation, since God has guaranteed the immunity of Sarah and Abraham from the beginning (cf. v. 6).

All the same, the introduction of the backward reference in v. 13 sounds odd. Elohim is said to have caused Abraham to "wander" from his father's house! Both the words used and the plural form are disturbing. Is the so-called election of Abraham (12:1) being paraphrased here and attributed to (several?) Elohim (gods)? The Samaritan Pentateuch at this point already smoothed the text into the singular. Then the wanderings seem to refer to the stages of abiding in foreign lands that make this false declaration "necessary."

The last addition by the redaction is found in vv. 16, 17a. Corresponding to the double quotation of husband and wife (v. 5), now not only is Abraham addressed and excused, but Sarah as well. In the dream-revelation God had made Abimelech's life depend not only on his giving back the woman, but also on the prayer of the prophetic bearer of the promise. So now a notice of the fulfillment of this instruction precedes the healing. Only then does God intervene on behalf of Abimelech. The restoration of fertility to the house of Abimelech is evidence that the prayer has been heard!

Much like the redaction in Genesis 16, that in Genesis 20 has introduced features into the original story that are not only foreign to the basic story but are even contrary to it. Nevertheless, the traces of redaction are not entirely erased; the disruptions remain, and it seems that some of them were deliberately left obvious (e.g., repeated introductions to speeches). The intentions of the old narratives peek through, like paintings that have been partly painted over. The redaction of Genesis 20 has primarily pedagogical purposes. The ancestors of Israel became, in the later tradition, figures to identify with and models of the path of faith. Especially in the case of Abraham this process, because of the binding of Isaac, the Akedah (Genesis 22), is especially powerful. The fact that an alteration of the sense was undertaken just here, in Genesis 20, had well-considered grounds. The (older) version of Gen 12:10-20, which in principle worked with the same narrative material and had Pharaoh as the foreign king, was sharpened in the canonical final text because later the people had endured the most massive oppression from the court of the Pharaoh (Exodus 1–14). Genesis 26 tells a toothless story in which Rebecca is never separated from Isaac. The very prominent placement of Genesis 20 between the announcement of the birth and its fulfillment, on the other hand, gave rise to special efforts to smooth out the offensive features. After all, the faith-filled patriarch could not be so careless as to gamble, by abandoning his wife, with the affirmation, just received, of the fulfillment of what he had longed for all his life!

11. Isaac, the son who makes them laugh

In Gen 18:14 Yhwh had announced another visit after a year; at that time Sarah would have a son. The announcement of a birth within a year's time is repeated from Gen 17:21. After such an announcement in both Genesis 17 and Genesis 18, one would expect an extensive narrative of the birth, concluding with the return of the guest to make sure that what he promised has been accomplished.

Instead, Gen 21:1-7 gives a brief account of the fulfillment of the promise of a son. The older narrative from Genesis 18 is continued only in Sarah's joyful reaction to this late birth; the guest does not return. Genesis 21:1-7 reads like a notice of fulfillment both of Genesis 17 and of Genesis 18:

> YHWH remembered Sarah, as he had said. And YHWH did for Sarah as he had promised. Sarah became pregnant and bore Abraham a son for his old age, at the time God had announced to him. And Abraham called the name of his son, who was born to him, whom Sarah bore to him, "Isaac." And Abraham circumcised his son Isaac when he was eight days old, as God had commanded him. Now Abraham was a hundred years old when his son Isaac was born. (Gen 21:1-5)

First comes YHWH's action on behalf of Sarah, which is twice emphasized. The use of the divine name as well as the concentration on the woman show that this verse is connected to Gen 18:15. The backward reference to Elohim's announcement to Abraham in v. 2b, the naming of the child by his father, the circumcision on the eighth day, and the reference to the father's age at the time of the birth are all to be read as the resolution of the word of God to Abraham in Genesis 17. The section in vv. 2b-5 never tires of emphasizing that Abraham is the father of the child and Isaac is *his* son. Thus it is obvious that the passage was never located anywhere but after Genesis 20. The seven suffixes that relate Isaac to Abraham exclude as clearly as possible any notion that Abimelech, for example, could be the father of the child.

In v. 3 the father names the child, without giving any further explanation of the name. In vv. 6-7 the mother does it, although not, as we would have expected, with a reference to her laughter when the birth was announced.

> Then Sarah said: "God has made laughter for me! All who hear of it will laugh for me." And she said: "Who would have said to Abraham: 'Sarah will nurse children!'? And yet I have borne a son for him in his old age!" (Gen 21:6-7)

Sarah expresses her joy over the late birth, one that was no longer possible in human terms.[40] Her joy is infectious. Not only she can laugh after a life of infertility, but all who hear this joyful message can laugh with her. If

---

40. May, "Saras Lachen," 36–37, interprets the laughter as praise of God.

anyone had conceived the idea that she could possibly give birth, he or she would have been laughed at. But now the unbelievable thing has happened. Sarah, at her great age, has borne a child for her old husband! Sarah's double speech expresses nothing, absolutely *nothing* of a laughter born of shame. The idea that one would be ashamed to give birth so late,[41] because it lays bare the taboo of sexuality in old age, is the product of a culture hostile to children, old people, and sexuality; there is no basis for it in the text. Ancient Israel was unreservedly positive toward children. Offspring were always a blessing. How much more when this is a son of the promise, awaited throughout a long life!

12. *"Drive out this servant woman and her son!"*

Two traditions are connected, in the Torah, with the firstborn.[42] The *firstborn child of every woman,* according to the cultic law concerning firstlings ("everything that opens the womb" cf. Exod 34:19-20), must be redeemed before YHWH. The *firstborn of the man* receives preference in the law of inheritance over his younger brothers (Deut 21:17). Sons of free (principal) wives have the right of inheritance. The offspring of a free man with slave women, according to the notions of law in the ancient Near East, must be acknowledged as sons by the legator in order to be able to make any claim to inheritance.

The son born to Sarah through divine intervention is not Abraham's firstborn. That precedence belongs—at least according to the Priestly writing's presentation—to Ishmael, whom the slave Hagar bore *for* Abraham. But the story of the second explusion of Hagar from her master's house, Gen 21:8-21, also presupposes the acceptance of Ishmael as Abraham's legitimate son.

Genesis 21 is a double tradition with Genesis 16 (just as Genesis 20 doubles 12:10-20). Both stories tell of the separation of Hagar and her son from the ancestral couple. In Genesis 16 Hagar flees from her severe mistress of her own volition. In Genesis 21 she is driven out with her son. So that this story can be told, in Gen 16:9 Hagar is given an order to return. Thus she is brought back into the house of the ancestral couple and bears her son there. When Sarah herself bears a son in her old age, the problem arises: Sarah's son is in the position of the second-born.

---

41. Thus, for example, the argument of Hermann Gunkel, *Genesis,* 227: "... the old woman is ashamed to have become a mother."

42. For the firstborn and the law of inheritance see Fischer, *Erzeltern,* 104–11. Daughters normally did not inherit within their own families because of the patrilocal form of marriage. If a family had no male progeny, the inheritance passed to the daughters (cf. the rule on behalf of Mahlah, Noah, Hoglah, Milcah, and Tirzah, the daughters of Zelophehad in Num 27:1-11; 36:1-12).

As the toddler grows and is weaned, Abraham gives a great feast in honor of the mother and child (21:8). On this occasion Sarah sees the son of the Egyptian Hagar, whom she had borne to Abraham, laughing (21:9; see the synopsis in the next section for the text). Hagar and Ishmael are not portrayed here as dependent on Sarah, and Sarah does not speak of "my slave," but rather of "this servant woman," and by the use of the demonstrative pronoun indicates something demeaning about the status of Hagar in relation to Abraham and within the family.[43] The express statement that the son was born for the paternal ancestor indicates his claim to inheritance as the oldest.

The fact that Ishmael takes part in the feast "laughing" is frequently interpreted, in the history of exegesis, as something against the boy. He must have done something that displeased Sarah.[44] Isaac's name echoes in the behavior of Hagar's son (מצחק—יצחק). Is what Sarah is seeing the laughing superiority of the firstborn? At any rate, it is clear to her from Ishmael's behavior that her son will not be the principal heir. Therefore, after seeing this, she demands that Abraham drive out "this servant woman and her son," for the son "of this servant woman" shall not inherit with her son, Isaac. On Sarah's lips Ishmael has no relationship to his father, and Hagar—as before in Genesis 16—has no name, but again only a subordinate social status. Ishmael is exclusively the son of this servant woman. But Isaac, too, according to Sarah's words, is not Abraham's son; he is *her* son. Sarah's representation of the situation is biased. If Ishmael is recognized as a son, and there can be no doubt of it if he was born *for* Abraham, he is the principal heir.[45] It is not Ishmael who inherits with Isaac, but the other way around. The second-born has the lesser claim!

In Gen 21:8-21 we can show the presence of the same level of redaction that had already intervened, in Gen 16:10 and Genesis 20B, to present

43. For the distinction between slave woman and servant woman (אמה/שפחה) see the section "Personenrecht für Unfreie" in Fischer, *Erzeltern*, 90–103. The slave woman is in the lowest social position; the servant woman is one rung higher (here I am following Karen Engelken, *Frauen im alten Israel*. BWANT 130 [Stuttgart: Kohlhammer, 1990] 185). "Servant woman" describes in Genesis an unfree woman who has children with a patriarch, if her status within the family is given. As such, however, she does not leave her position as slave of the wife (cf. *Erzeltern*, 91–97).

44. Thus, for example, the Luther translation: "doing mischief." The Septuagint already inserts "with Isaac, her son," and thus causes it to appear that Sarah's son was being harmed by Hagar's child. Milton Schwantes, "'Lege deine Hand nicht an das Kind,'" in Frank Crüsemann, et al., eds., *Was ist der Mensch? FS Hans Walter Wolff* (Munich: Kaiser, 1992) 164–78, at 170, also starts his interpretation, which is worthy of consideration, from the root צחק: "He makes himself such, i.e., in light of v. 10, the heir."

45. Arie Troost, "Reading for the Author's Signature: Genesis 21.1-21 and Luke 15.11-32 as Intertexts," in *Feminist Companion to Genesis*, 251–72, at 263, interprets differently: The two sons do not inherit together; each inherits through the mother. The promise to Hagar (21:18) will guarantee Ishmael's inheritance.

a more favorable picture of the ancestral couple. The section in 21:11-13 is part of the same strand. We will speak below of how this strand alters the basic narrative; first I would like to describe the original narrative and its intention.

In the basic narrative Abraham obeys Sarah's command immediately, on the morning after the weaning festival (v. 14). He drives out the woman who had borne him his first son, and the son with her. The patriarch sends mother and son out with a measly day's ration. The narrator makes the harshness of Abraham's action clear by contrasting what is done for the two mothers and their sons: a sumptuous banquet of food and wine for Sarah and Isaac, and for Hagar and Ishmael only as much bread and water as a woman with a child in arms can carry. The principal heir and the mother of the firstborn truly deserved a different compensation! The sequence of narrative verbs in v. 14a, all of them with Abraham as subject, emphasizes the activity of the man in the expulsion. The ancestral father now, for the second time, casually abandons Hagar and their child, thus disowning his son.

This time Hagar does not leave the house of her oppression of her own accord, but is driven out against her will.[46] She does not find a watering hole as she had when she fled (16:7), but wanders aimlessly in the wilderness. When the waterskin is empty, both the expelled refugees are facing death from thirst. The child is affected first. Hagar places him under a bush to protect him from the burning sun. Then she goes and sits down at a distance. The mother cannot bear to see the child die.[47] She lifts up her voice and wails (vv. 15-16). While the events up to her expulsion were marked by superfluity and festival, as well as activity, now every action comes to a stop. The narrator describes a single scene in the utmost detail and thus paints the scenery of death in the darkest colors. Hagar can do nothing more for her son; she can only wait for his death.

The reversal comes unexpectedly. God hears the voice of the child, who is crying with thirst. An angel of God speaks to Hagar from heaven, calling her by name. In the form of the oracle of salvation, "Fear not!" he assures her that God has heard the boy where he lies, where she had thought he would die. Although v. 16 only reported Hagar's lamenting, here it is twice emphasized that God hears the voice of the boy (שָׁמַע). There is a clear allusion to Ishmael's saving name (יִשְׁמָעֵאל). According to Genesis 16, YHWH heard the mother in her oppression, thus suggesting the naming of the child in gratitude: Ishmael already bears a name signifying that God hears him!

Every action Hagar did when she expected her child to die is now reversed. The messenger tells her to get up, pick up the child, and take him

---

46. Wacker, "Hagar," 26, 29 emphasizes this difference.

47. Annemarie Ohler, *Mutterschaft in der Bibel* (Würzburg: Echter, 1992) 88 points to the correspondence of רָאָה, see, in v. 9 and v. 16.

by the hand. Hagar, who had been entirely sunk in the passivity forced on her by the situation, is to become active. The threat of death is ended; now the rescued child has a great future before him. God will make of him a great nation (v. 18b). The rescue is not only for the moment; it is promised to run deeply into Ishmael's future.

The messenger makes the resolution of the immediate crisis possible by opening Hagar's eyes (v. 19). She sees a spring, goes to it, fills her water-skin, and gives the boy a drink. The tension set up when the water in the skin was exhausted is resolved. Now it is full again, and life can continue!

The narrator makes a quick time-lapse fade, jumping years ahead. The boy grows up, and God is with him. When he is grown, he settles in the wilderness of Paran. Hagar takes a wife for him from her own people and marries Ishmael to an Egyptian woman.

Genesis 16 was the rescue narrative of a woman who had been oppressed. Hagar had fled of her own accord and put an end to her oppression. The messenger who met her at the well had legitimated her flight by his gracious word. Why, then, is a similar story told again, sharpening the situation in many respects and also accepting that by this means a story of rescue would be reinterpreted as a story of oppression? What is the underlying purpose when Hagar is now driven out against her will, her son disinherited, and the rejection without sustenance escalates to a threat of death? What group is addressed when the ancestral couple is portrayed as inhuman, as people who, by disowning Ishmael, have also violated their own law? Genesis 21 is also a story of rescue, but God only rescues the barest remaining minimum of life at the last minute and does not set aside the life-threatening crisis. Such a message was directed at the people during the exile. In order to deal with the catastrophe of the destruction of the city and Temple and their own exile, they had to admit that the sin was to be sought in their own ranks. Inhuman exploitation of the socially marginal, which contradicted Yhwh's concept of a blessed life in the land, had to have consequences. That the eruption of such a catastrophe also destroyed the lives of many innocent people is in the tragic nature of such events. God not only rescues from threat, but even through catastrophe.

But Genesis 21:8-21 was not conceived as an individual text. It has a partner: Genesis 22, the so-called "sacrifice of Isaac." Only the two texts taken together yield the message of the ancestral narratives for the people of the exile.

13. "Sacrifice your son, your only son!"

Abraham had casually driven his older son away (Gen 21:14). Now only Isaac remains to him. He is the only one he loves; he is Isaac, the son of the lifelong awaited promise. Now God, with his command of sacrifice in Genesis 22, reaches out to take this child, the token of the divine promise. Abraham is presented with the resumé of his life. He has abandoned every human being who was close to him: Sarah, when she was young and beautiful, in Egypt (Gen 12:10-20), and Sarah again as an aging woman, at the time when she had been promised pregnancy and birth within a year (Genesis 20). Hagar he had given into the hands of his oppressive wife (Genesis 16) and hunted her out of the house without any provision, because Sarah wanted it that way for her son. He had thus placed mother and son in danger of death (Gen 21:8-21). The only one he has not yet abandoned is Isaac. Abraham is old, beyond the biological possibility of having other children. Hence all his hopes for the future rest on Isaac. Now it is this son whom God demands of Abraham, as a sacrifice to God.

The test to which God puts the patriarch is not whether he will now betray the last not-yet-abandoned person in his near vicinity. In Genesis 22 the issue is not Isaac; it is Abraham. The death of an old man means the expiration of his life. If God wants to attack Abraham himself, he must attack his only future, Isaac. With the command to sacrifice, God tests Abraham to see if he is ready to do to himself what he has already done to every person around him.

God does not desire human sacrifice. The narrator makes that clear in the first verse. This is a test. The readers may hope from the outset that the sacrifice will be averted. But if Abraham were to refuse, nothing at all would happen to the son. Genesis 22, in its original intent, did not tell about the fate of Isaac, but rather, as the narrator emphasizes at the beginning and end (vv. 1, 12), about the testing of the promise-bearer, Abraham.[48]

This interpretation of Genesis 22 is closely connected to the narratives of abandonment and the Hagar stories. That this is not an accidental association, but a deliberate intention, is shown by the text of Gen 21:8-21, which is similar both in its choice of words and in its narrative structure. In order to make the argumentation easier to follow I will place the two texts side by side in the form of a synopsis, with the parallel passages in bold and the later editing marked by square brackets:

---

48. For the discussion of Genesis 22 and a more extensive analysis of the common features of Genesis 22 and 21 see Irmtraud Fischer, "Möglichkeiten und Grenzen historisch-kritischer Exegese: Die 'Opferung' der beiden Söhne Abrahams," in Ansgar Franz, ed., *Streit am Tisch des Wortes?* PiLi 8 (St. Ottilien: EOS Verlag, 1997) 17–36.

Genesis 21

8 The child grew and was weaned. On the day when Isaac was weaned, Abraham made a great feast. 9 And Sarah saw the son of Hagar, the Egyptian, whom she had borne to Abraham, laughing.
10 Then she said to Abraham: "**Cast out** that servant woman there with her son! For the son of this servant woman shall not inherit with **my son, Isaac!**" [11 It was evil, very evil in Abraham's eyes because of his son. 12 Then God said to Abraham: "Let it not be evil in your eyes because of the boy and because of your servant woman! In everything Sarah says to you, listen to her voice! For from Isaac shall offspring be named for you. 13 But also the son of the servant woman will I make to be a nation, for he is your offspring."]
14 **And Abraham rose in the morning,**

took bread and a skin with water and gave it to Hagar, **laid** it on her shoulder—with the child—and sent her away. And she **went** and wandered in the wilderness (of Beersheba).

Genesis 22

1 And it happened after these things: God tested Abraham. And he said to him: "Abraham!" And he answered: "Here I am!"

2 And he said: "**Take your son,** your only son, whom you love, **Isaac,** and go to the land of Moria and sacrifice him there as a burnt offering on one of the mountains that I will tell you!"

3 **And Abraham rose in the morning,** saddled his donkey, took two servant men and Isaac, his son. And he split the wood for the offering and rose and went to the place God had told him. 4 On the third day Abraham lifted up his eyes and saw the place in the **distance.** 5 Then Abraham said to his servants: "Stay here with the donkey! I and the boy will go on farther and worship and then return to you!" 6 And Abraham **took** the wood for the sacrifice and **laid** it on Isaac, his son. And he took the fire and the knife in his hand. So the two **went** together. 7 And Isaac spoke to Abraham, his father. And he said: "My father!" And he said: "Here I am, my son!" And he said: "See, the fire, the knife, but where is the lamb for the burnt offering?" 8 And Abraham said: "God will provide the lamb for the burnt offering, my son!" So the two went on together.

15 When the waterskin was empty, she laid the child under one of the bushes. 16 And she went and sat down alone nearby, a bowshot **distant,** for she said: "I cannot behold the death of the child!" So she sat opposite and lifted up her voice and wailed.
17 But God heard the voice of the boy, **and the messenger of God called to Hagar from heaven, and he said to**

her: "What is wrong, **Hagar? Do not** fear!

For God has heard the voice of the boy, there where he is. 18 Stand up, take up the boy, and take him by the *hand!* For I will make him a great nation!"
19 And God opened her **eyes,** and she **saw** a well.

And she **went,** and she filled the skin with water and gave it to the boy to drink.
20 And God was with the boy, and he grew up and settled in the wilderness and became an archer.

21 He **settled** in the wilderness of Paran. And his mother took for him a wife from the land of Egypt.

9 And they came to the place that God had told him of; and Abraham built an altar there, piled the wood on it, bound Isaac, his son, and laid him on the altar, on top of the wood. 10 And he stretched out his *hand* and took the knife to slaughter his son.

11 **And the messenger of Y**HWH **called to him from heaven, and said: "Abraham! Abraham!"** And he said: "Here I am!"
12 And he said: "**Do not** stretch out your *hand* against the boy, and do nothing to him! **For** now I know that you fear God! You have not withheld from me your son, your only son!"

13 And Abraham lifted up his **eyes** and **saw.** And see, a ram was caught in the bushes there. And Abraham **went,** took the ram, and sacrificed it as a burnt offering in place of his son.

14 And Abraham called the name of the place "Y HWH sees." As they say even today: "On the mountain where Y HWH let himself be seen."
[15 And Y HWH's messenger called to Abraham a second time from heaven. 16 And he said: "By myself I swear— word of Y HWH—for while you have done this and have not withheld from me your son, your only son, 17 there-fore I bless, yes, I bless you; I will in-crease, yes, increase your offspring like the stars of heaven and like the sand on the shore of the sea. And your offspring will inherit the gates of their enemies. 18 And through your offspring the nations of the earth will bless you, for this reason, because you listened to my voice."]
19 And Abraham went back to his servants, and they arose, and they went together to Beersheba. And Abraham **settled** in Beersheba.

Both texts tell of the separation from a son. While the first was casually driven away, the second must be sacrificed with a heavy heart. Isaac, in both texts, is the son to whom the ancestral couple have a close tie (21:10; 22:2). Both times there is a challenge to the father to separate from one of his sons. In Gen 21:10 the command comes from Sarah, in Gen 22:2 from God. Both times, Abraham obeys what is said to him. The very next morning he gets up (21:14; 22:3) and makes preparations. The separation is introduced by the same sequence of actions: taking (לקח), loading (שִֹים עַל־), and going (הלך) (21:14a; 22:6, 9). In each case one parent goes with the child who must leave the home. Hagar is driven out with her son; Abraham must accomplish the separation himself, through the sacrifice. Both sons are threatened with death. In this situation, both times, the parent is alone with the child. While Hagar cannot look at the death of her boy and sets herself at a distance from him, Abraham sees the place of sacrifice from afar with a resolute eye (ראה, רחק: 21:16; 22:4). At the moment when death is imminent, when Ishmael is about to die of thirst and Isaac lies bound on the altar, an angel of God appears from heaven and addresses the parent by name (21:17; 22:11). The messenger's speech consists of a negative command (in the jussive) followed by an explanation (21:17; 22:12). The liberation from the threat of death is accomplished through Hagar and Abraham's seeing, followed by going (21:19; 22:13); by these actions they make possible the survival of their children. Both narratives close with a notice about settling in a place (21:21; 22:19).

So many common features in two narratives within the immediate context cannot be accidental. The two texts are planned as twins and, as such, they tell of the threatened deaths of Abraham's two sons. Genesis 21 is anything but a comforting story.[49] Only someone who trivializes female experience can read it that way. It is true that Hagar is neither self-guided nor acting under divine orders. Her suffering is rooted in the hard-hearted action of Sarah in driving her out, and in the miserable provision provided by Abraham. She and her son are victims of the ancestral couple's machinations. For Abraham the journey to the place of sacrifice is the testing of his life. In his social and family connections he has shown himself to be a man who would take the line of least resistance, at the expense of others. But he has believed his God to the letter, against all his mature experience of life. Now God tests whether the ancient patriarch can bring "faith and works" into harmony. Abraham passes the test. And God rescues what is now his only son, the one he loves, Isaac, just as God had rescued his expelled firstborn. But God does not rescue *from* danger; the rescue comes

---

49. As, for example, in Gunkel's interpretation (*Genesis*, 228) or that of Blum (*Komposition*, 314), who sees some common features in the narratives but regards Genesis 21 as a "practice run" for Genesis 22.

in the time of most intense threat. Thus the testing becomes for Abraham an opportunity to bring his love for God and neighbor into agreement by his readiness to take upon himself what he had demanded of his two wives.

Genesis 22 is exclusively about the testing of Abraham. There is not a word about Sarah, even though it was she who had called for the expulsion of Hagar and her son. But Sarah has already been tested. She was twice abandoned and has already lived through the danger of being cut off from the current of life. God had taken her part and rescued her. Therefore Sarah need not be tested. But it is also *her* son who is in danger of suffering death because she had behaved as inhumanly to Hagar and Ishmael as Abraham did.

For the people of the exilic generation the message of these twin texts was, on the one hand, a critique of an unsolidary life that had led to catastrophe. On the other hand, there is encouragement here. The author of the two texts wrote for escapees who had not been preserved *from* the collapse of all the bases of their lives, but *in* that collapse. And both stories encourage the people to hold fast to God, even when God does not preserve from the danger of death and is responsible for things that are incompatible with the saving God of Israel: God does not test beyond endurance. Through and beyond catastrophe, God holds to God's promises!

14. God tests the righteous

These twin texts were expanded by a hand that was already visible in Gen 16:10; 18:17-21*, and in the redactional layer in Genesis 20. The author of this layer is polishing the image of the ancestral father. The theological problems have changed. In his time people are no longer asking whether the loss of the promised goods of the land and the great nation was a result of unrighteous living. The questions now at issue were about the suffering of the righteous. The dramatic stories about Abraham offered the best points of reference for treating this new set of questions. The accents simply had to be applied somewhat differently.

In the postexilic period Abraham became increasingly a model of faith. The high-theological texts of the exilic layer (12:1-4a; 21:8-21; 22) cooperated decisively in beginning this development of tradition. The reinterpretations undertaken with respect to the final major layer of the Abraham-Sarah cycle, however, should not be seen as falsifications of the original intent of the texts. Instead, they are a witness to the vitality of the message of earlier generations. The late author updated the traditional written material, which by now was already binding, for his own time. He writes with didactic purpose: Abraham is to be the great model for those in his generation who seek God.

The basic narrative in Genesis 21, much like that in Genesis 20, draws a critical picture of the ancestral couple. In order to make the text service-able for his intentions, the editor therefore inserted vv. 11-13 immediately after Sarah's demand. The ancestral father is troubled about his son (not, however, about Hagar!). Sarah's words are entirely despicable in his eyes. Therefore a divine speech is necessary in order to persuade him that even his ejection of the mother and child will not put an end to God's concern for them. Unlike Abraham, God also has the servant woman in mind, al-though her name is not mentioned (v. 12a). God agrees with Sarah and ap-proves her command to drive them out. But at the moment when the patriarch is threatened with losing sight of Ishmael forever, God assures him that God will make him, too, a great nation *because* he is Abraham's son. But the line of the promise will continue with Isaac. He is the heir, as Sarah has recognized. In v. 14b the editor adds "of Beersheba" after "wilderness." He thus has Hagar wandering in a region that, it is clear from the outset, is not waterless. Anyone who reads to the end of the chap-ter (21:22-34) realizes that Ishmael was rescued from dying of thirst by water from the well his father had dug.

These insertions into the basic narrative make a crucial alteration in the original message. The ancestral couple are no longer harsh people who cast out the firstborn for reasons bound up with family politics. Sarah's will re-ceives divine sanction, and Abraham shows strong feelings for Ishmael. The expulsion of the two is part of the divine plan of salvation, in which Ishmael is not forgotten. The father receives a promise on behalf of this son, and only after that does he send Hagar and Ishmael out of the house. The drama of Hagar's aimless wandering is dissipated by the description of the landscape as "the wilderness of Beersheba." Readers of the canonical final text see this as already a signal of divine protection. In order that Ish-mael need not die of thirst close by his father's well, Hagar's eyes, which had been prevented from seeing, are opened. The promise for the son that is given to the mother sounds like a repetition (vv. 13, 18; cf. 17:20).

The editor has thus deprived the characters in the basic narrative of their edge. God promises support to both sons even before they are in peril. God's rescuing the boy from dying of thirst is the fulfillment of the promise to Abraham that persuaded the patriarch to separate from Ishmael.

In Genesis 22 the editor inserts a second speech by the angel, vv. 15-18. In this way Abraham's passing the test becomes the basis of his exalted position in both Jewish and Christian tradition. He is the father of faith, having himself withstood such a great temptation. What Abraham had been prepared to do effects blessing through all generations, as the promise is renewed because of the merits of the ancestral father. However, Abraham's listening to the voice of God not only has a saving effective-ness for *his* nation; through it, it is effective for *all the nations* of the earth.

Because he attended to God's instructions, the promises are passed to his son, Isaac (cf. 26:5). Thus for the people of the post-exilic epoch Abraham also became a model for keeping the Torah.

Genesis 22 is a much-disputed narrative, even in its final form. The massive challenges posed to the image of God, especially since the European Enlightenment, and to Abraham's unquestioning and obedient faith, have not fallen silent even in our own time. The story is scandalous, and the best explanation dare not render it harmless. The vitality of this text lies precisely in this, that throughout its entire history it has evoked resistance, while also offering the possibility of identification with it. In the most gruesome epochs of the persecution of Jews, for which Christians are responsible, this inconvenient narrative was especially fruitful.[50] Jews were able to interpret their own history of horrors in light of Isaac, who was bound and then released, and in spite of the necessity of refusing to make peace with the horror they could go on living with and toward their God. The challenges to the "binding of Isaac," as Judaism calls the story— more accurately than the Christian designation "the sacrifice of Isaac"— therefore have their clear limits where they become anti-Jewish polemic against a cruel God in the Hebrew Bible!

15. A grave for Sarah

The burial place of the ancestral couple in Hebron, revered to this day, can be derived from biblical tradition. The tradition, however, is not ancient. Ancient Israel, in distinction from the cults in its environs, had a difficult time with graves as memorial places. Hence they retained only a few ancient burial traditions, and they are all places honoring the memory of important women. Rachel's tomb near Bethlehem and Miriam's grave in Kadesh are among these traditions.

The burial site of the ancestral couple in the cave of Machpelah near Mamre played no role in the ancient texts. When Genesis gives the impression that a succession of patriarchs and their wives were buried there (cf. 25:9-10; 35:27-29; 46:29-32), that is the work of the redaction associated with the combining of the Priestly texts with the older traditions.[51]

---

50. On this see the collected volume edited by Willem Zuidema, *Isaak wird wieder geopfert* (Neukirchen-Vluyn: Neukirchener Verlag, 1987).

51. The arguments against associating Genesis 23 with **P** have been collected by Blum, *Komposition,* 441–46. In my opinion Genesis 23 should be linked with Genesis 24. Cf. being a foreigner among the Canaanites (23:4; 24:3), the exhaustiveness of the negotiations and the reference to Sarah's death in 24:67. Genesis 23 takes place at the gate, the men's meeting place and the place for legal business, Genesis 24 at the well, where the women congregate. Also the words "speak" and "answer" (דבר, ענה), relatively rare in Genesis 12ff., with which conversations are introduced in both these texts, favor this. Probably the identifications of the various place names in vv. 2 and 19 can also be traced to the latest layer.

> Sarah lived one hundred twenty-seven years. And she died in Kiriath-arba, that is, Hebron, in the land of Canaan. Then Abraham buried his wife Sarah in the cave in the field of Machpelah near Mamre, that is, Hebron, in the land of Canaan. (Gen 23:1-2a, 19)

By her death notice Sarah is brought to the forefront of all the ancestral women of Israel. The Priestly writing, with its interest in life-dating, here gives an indication of her age. In the second and third generation only the ages of the patriarchs are given.

The place of Sarah's death also becomes her burial place. Abraham negotiates with the men resident in the place about the purchase of a cave. The grave is not to match his status as a foreigner. He does not want to use any of the grave-places of the inhabitants of Canaan, but to buy the land in which the grave will be located in regular fashion. Thus the grave becomes the first piece of land that belongs to the ancestral couple as heritable property. The first burial there is that of the ancestral woman. Read in the context of Genesis 12–23, this means that Sarah, by her death, becomes the first heir of the promise of the land.

Chapter Three

Rebecca:
A Strong Woman With a Colorless Husband

1. A woman in the male family tree

From the beginning of the story of the ancestral couple, Sarah and Abraham, threads are woven into the narrative to connect to the genealogy of their family remaining behind in the East: Abraham had a brother named Nahor who married Milcah, one of the daughters of Haran (Gen 11:29).[1] Toward the end of the story of Sarah and Abraham the family tree of these related couples is given (22:20-24), introduced and concluded by notes on Milcah's childbearing (vv. 20b, 23b). Of the eight sons she bore to Nahor, interest falls on the last, named Bethuel. With him the genealogy is lengthened into the next generation: "Bethuel begot Rebecca" (22:23a).

This is the only statement in the ancestral narratives about the begetting of a *daughter*. Normally such notices are given only for sons.[2] Rebecca is thus emphasized in a most unusual way.[3] If we note also that the readers of Genesis up to this point have been able to take the end of a genealogy as a signal about which person will carry the story onward in the next part[4]

---

1. On this see above, Chapter Two, section 1, n. 2.

2. Cf. the section "Gebär- und Zeugungsnotizen," in Irmtraud Fischer, *Die Erzeltern Israels.* BZAW 22 (Berlin: Walter de Gruyter, 1994).

3. Thus now also Lieve Teugels, "'A Strong Woman, Who Can Find?' A Study of Characterization in Genesis 24, with some Perspectives on the General Presentation of Isaac and Rebekah in the Genesis Narratives," *JSOT* 63 (1994) 89–104, at 91: ". . . the genealogy seems to be specially written to introduce Rebekah."

4. Thus, for example, in Cain's family tree (Gen 4:17-24), concluding with Lamech and then continuing with notes on his life. Likewise the family tree of Seth, ending with the begetting of Noah (Genesis 5), is shaped in the same fashion, as is the line of Shem, concluding with the begetting of Abram and Nahor (Genesis 11).

47

we can see that the notice of Rebecca's begetting creates interest in her story.

However, the family tree of Milcah and Nahor is introduced as news brought to Abraham (22:20a), and the father of the clan, Nahor, is twice mentioned as Abraham's brother (vv. 20b, 23b). Thus the link to Abraham is written into the genealogy from the outset and allows us to conclude that the rest of the story will concern the two people so irregularly emphasized in this family tree, namely Abraham and Rebecca.

2. *The bearer of the promise seeks a daughter-in-law*

Just as the couple had been characterized, before the announcement of the birth of their son, as "old and advanced in years," so now the same is said of Abraham (24:1; cf. 18:11). He is facing an equally crucial event in his life. The ancestral mother, Sarah, has died and been buried (Genesis 23), and her son Isaac is not yet married. If the promise is to continue in him, he must found a family. His father takes over the arrangements (Genesis 24). These are the preconditions for the story that develops out of the hints in the family tree of Milcah and Nahor: Abraham's and Rebecca's paths are drawn together.

Genesis 24:1-9 tells of Abraham's commission to his oldest servant to seek a wife for Isaac. In the canonical final text this introduction to the narrative fulfills a number of functions:

Within the Abraham-Sarah cycle the speech at 24:7-8 is to be read as Abraham's commission.[5] It is his last direct speech before his death (25:8), and thus constitutes a confirmation of the fulfillment of the promise: Abraham is living in the land promised him by God, even though it is not yet his own.[6] He has been blessed in everything (v. 1; cf. 12:2) and has an offspring of his own body. The center of this concentrically constructed section, v. 7, not only refers, in the predicate it gives to YHWH, to the beginning of the narrative cycle, but directly quotes some passages from the text:

> "YHWH, the God of heaven, who took me *from my father's house and from among my relations (cf. 12:1),*[7] and who said and swore to me: *'To your seed I will give this land!' (cf. 12:6)* . . ."

---

5. Winfried Jüngling points out this aspect. He was kind enough to make available to me his manuscript on Genesis 24 from the lecture series *Eating and Drinking* (Frankfurt: SoSe, 1993) 44.

6. Abraham lives in the promised land under the Canaanites (v. 3b), but calls the land of his origins "my country" (v. 4a).

7. The local designations "from my father's house and from among my relations," however, are in reverse order from those in 12:1, where they are found in a challenge within a divine speech. Noteworthy is the subject of Abraham's separation from his family: in 12:1 it is Abraham; in 24:7 (as already before in 20:13) it is God.

In this way a frame is constructed around the ancestral father's life. The first speech to him, which incorporated the divine promises, is confirmed in this confession as having been fulfilled.

Within the ancestral narratives Genesis 24 links the two great narrative cycles surrounding Abraham and Jacob still more closely together and, with this narrative, creates an extensive Rebecca-Isaac cycle.[8]

Within the canonical final text the prohibition of mixed marriages, sustained in the Jacob cycle (cf. 27:46–28:5), points to the program that Ezra (Ezra 9:1-4; 10) and Nehemiah (Neh 13:23-31) attempted to enact, and against which the book of Ruth was probably written. The position adopted by Genesis 24 in this question is that of the absolute priority of the Land[9] over endogamous marriage. Isaac dare not leave the Land,[10] not even to obtain a bride. Therefore the servant takes on the journey to the relations. If the bride should refuse to leave her land and accompany him back to *this land* (vv. 5, 7), the servant is freed from his vow.

The theme of the oath imbues the whole section in vv. 1-9. A demand that he swear an oath introduces the commission to the servant, and his carrying out of what he had promised concludes it. At the center, in v. 7, is Yhwh's oath to give Abraham *this land*. The primary interest of vv. 1-9 is in the choice of the right bride for the son, but still more important is the right land. In essence this means that the right wife for the son is living in the wrong land, and the right land has no right wives for him.[11] The wife Abraham desires for his son must not only come from his own family. She must also be prepared, like Abraham, to leave her family and her land in order to move to *this land*. In this Abraham attributes to the woman the ability to decide, not to her family. He decides for his son. As regards the woman he seeks, he assumes that she will do it—and not her father. Abraham puts the woman on a level with himself, not with her future husband Isaac, for whom the decision is made.

---

8. An earlier literary stage linked the two narrative cycles of the ancestors of South and North by joining the son of the South with the mother of the North into a single couple. Isaac's tradition-historical locus is clearly in the Sarah-Abraham cycle, where his name is repeatedly given an etiological explanation (Gen 18:1-15; 21:6-7). Rebecca, however, was originally associated with the Jacob cycle. Her origin also indicates this. (For tradition-critical questions regarding an independent Isaac cycle see Fischer, *Erzeltern,* 216–23.)

9. For the significance of the land in the ancestral narratives see Erich Zenger, "'Deinen Nachkommen gebe ich dieses Land . . .' (Gen 12,7). Überlegungen zum christlichen Umgang mit den Landverheißungstexten des Ersten Testaments," in Ferdinand Hahn et al., eds., *Zion, Ort der Begegnung. FS Laurentius Klein.* BBB 90 (Bodenheim: Athenäum Hahn Hanstein, 1993) 141–61.

10. An express prohibition on Isaac's leaving the land is found in Gen 26:2.

11. On this see Susanne Bucher-Gillmayr, וְהִנֵּה רִבְקָה יֹצֵאת. *Eine textlinguistische Untersuchung zu Gen 24.* Dissertation, Innsbruck, 1994, 215.

3. Encounter at the well—this time without a bridegroom

In ancient Israel there were a number of ways in which a marriage could come about. The marriage of two young people could be arranged by their families. Or the man could apply to the bride's father for the young woman's hand. And there was also the spontaneous encounter between a woman and a man who fell in love and married. A typical place for such encounters was the well. In ancient Israel if you wanted to meet a man, you went to the city gate; if you wanted to meet a woman, you went to the well, where the women drew water.[12] But in Genesis 24 we do not find a man seeking a bride sitting and waiting at the well, but a servant who seeks a daughter-in-law for his master.

With the assurance that the angel of YHWH will be a companion on the journey (v. 7), and with precious gifts and a great caravan, the servant goes forth (v. 10). That he arrives at the goal of his journey precisely at the time of day when the women come to the well outside the city to draw water is already a stroke of good luck (v. 11). Before the servant carries out his commission he prays to YHWH that his purpose may succeed, asking that God show steadfast love (חסד) for Abraham. He suggests a sign by which God can make the right wife for Isaac known to him. She should be the one who, when asked to give him a drink, also offers to water his camels. Through her (בה) he will know that YHWH will show steadfast love for Abraham. The servant thus expands the demands to be made of the future wife to a further dimension. The criteria are not only the right origins and a readiness to abandon her family. The servant seeks a woman who is prepared to give more than is demanded, one who knows what is lacking and acts where there is need.

> And it happened, even before he had stopped speaking: And see, Rebecca came out, she who was born to Bethuel, the son of Milcah the wife of Nahor, Abraham's brother—with her jar on her shoulder. (Gen 24:15)

The simultaneity of the prayer and the appearance of Rebecca creates the awareness: This is how swiftly YHWH hears the prayers of those who love him! But the servant must still test whether this is true or not.

---

12. For this see, in the next chapter, the meeting between Jacob and Rachel and the encounter between Moses and the priest's daughters. In the NT Jesus' encounter with the Samaritan woman at Jacob's well (John 4) reflects the same scene. There, too, there is talk of the woman's husband. Although she apparently lives in an illegitimate marriage, he does not refuse her *communio*, but reveals himself to her as the Messiah. Susanne Bucher-Gillmayr, "Begegnungen am Brunnen," *BN* 75 (1995) 48–66, thinks to the contrary, that meetings at wells had "an accidental character" (ibid. 65). Esther Fuchs, "Structure, Ideology and Politics in the Biblical Betrothal Type-Scene," in Athalya Brenner, ed., *A Feminist Companion to Genesis* FCB 1/2 (Sheffield: Sheffield Academic Press, 1993) 273–81, reads the encounters of the couples at the well in their canonical sequence and observes a successive diminution of the value and activity of the women. I cannot agree with her notion of the passive, obedient Rebecca (ibid. 275, 279).

Rebecca's daily trek to draw water is presented as an appearance.[13] She is not portrayed (as in v. 14) as a girl who comes out to draw water. Her name is presented as if it must be known to everyone. The presentation with her family tree gives this appearance a solemn note. The genealogical information conforms to 22:22—here again she is linked to Abraham. That she is also very beautiful and still a virgin are facts that make her an ideal bride in the eyes of the readers, who have the advantage of this information before the servant knows it.

The servant takes the initiative and approaches the girl with his request, although he presents it in more modest fashion than in his conversation with YHWH. Rebecca answers: "Drink, my lord!" (24:18). The servant slakes his thirst—and the tension grows. She has not yet said anything about watering the camels! Only when the servant has finished drinking does she speak the words that relieve the tension: "I will also draw for your camels until they finish drinking!" (24:19). With this, Rebecca shows the servant that she is the one he is seeking. She carries out her work to the fullest.[14] Only when she has *entirely* satisfied his thirst does she water *all* his animals, until they, too, have drunk their fill. The servant, as a silent but attentively observant witness, is contrasted with the hard-working woman manipulating the full water jars. Drawing water for household use is women's work. But that the man does not help her as she waters the camels is connected to the fact that he wants to know whether this woman answers his expectations, and whether YHWH is allowing his journey to succeed. When he sees that his own criteria have been fulfilled he gives a gift to the woman, who is still unknown to him, after she has finished her work. The gold ornament is not a payment. It is part of the bridal gifts the servant has brought with him—*she* is the woman *he* has chosen. Only after this does the servant inquire about the conditions desired by his master. He asks the woman's origins and, in order to pursue the matter, invites himself into her house as a guest. The young woman's answer meets both conditions: She comes from the desired family, and she also thinks, with regard to the overnight stay, about fodder and straw for the camels. That is more than the servant could expect.

The encounter began with a prayer, and it concludes with a prayer. While Rebecca runs to her mother's house, the man blesses YHWH, the God of his master Abraham. *He* has chosen Rebecca as the bride![15]

---

13. After the presentation, "and behold!" the inverted verbal clause places the personal name of Rebecca, who is not yet known to the narrative, at the apex.

14. Bucher-Gillmayr, *Gen 24,* 159, and Jüngling, lecture manuscript 68–69, point to this aspect, which is expressed through the repetition of the root כלה, complete, in a word-play with כל, all. (See also what follows.)

15. That is the servant's interpretation in retrospect at 24:44.

4. Rebecca's decision: "I will go!"

A male guest must, for decency's sake, be invited by the master of the house. Laban, Rebecca's brother, hurries out of the city to welcome the generous, rich man to his house. After he has been cared for according to all the rules of hospitality, they are seated at a common meal. But the guest will not eat until he has presented his cause (24:33). Now, for the first time, he reveals the secret of his identity: He is only the servant of his master Abraham, whom YHWH has richly blessed—as is evident already from the gifts he has brought. The man relates the basic facts of Abraham's story that are essential for Rebecca's family to know, ending with his commission to find a bride.[16] Here he alters the exception clause he had negotiated with Abraham when swearing his oath. While his master had allowed it in case the woman herself should refuse to come with him, the servant introduces a doubt about whether the family will give him the bride. The messenger, with his commission, knows who he is talking to and targets his speech accordingly. After a detailed retelling of the events of the day (24:42-48),[17] framed by his account of his own prayers, the servant poses the crucial question. However, it is not formulated as a request for a bride; instead, it is about graciousness and fidelity (חסד ואמת) toward Abraham. The servant thus appeals again to family solidarity. Nevertheless, the answer argues in terms of YHWH's choice, which frames the assent:

> "The matter comes from YHWH. We cannot decide positively or negatively. See, here is Rebecca before you. Take her and go! She shall be the wife of your master's son, as YHWH has spoken!"

When the servant hears these words of submission to God he gives double thanks: first to YHWH, then to the family. He gives his treasures to Rebecca, her brother, and her mother. Only then does the man accept hospitality, eating and drinking with the family.

The servant is in a hurry.[18] The very next morning he asks to be excused. Brother and mother want to keep the bride a few more days, but the servant wants to bring the path YHWH has blessed to a rapid end. So the family lets Rebecca herself decide.

16. This speech, like Gen 24:1-9, is full of allusions to and direct quotations of Genesis 12–24, their sequence attesting to the canonical ordering of the texts: Abraham has been blessed (12:3), has become great (12:2), possesses wealth in the form of herds, servants, and precious metals (12:6; 13:2). Sarah has borne him a son even in his old age (21:7), who will be the sole heir (cf. 21:10-13). Finally, the speech ends with a paraphrase of 24:1-9.

17. For the technique of looking back through subsequent narrative as well as the minute differences in the servant's retelling see chs. 4 and 5 in Bucher-Gillmayr, *Gen 24*.

18. The whole story is shot through with haste: "run" and "hurry" are key words in the scenes that take place outside the Land. Haste in hospitality is also emphasized in the scene with guests in Genesis 18.

Then they called Rebecca and said: "Will you go with this man?" And she said: "I will go!" (24:58)

The question Rebecca so decisively answers is not just about the time of her departure; as agreed with Abraham, it also contains her assent. With her simple and clear "I will go!" Rebecca puts herself alongside her future father-in-law.[19] He, too, answered the call from YHWH to leave his country and his family with sober action: "And Abram went, as YHWH had said to him" (12:4a).

The family cannot resist such a firm life-decision. It releases its daughter with a blessing:

"Our sister,
you will become a thousandfold multitude!
May your seed inherit the gates of those who hate him!" (24:60)

This saying ties Rebecca's past and future together: It emphasizes the enduring relational bond and wishes fertility for the bride. The formula "your seed" (זרעך) is unusual for a woman and—corresponding to the "begetting" passage in 22:23—normally only stands for the offspring of a man, since in patrilineal genealogies origins are traced through the father. But this blessing of the bride traces the children from their mother. Here the root of the narrative thread that will be continued with Jacob in the same house is woven in. The son, defined by his mother, will present himself in Laban's house (29:12). But the readers of the canonical final text perceive something else as well: through the wish that her seed may inherit the gates of the enemies, Rebecca is presented as the heir of the promise to Abraham (cf. 22:17).[20]

The departure for the journey back to the Land is reported first from Rebecca's point of view and that of her maidservants (24:61a), then from that of the servant, who takes Rebecca and goes. The man, who is traveling under divine guidance, *takes* the woman YHWH has chosen, just as once YHWH had *taken* the father Abraham from his family (לקח, vv. 7, 61).

---

19. This is clear also to Teugels, "Strong Woman," 97–98. I only learned of this publication after completing the chapter. She, too, starts from the final text and arrives, both in regard to contextual relationships and in the general evaluation of the strong wife at the side of a weak husband, to similar conclusions.

20. The formulae differ only in the designation of the enemies and in the suffix that on the one hand designates the seed of the woman, on the other that of the man: 22:17; 24:60: איביו/שׂנאיו
.וירשׁ זרעך את שׁער

5. "Who is that man?"

The closing scene, 24:62-67,[21] dissolves back into the land to which the bride and her entourage are traveling. Isaac sets out from the extreme south, and toward evening he is taking the air. Lifting up his eyes, he sees camels approaching. Rebecca, too, lifts up her eyes. She sees more clearly; she sees Isaac (24:63-64). In order to sharpen the view for the one approaching, she descends from her camel[22] and asks the servant about the man. When she learns that it is Isaac who is approaching her, Rebecca veils herself. She goes alertly and consciously to her first meeting with her husband.

Isaac, who here appears for the first time as subject in the narrative, does not shape the encounter. Although the encounter takes place here also at the classic meeting-place for couples, at a well (24:62),[23] no erotic tension is established. The bridegroom first receives information from the servant. Then, speechless to the last, he takes Rebecca into the tent of his mother, Sarah. There she becomes his wife. He loves her, and so he is consoled for the death of his mother. Rebecca takes Sarah's place.[24]

The father who had sought a wife for his son has nothing to say in this scene, in which the successful plan comes to a good end. Isaac is viewed entirely in terms of Sarah. It is *her* tent to which he goes (cf., in contrast, Gen 18:2-15). And Rebecca consoles him for *her* death (24:67b). The emphatic "my son" in the scene with Abraham (vv. 1-9) finds no corresponding resonance with Isaac. His point of reference is his mother, and his point of reference will be the woman who replaces his mother. After Abraham's death, Rebecca will make decisions for him!

6. Rebecca questions Yₕwₕ

Genesis 24 is so placed in the ongoing text of Genesis that afterward we are brought back to Abraham again. His marriage to Keturah and her

---

21. For a detailed study of this section see the stimulating article by Magdalene L. Frettlöh, "Isaak und seine Mütter," *EvTh* 54 (1994) 427–52.

22. Frettlöh, "Isaak und seine Mütter," 432–41, reads נפל in terms of its basic meaning, "fall," and thinks that Rebecca falls from her camel in fright and veils herself, since Isaac, who is approaching her, is marked by the Akedah and the death of his mother. Frettlöh examines critically and in detail the usual view of Rebecca as a chaste, submissive bride.

23. The encounter is localized at the well of Beerlahairoi, named by Hagar in Gen 16:13 after her rescue. Frettlöh, "Isaak und seine Mütter," 447–50, pursues the key-word "see" and concludes that, through the intertextuality with Genesis 16, Rebecca comes to the sorrowing Isaac as a messenger from God, and ultimately is able to console him (cf. ibid. 449).

24. Frettlöh, "Isaak und seine Mütter," 441–47, takes a critical stance toward the attempts of exegetes to remove Sarah from Genesis 24 and insert the death of Abraham instead. She sees Gen 24:62-67 as a narrative about "paths of mourning" (ibid. 451).

family tree are inserted before the notice about his death and burial (25:1-11). Then there is an account emphasizing the fertility of Hagar's son, Ishmael, as his family tree is given.[25] Only after this does the scene shift back to Isaac and Rebecca. Very much in the style of the Priestly writing, what follows has the superscription "The Descendants *(toledot)* of Isaac."[26] An indication of his age introduces the notice of his marriage, which, however, describes Rebecca only in terms of her male relatives. Unconnected to the narrative thread we find here—as with Sarah, and later with Rachel—a notice of Rebecca's barrenness (עָקָר, 11:30; 25:21; 29:31). While there are narratives connected to this in the cases of the older and younger ancestral women, the infertility of Isaac's wife is immediately removed when he prays for her to YHWH.[27]

Rebecca's pregnancy is not easy. The readers are given an advance notice: she is carrying twins. Rebecca cannot interpret her complications, and in her irresolution she goes to inquire of YHWH. Normally one would go to a sanctuary and obtain an oracle from a priest. But it is not said where Rebecca goes.[28] YHWH speaks directly to her. The divine speech is a popular oracle about the common origin of two rival tribes stemming from the same mother. Since the ancestral narratives tell the history of peoples as a family history, the saying is given to the mother-to-be. This is how Rebecca learns that she is pregnant with twins. The complications come from the fact that the children are already fighting in their mother's womb. YHWH tells her that the older son will have to serve the younger.

It comes to pass as YHWH has told her. When she gives birth, she has two sons. The older is described and named according to his appearance: Esau, the "hairy one," the "red one." With regard to the younger, we learn of an action: During the birth he grasps the heel of his brother and is therefore called "Jacob," "heel-holder."

25. Genesis 25:12-18 presents the *toledot,* the descendants of Ishmael, and is to be read, with its listing of twelve sons, called twelve "princes" in v. 16, as a notice of the fulfillment of the promise in Gen 17:20. From the point of view of **P**, Ishmael is introduced as "the son of Abraham, whom Hagar, the Egyptian, Sarah's slave, bore to Abraham." Thus the Ishmaelites, like most of the genealogical sub-lines of the ancestral couple, are traced to both father and mother (25:12; 36:1-5, 9-14; cf. 25:1-4). In contrast, the *toledot* of the line of the promise contains only the father of the tribe (cf. 11:27; 25:19).

26. For the unique features of the Isaac *toledot* and the lack of any Abraham *toledot* see Fischer, *Erzeltern,* 40–44.

27. This notice is not part of the older narratives about Rebecca. Barrenness seems to have become, at a later time, a fixed element attached to the motif of the late-born, chosen child. On this see Irmtraud Fischer, "'. . . und sie war unfruchtbar.' zur Stellung kinderloser Frauen in der Literatur Alt-Israels," in Gertrude Pauritsch et al., eds., *Kinder machen.* Grazer Projekt "Interdisziplinäre Frauenstudien" 2 (Vienna, 1988) 118–26, at 120–21.

28. The expression "ask of YHWH" presupposes an institutionalized cult. But the cultural milieu of the ancestral narratives is unacquainted with any temple or cultic personnel; the fathers build their own altars.

Although the whole section 25:21b-26 is about Rebecca, the statement about Isaac's age at the time of their birth locates the sons in the life-story of their father, not in that of their mother.[29]

Within the context of Genesis 12–36, this birth narrative begins the Jacob-Esau cycle. The next segment, 25:27-28, presents the two brothers in their preferred environment. Esau is a hunter, a man of the woods and fields. Jacob, however, prefers to remain among the tents. Has the heel-holder become tame? The father's love belongs to the elder, because he brings him wild meat to gum. Rebecca, however, loves Jacob—without explanation.[30] Of course, the mother knows YHWH's birth-oracle!

One day Jacob, the "home boy," is cooking lentil stew (25:29). When Esau, who is described in a typical male role, comes tired and hungry from the field, the birth-oracle begins to be accomplished (25:29-34). Jacob takes advantage of his brother's current plight and buys the right of the firstborn for the price of a meal. For Esau, only the moment counts. The right of the firstborn doesn't meet his momentary needs. So he swears to his brother, eats and drinks, gets up and goes away as if nothing had happened.

7. A marriage between tenderness and betrayal

As if Jacob needed to be given time to establish his dominance over his brother, in the meantime the readers are confronted with stories about their parents. The two sons disappear from the stage. In Genesis 26 it seems as if Rebecca and Isaac are traveling alone, even though the story speaks of a state of things in which one would certainly not leave children behind, alone.[31]

A famine comes over the land (26:1). That is how the narrative about the abandonment of Sarah by her husband Abraham, in 12:10-20, began. We are immediately reminded of that story when the narrator explains that this was a different famine from that in Abraham's time. Like his father before him, Isaac also leaves his home, with his wife, and goes to Abimelech, the king of the Philistines, who dwells in Gerar. Isaac receives a vision of God: YHWH appears and speaks to him:

> "Do not go down to Egypt!" *Dwell in the land I will tell you of!* Dwell as a stranger in this land, and I will be with you! *And I will bless you, for to you*

29. The **P** notices at 25:19-20, 26b thus frame the episode of pregnancy and birth.

30. The parents' preferences are also introduced in different styles in v. 28. For the father, there is a normal verbal clause with explanation. For the mother the subject is inverted, and there is no explanation.

31. Such breaks in the narrative thread make the growth of the Rebecca-Isaac cycle obvious. In the older layer the narrative about the sale of the birthright (25:27-34) is followed immediately by that of the betrayal over the blessing, Genesis 27. Genesis 26 was written into the context when the two narrative cycles of the ancestors of south and north were combined (on this see Fischer, *Erzeltern*, 354–56).

and your seed I will give all these lands. I will bring to pass the oath that I swore to your father Abraham. And I will increase your seed like the stars of heaven. To your seed I give all these lands. Through your seed all the nations of the earth will be blessed, because Abraham listened to my voice and kept my charge, my commandments, my ordinances, and my instructions." (Gen 26:2-5)

This extensive divine speech has two different aims. On the one hand it gives concrete instructions for how to act in the situation of famine that was already described. On the other hand it transfers all the promises that had been given to Abraham to his son Isaac, but without reference to the concrete situation. Thus, for example, the promise of the land is given at the moment when Isaac has just left it. The length of the speech also stretches the narrative thread so much that the continuation in v. 6 appears to be a new introduction. These tensions can be explained if we suppose that the divine speech was expanded at a later time (by addition of the passages given in italics above).[32]

In the basic narrative YHWH speaks to Isaac when he is already in Gerar. He forbids him to go on into Egypt and promises to be with him during his sojourn as a stranger in Gerar. After that, Isaac settles in Gerar (v. 6).

In the edited version the positioning of the instruction to dwell in the land that YHWH will tell him about (v. 2b)[33] creates the impression that Isaac is still on the way and will only settle in Gerar in response to God's order. But in its content, v. 2b must be read as part of the secondary passages. In their allusions they all presume Genesis 12ff. and are to be regarded as belonging to the same literary layer as Gen 22:15-18.[34] Since the Abraham cycle does not report any deathbed blessing by the father and thus says nothing of a conveyance of the promise to the son, the expanded divine speech takes over this function. In Isaac, YHWH carries forward all his blessings to Abraham, because the father lived according to his instructions. Isaac is the heir of the promise because of God's fidelity to God's promises, and because of the merits of his father.

At God's command, the patriarch settles in Gerar (v. 6). When the men of the place ask him about his wife, he answers: "'She is my sister!' because he was afraid to say: 'my wife! May the men of the place not kill me because of Rebecca! Because she is beautiful to look at'" (26:7). The question by the men of Gerar was apparently intended only to gain information. Although Isaac pretends that his wife is a marriageable girl, no one desires her. The couple lives in Gerar, completely unnoticed, for a long time (v. 8a).

32. Ibid. 176–82.

33. The formulation alludes to Gen 12:1, but uses the vocabulary of 22:2.

34. The following texts of the Abraham-Sarah cycle should be included in this later layer: Gen 16:10; 18:17ff.; 20B; 21B; 22:15-18.

But the question alone freezes the husband with the fear of death. This fear, which is shown in the very next verse to be completely baseless, causes the husband to deny his wife. Isaac does not stand by the woman who had spontaneously left her land and her family for his sake.

Only after a long time does the husband's lie lead to problems. The king of the place commits an indiscretion that is completely implausible for someone in his position. He looks through the couple's window, and behold! Isaac is being tender to his wife Rebecca (v. 8b). This surprising discovery makes Abimelech very upset. He calls Isaac and says to him:

> "So, she is your wife, after all! Why did you say: 'She is my sister!'?" Then Isaac answered him: "I said to myself: 'May I not be put to death because of her!'" (26:9a)

The king's demand for an accounting sets the truth in sharp contrast to the lie, which is given in a direct quotation from Isaac. In his answer, the ancestor admits that the reason for the lie was his alone. In all honesty, he makes no reference to the question posed by the men of the place. At this Abimelech changes his tone. He points out what could have happened because of the lie (v. 10): How easily it could have happened that one of the people would have lain with Rebecca and thus brought guilt on everyone! Since (so far) nothing has happened, the king naturally does not mention himself as a potential evildoer (as in Gen 12:10-20; 20:1-18), but some XY from among the people. The opening formula of accusation: "What have you done to us?" shows that in case of an offense the real culprit would have been Isaac himself. But the king does not punish the stranger; instead, he offers public protection to him and his wife: "Abimelech commanded the whole people: 'Anyone who touches this man or his wife shall die!'" (26:11). The one who had feared he might die is now so protected that others will die if they touch him. Rebecca, the betrayed wife, the chief person threatened, is only in second place with regard to the protective command. But she had not been bothered by the Gerarites. It was *her husband* who had betrayed her out of fear. By his lie about their brother-sister relationship he had exposed her to the danger of adultery.

That the matter turned out so swimmingly owed nothing to the primary actors. Yhwh had promised protection in Gerar. He had preserved Rebecca from attacks, and also preserved Isaac from prosecution under the law. Yhwh remains true to his promises. This is illustrated by the abundant harvest Isaac, the protected alien, is able to gather in Gerar (26:12). In this version of the story about the abandonment of the ancestral mother the great wealth does not accrue through a betrayal of the foreign ruler,[35] but through the obvious blessing of God.

35. Abraham's great wealth, acquired as gifts from betrayed rulers (Gen 12:16; 20:14), was apparently a fixed feature of the narrative material, and so it is not lacking in this story transferred

As in the other stories of abandonment, the wealth thus acquired causes rivalry within the social environment (26:12-33; cf. Genesis 13; 21:22-34). The patriarch's wealth in flocks leads to strife over the life-sustaining water wells. This story, like the abandonment narrative, is modeled on the one in the Abraham cycle. The father's actions and memory are constantly at the forefront (26:1, 5, 15, 18, 24). Even the etiology of Isaac's locale, Beersheba, is taken as an agreement regarding a well, again modeled on the narratives about his father. The son is thus clearly distinguished as a generation in himself. The transfer of stories from father to son leaves no possible doubt about Isaac's rootedness in the narrative cycles of the South, but Rebecca, the strong ancestral woman of the North, loses her powerful profile precisely in these stories.

At the end of the chapter, at Gen 26:34-35, there is an abrupt dissolve back to the father's favorite son. As a signal for a new narrative cycle, Esau's age is given as forty at the time of his marriage. He is thus the same age as his father when he married (25:20). Esau marries two women from among the inhabitants of the Land. Judith and Basemath are portrayed as Hittites.[36] Immediately, and without any reason given, we read that these two wives made life bitter for Isaac and Rebecca. It is clear that only people who have already read Genesis 24 would understand such a statement. The bitterness is grounded in the firstborn's exogamous marriages. The father's favorite son, after having already despised his birthright, has now disqualified himself a second time!

8. The mother's favorite son

The son has married, the father is old and fragile. The sequence of generations must continue. It is time for the "handing over of the estate," for the father's blessing on his oldest son. We already recognize the voice with which the father calls his son:

And he said to him: "My son!" And he answered: "Here I am!" (27:1)

---

to Isaac. But since in this version there is no occasion for gifts, while Y<small>HWH</small> had promised protection from the outset, Isaac comes to his wealth through Y<small>HWH</small>'s blessing (cf. Fischer, *Erzeltern,* 203–204).

36. The canonical final text has two different traditions about the three wives of Esau (26:34-35; 28:9; 36:1-5). The older is apparently found in Genesis 36: there Adah is the daughter of the Hittite Elon, Oholibamah is of Hivite descent, and Basemath is the daughter of Ishmael. The Edomite genealogy in Genesis 36 indicates a relational tie with Seir (for which see Fischer, *Erzeltern,* 56–61). It has no problem with the foreign lineage of the women. The newer layer knows of two Hittites, although one of them bears the Jewish name Judith, and a daughter of Ishmael named Mahalath (28:9). In this line the problem of exogamous marriage assumes the same seriousness as in Genesis 24.

Anyone who has been reading the ancestral narratives knows of a similar intimate dialogue between father and son, from Gen 22:7. The old father is about to die. He wants from his favorite son, just one more time, the thing he values most from him (25:28). Esau is to bring him wild game. With this favorite food the father will experience once more, in eating, the full pleasure of life, before he gives his dying blessing and surrenders himself to his final destiny (27:2-3). Before being told that Esau went out to hunt (v. 5b), the readers are informed of a simultaneous occurrence: "Rebecca, however, heard what Isaac said to his son Esau" (27:5a). The deliberate placement of her name first in the sentence in Hebrew draws all attention to her.[37] In contrast, the next sentence telling of Esau's action has an ordinary structure. The narrator calls Esau the son of Isaac. Although it is his mother who is listening, Esau is not *her* son. *Her* son is Jacob (v. 6); to him she turns as soon as the older son has left the house. She tells *her* son about the conversation between the two men, whom she calls "your father" and "your brother." Rebecca does not relate these two to herself, even though she is respectively their wife and mother. She quotes what she has heard in direct discourse (v. 7), but changes it at a crucial point: Isaac is going to give his son his dying blessing. Rebecca identifies this blessing before death with a blessing before YHWH! She thus gives the story about to unfold a significantly deeper dimension, a decisively greater weight. With vehemence and determination she urges Jacob:[38]

> "But now, my son, listen to my voice, to what I command you! Go to the flock and take for me two good kid-goats from it! I will prepare them as a delicacy for your father, just the way he likes it. Then you will take them to your father and he will eat, so that he may bless you before he dies!" (27:8)

The mother commands *her* son to bring two kids *for her.* She will prepare them like Isaac's favorite dish. In her choice of words Rebecca avoids any reference to a relationship between herself and the two she is about to betray. Isaac remains Jacob's father and Esau, Jacob's brother. But Jacob relates himself to all the members of the family (v. 11): He admits to Rebecca, *his mother,* that he is afraid *his father* might recognize him, since he is not hairy like *his brother.* Jacob fears the curse that his blind father might utter, instead of a blessing.

---

37. For the stylistic emphasis in v. 6 and the caesura that results see Ina Willi-Plein, "Genesis 27 als Rebekkageschichte," *ThZ* 45 (1989) 315–34, at 327–28.

38. Rebecca's powerful position causes Adrien Janis Bledstein, "Binder, Trickster, Heel and Hairy-Man: Rereading Genesis 27 as a Trickster Tale Told by a Woman," in Athalya Brenner, ed., *A Feminist Companion to Genesis,* 282–95, to posit a female author for the Rebecca cycle. Willi-Plein, "Genesis 27," 332–33, is critical of the idea of female authorship, but acknowledges a layer that writes the stories of the fathers as stories of the mothers.

> But his mother said to him: "May your curse fall on me, my son! Now, listen to my voice! Go and get it for me!" (v. 13)

Rebecca sticks with her decision, commands him just as she had at the beginning of her speech, and brushes aside his objection. She herself takes responsibility for what her son is about to do.[39] She, who has connected Isaac's dying blessing with YHWH, does not fear a curse. Is Rebecca lacking in fear of God? If the father's blessing conveys the blessing of YHWH, is the case not the same with his curse? But the mother knows the words YHWH had spoken before the birth of her children:[40] "'The older will serve the younger!'" (25:23). Rebecca knows for sure who the blessing belongs to. But in a patriarchal society she herself cannot give it. The mother's blessing or curse is just as effective as that of the father (cf. Sir 3:9), but the blessing that continues the legitimacy of the family must come from the patriarch.

Now Isaac is about to bless the older son. Rebecca prevents it, with divine support at her back—but not in confrontation with her husband; she employs deceit. Her husband is blind. He can no longer see; but he is also blind to the divine dimension of his blessing. He has denied his wife by calling her his sister. She was supposed to be someone else. Now she pretends that her favorite son is the one he loves. He had betrayed her and put her in danger by his fruitless pretense that she was his sister; she now contrives betrayal between the brothers. As Isaac had tried to deceive Abimelech with a false statement about her identity, so now Rebecca deceives him in the same way.

Rebecca's plan succeeds, even though the blind man has some doubts. Isaac uses all his senses—save for the one he has lost—to make sure of the identity of his son: He hears the voice, which is not that of Esau (v. 22); he smells his son's clothes (v. 27), touches his hands (v. 21), and tastes the delicacy of the hunt (v. 25). All the father's efforts at certainty are accompanied by questions. Thus it is *not just one* lie that Jacob must tell in order to get the blessing.

The blessing Isaac gives is, on the one hand, the hope of fertility; on the other hand the oracle of the nations that YHWH had given the mother before she gave birth is also echoed here:

---

39. This lofty statement is often viewed negatively: Susan Niditch, "Genesis," in Carol A. Newsom and Sharon H. Ringe, eds., *The Women's Bible Commentary* (Louisville: Westminster John Knox, 1992) 10–25, at 20 sees Rebecca here in the typical female role of self-sacrifice. Willi-Plein, "Genesis 27," 330–32, thinks Rebecca can speak this way because of the "juridical freedom of fools" belonging to women, who have "nothing to say" in a patriarchal society; she bears no responsibility.

40. For this connection see also Willi-Plein, "Gen 27," 318–19.

> "May God give you the dew of the heavens
> and the fatness of the earth,
> grain and new wine in abundance!
> Nations shall serve you
> and peoples bow down before you!
> Be lord to your brothers,
> they shall bow down before you,
> the sons of your mother!
> Those who curse you, let them be accursed,
> those that bless you, may they be blessed!" (27:28-29)

The recipient of the blessing is set over his brothers, who are to serve him. The promises set brothers and nations in parallel. Thereby the father achieves against his will what YHWH had spoken in Rebecca's birth-oracle. Through betrayal, the promise is fulfilled for the right son. And it sounds like irony when Isaac defines the blessed son in terms of himself, and the serving sons in relation to the mother. By a trick *she* has caused the paternal blessing to fall on *her* son, making him immune to every curse (cf. vv. 12-13).[41]

When Esau returns home with the prey of the hunt he still suspects nothing of what has happened. His mother and brother let him go in un-suspecting to his father—the narrator makes them absent. The shock of realization is for both the firstborn and the father bitter and full of tragedy. Esau, dumbfounded, asks whether his father has only *one* blessing to give. His pleas evoke a saying that is equivalent to a diluted blesing.[42] As a ray of light, the father offers the prospect that the younger son's yoke will not be forever.

If Esau took lightly the sale of his birthright, the loss of his blessing makes clear to him the weight of the situation. He waits for his father to die before taking revenge on his brother (27:41).

> Rebecca was told of the words of Esau, her elder son. And she sent and called Jacob, her younger son, and said to him: "Look, Esau, your brother, is thinking of revenge, to kill you! But now, my son, listen to my voice! Get up and flee to Laban, my brother, in Haran! Stay there with him until your brother's wrath is turned away, until your brother's rage turns from you and he forgets what you have done to him. Then I will send for you and take you from there. Why should I become childless, losing both of you in a single day?" (27:42-45)

41. The theme of "blessing and curse" is firmly fixed in this narrative. Genesis 12:3 probably refers back to the formula in Gen 27:29b, and not the other way around.

42. Willi-Plein, "Genesis 27," 320–25, rightly rejects the interpretation that Isaac has only one blessing and therefore would curse Esau.

Again it is Rebecca who correctly evaluates the situation. Now it is not only Jacob who is *her* son; so is Esau. She cares for both of them, and does not want to lose either one.[43] Rebecca is aware of Esau's justified, helpless rage. She does not speak a word of judgment against him. To prevent anything bad from happening, her beloved son must leave, while Esau can remain. The bearer of the blessing must leave the family. The one betrayed can then, in his absence, take the place that was his by right. Rebecca hopes for a temporary state of things; she wants to bring Jacob back as soon as Esau's rage has quieted. The tragedy of the mother who devised the betrayal is that she does not send for him. When Jacob returns, half a lifetime later, he still fears his brother (32:4-12). It appears that the mother is already dead by that time (35:27-29). They never see each other again.

9. Rebecca seeks a daughter-in-law

The mother knows that her beloved son must flee. He is to go to her relatives; there he will be safe and will be received. The original narrative thread continued the story (27:1-45) right away with Jacob's flight (28:10-22). A much later layer pursues a different line in 27:46–28:9, with reference to Genesis 24. Here, as in the earlier story, the problem is that of mixed marriage and the intention is that the son of the blessing should marry a woman from within the family.

In the context of Rebecca's speech to her son, this means that for Jacob she puts a good face on this serious situation. To her husband Isaac, though, who is blind to everything around him, she speaks differently. She has to make it clear to him why their son must leave. So she puts forward a different reason for sending Jacob on a journey. But she begins her argument with Esau. The two Hittites he has married are an offense to her (27:46; cf. 26:35). If Jacob were to marry such a wife, it would be a catastrophe for her. So Isaac, like his father Abraham before him, takes the initiative and orders his son not to take a wife from the daughters of Canaan (28:1; cf. 24:3). He deliberately sends Jacob to the house of Bethuel, his mother's father, to find a wife among Laban's daughters. Isaac no longer defines the relationship through his father Abraham (cf. 11:27-32; 24:4), but instead through the line of Rebecca, which is now closer. In this way both Rebecca's father, Bethuel, and her brother Laban are integrated, through the female line, into the family genealogy (28:2, 5).

The father, who in this scene no longer appears as an aged man, gives his son a blessing for the journey, one that in its theological dimension is

---

43. The saying has the institution of blood vengeance in view. The one who kills his brother must in turn be killed by his relatives (cf. Benno Jacob, *Das Erste Buch der Tora. Genesis* [Berlin: Schocken, 1934] 572).

far beyond the desired and cunningly obtained deathbed blessing. In literary terms it is a summary of a number of promises traced to Abraham. It is probably part of the same layer that, in 26:2-5*, also transferred the summarized promises from father to son as he left the Land.

Genesis 28:6 makes another narrative beginning, first giving a short recapitulation of the previous scene and then reporting an action of Esau's that is intended to reconcile him to his father and mother: He goes and gets Mahalath, a daughter of Ishmael, as his wife. The link to Ishmael, who is explicitly called the son of Abraham (28:9), is apparently intended to sanitize his exogamous marriages. But in fact it indicates that Esau, like Ishmael before him, is now associated with a genealogical sideline.

10. YHWH confirms Rebecca's choice

Rebecca did not want to lose both her sons on the same day (27:45). Now, as she recommends to Jacob that he flee from *the* Land and seek an interim exile with her brother, she rescues him from the intentions of the betrayed Esau. For herself, however, she does lose both sons on the same day. The remaining narratives are deliberately silent about any further communication between her and her two children. The mother did not decide for herself, but for her favorite son, who from now on will spend his life blessed, but far from her.

The first scene of the flight (28:10-22) gives us a glimpse of the life of a fugitive. Jacob arrives in a place where he has to spend the night, because the sun is sinking. He, who always used to remain among the tents (25:27), finds a stone for his pillow. Now he has become a man of the fields, spending the night in the open. But it is precisely the open sky that in turn opens his eyes. Jacob dreams during the night. He sees the heavens open. A ladder joins heaven and earth, and God's messengers are going up and down the ladder. And see: YHWH stands over him and speaks to him. He promises to be with this now homeless wanderer and to shelter him in all his ways, and he assures him that he will return to *this* piece of earth (אדמה, 28:15). When Jacob wakes it is clear to him that the place he had chosen for his overnight stay is one where God is present. The stone he had used as a pillow he now sets up as a memorial, anoints it with oil, and designates the place of his encounter with God in a dream Beth-el, the house of God. He chooses this place as a new starting point for his life. Jacob swears to build a house for God in this place if the God who has revealed himself to him will protect him on his way, assure him survival, and bring him back in peace (28:20-22). The fleeing betrayer recognizes that

---

44. For the literary layering of the divine speech see Rolf Rendtorff, *Das überlieferungs- geschichtliche Problem des Pentateuch.* BZAW 147 (Berlin: Walter de Gruyter, 1977) 54.

Yhwh is present, even when he does not expect it. But he is only prepared to acknowledge this God as his own God if the vision of the ladder of heaven proves to be a ladder to his own success!

After the revelatory dream in Bethel, Jacob is for the first time standing on his own feet. Up to now, Rebecca had decided for him and protected him. Now, however, *her God* presents himself to the son as the God of his ancestor Abraham and the God of Isaac, and so confirms for him that he will be the bearer of the promises of the Land and a great progeny. Rebecca's choice, which was based on the birth-oracle but which she could only effect through betrayal, is thus confirmed by Yhwh at a moment when it appears that Jacob has lost everything: family, land, and thus the apparent blessing. The blessed one is not established in his rights; he is underway toward promise!

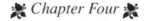

Chapter Four

Rachel and Leah:
The Founders of the House of Israel

1. The stone of opening, the stone of stumbling

Bethel was the starting point for Jacob's new life, far away from his mother. From there he now travels eastward (29:1). The well at which he arrives is introduced, through the twofold "and behold" (והנה, v. 2), like a "revelation":

> And he saw—and behold: a well in the distance. And behold: there were flocks there, for the herds were watered from the well. And there was a great stone covering the well. (29:2)

Jacob had set up the stone (אבן) that had served as his pillow at the place of revelation as a memorial of the promise of support given him at Bethel (28:10-22). Now, as his gaze sweeps over the well and the flocks of sheep gathered around it, it comes to rest on the stone (אבן) that closes the well. These two scenes, so different in content, are placed from the outset in an intimate relationship through the linking word "stone." Whereas the one stone opened his eyes to his God, now the other opens his access to Rachel, and so to the house of his mother's brother. The promise in memory of which he had set up the first stone begins to be fulfilled in the story of the other stone: It will be the stone of new beginning in Jacob's new story, far from the protection of his mother.

The stone over the mouth of the well is a symbol of community in that place. It is only removed when all the flocks have gathered, and the animals are watered together. The readers are informed about this local custom even before Jacob speaks to the waiting shepherds (v. 3).

The address "my brothers" is meant to create familiarity between those who so far are strangers. In the following dialogue with the tight-lipped shepherds, Jacob assumes leadership step by step. To his question about where they come from, the shepherds answer with the place Jacob is seeking: Haran. When he asks about Laban, the son of Nahor,[1] they say, "We know him" (v. 5). The question about Laban's welfare finally opens the shepherds' mouths: "And they said: 'It is well with him! — See, here comes Rachel, his daughter, with the sheep'" (29:6).

At the very moment when Jacob turns the conversation to Laban, his daughter Rachel appears. Her appearance is emphasized not only by the presentation (הנה), but also by the structure of the sentence, which deliberately places her own name and her origins at the front. Jacob knows what kind of encounter is about to take place, and he wants to make it private. He tries to persuade the shepherds to water their flocks as quickly as possible and take them back to pasture; after all, it is not yet time to gather them together for the night (v. 7). Suddenly this stranger, who came and addressed them as brothers and questioned them, is giving orders to the local shepherds! They reject Jacob's appeal by instructing him in the local customs: The sheep are watered together, and the stone is not removed from the well until all the flocks have gathered (v. 8). From their speech Jacob acquires information the readers already got from v. 3. There are fixed customs in Haran—something Jacob will stumble on a second time, in a much more painful manner!

> And while they were still speaking, Rachel came with the flocks belonging to her father, for she was a shepherd. And it happened that as soon as Jacob saw Rachel, the daughter of Laban, his mother's brother, and the flocks of Laban, his mother's brother, Jacob went and rolled the stone from the mouth of the well and watered the flocks of Laban, his mother's brother. And Jacob kissed Rachel, and he lifted up his voice and wept. Then Jacob told Rachel that he was her father's brother and the son of Rebecca. And she ran and told her father. (29:9-12)

The meeting between these two, which Jacob wanted to make private, is narrated with an emphasis that is offputting at first: So much talk about animals, so little about the meeting of the couple! The narrator only gives the readers an indirect glimpse of the latter. While the dialogue with the shepherds was in direct discourse (vv. 4-8), we learn about this fateful meeting only through an indirect report. Our curiosity about this daughter of Laban is not satisfied. It is said that she is a shepherd and herds her

1. The disagreements with the family tree in 22:20-24 should not be overemphasized. Jacob traces his relationship through Abraham; elsewhere he speaks of himself as a brother of Rachel's father (v. 12).

father's sheep. It was probably unusual in ancient Israel for a man to kiss a woman in public (cf. Song 8:1-2). But the context of the kiss is not love at first sight; it is relatives meeting. Jacob weeps when, after kissing her, he introduces himself as Rebecca's son! Rachel makes no answer to her emotional relative. She runs away to tell her father what has happened. Doesn't it seem like a rather bungled first meeting between this pair, who are later to be such great lovers?

The narrator has more in mind in this section about Jacob's arrival in Haran than the moment of first meeting between Jacob and his beloved Rachel. The stone had already been a signal of the special customs in Haran. Jacob breaks those customs by removing the stone all by himself and then not watering all the flocks, but giving preference to Rachel's. Jacob will break other customs of animal husbandry (30:25-43). The young woman is keeping her father's sheep, something Jacob will soon be doing. By watering the flock he is already beginning to take over her tasks. The fourfold reference to their relationship through his mother extends a link back to Rebecca, who had sent her son to her own family.

In the context of the Rebecca cycle this encounter at the well acquires further dimensions of meaning. The man in flight arrives at the well without any caravan of his own (cf. Genesis 24). Unlike the man who came to seek his mother as a bride, he has no fine gold jewelry to give. He is not even, primarily, in search of a bride; he is seeking the house of his mother's brother, who will offer him asylum. At the well Jacob takes over Rebecca's role:[2] His mother had once drawn water for Abraham's servant. Now Jacob draws for the flocks that Rachel tends. Rebecca had thus proven herself to be the right bride; now Jacob must show himself to be the right bridegroom. He is in the same situation as the fugitive Moses (Exod 2:15-21), who also obtained access to the father by watering the flocks for the daughters, and thus found a place of refuge.

In the final text of the Jacob cycle this encounter at the well is used to link the two texts (27:41-45; 27:46–28:5) that offer differing motivations for Jacob's journey to Haran. On the one hand Jacob is in search of his mother's brother's house to find refuge there; on the other hand he is seeking it in order to get a wife from among Laban's daughters. When he meets Rachel, the daughter of Laban, both goals are about to be achieved.

2. Seven years of service for the wrong bride

In a patriarchal society it was not seemly for women to bring strange men home unannounced. Like Rebecca (Gen 24:28-32) and Raguel's daughters (Exod 2:18-20), Rachel also runs home (Gen 29:12b) without

---

2. On this see Susanne Bucher-Gillmayr, "Begegnungen am Brunnen," *BN* 75 (1995) 63.

offering an invitation to the man at the well. Laban had already gone to the well on receiving such a message from a woman in his household (24:29). That man had proved himself by his golden gifts to Laban's sister. Who he was, Rebecca did not know. The man who this time was waiting at the well for an invitation had no legitimation except his origins. Laban's daughter can already tell him who the man is. The meeting of the two men is cordial. Laban kisses and embraces the son of his sister and invites him into his house: "And Jacob told Laban of all these things. Then Laban said to him: 'Truly, you are my bone and my flesh!' And he stayed with him until the new moon" (29:13b, 14).

What would Jacob have told his mother's brother? Apparently he did not say anything about his deception over the blessing and the death threat that lay on him, since the response to his story is an acknowledgment of the relationship. At any rate, it is clear to the men that this is not merely a visit. With the new moon, the period of hospitality is over. Then Laban says to Jacob:

> "Since you are my brother, should you serve me for nothing? Tell me what your wages are to be!" Now, Laban had two daughters. The name of the older was Leah and the name of the younger was Rachel. Leah's eyes were weak. But Rachel was beautiful in form and lovely to look at. And Jacob loved Rachel. Then he said: "I will serve you seven years for Rachel, your younger daughter!" And Laban answered: "It is better that I give her to you than to another man. Remain with me!" And Jacob served seven years for Rachel. Because of his love for her, they were in his eyes like but a few days. (29:15-20)

The two men negotiate over wages. The narrator puts forward the question of compensation, but then moves out of the conversation in order to give some information. Our attention is directed to two daughters of Laban, and then first of all to Leah. She is the older of the two and has a problem with her eyes.[3] We already know Rachel from the previous narrative. But we do not know yet how beautiful she really is! All the women of the line of promise were beautiful (12:11; 24:16). When Jacob falls in love with the beautiful Rachel he is in the tradition of his fathers—or does love simply make people beautiful in each other's eyes?

As a fugitive, Jacob cannot offer an appropriate bride-price, so he offers his labor for seven years. We may see this as an indication of the high value of the bride or the low value of human work; for Jacob this offer is the only way he can earn his beloved Rachel. He describes the bride he

---

3. Klara Butting, "Rachel und Lea," *TeKo* 33 (1987) 25–54, interprets רך in light of Isa 47:1 as "tender, sensitive." In that case, Leah had the more beautiful eyes. She builds on this her thesis that Rachel was Jacob's subordinated concubine and Leah was reinforced in her power position as the older.

wants very precisely, by name and by her position as the younger daughter. Laban agrees without objection. He argues with the preferable endogamous marriage custom and invites Jacob to remain. The narrator simply omits the seven years: for Jacob they are like a few days, so much does he love the bride he is working for. What Jacob is here prepared to undergo for the sake of his love is diametrically contrary to his birth-oracle and the stolen blessing. Both times it was promised him that the role of serving would not be his (25:23; 27:29), but instead he would be the master. Now he serves the man whose brother he claims to be (29:11).

After seven years, Jacob's patience is at an end. He has to remind his father-in-law to give him the bride who now, after he has served seven years for the bride-price, is his wife: "'Bring me my wife, for the days are accomplished. I want to go in to her!'" (29:21). The narrator does not show Laban answering, only acting. On that very same day the father-in-law gathers all the men in the place and holds a banquet. After seven years of silence, the narrator gives a precise account of the events of that day:

> And it happened in the evening: He took Leah, his daughter, and brought her to him. And he went in to her. *And Laban gave Zilpah, his slave woman, to Leah, his daughter, to be her slave.*[4] And it happened in the morning: And behold—it was Leah! (29:23-25)

By the evening that has now arrived Jacob has waited seven years. The deception is related with sober brevity. Contrary to the clear agreement that the bride is to be Rachel, Laban takes his older daughter and brings her to Jacob. We wonder how it is that Jacob, who loves Rachel above all, does not recognize even in the midst of sexual intercourse that he has been betrayed.[5] Only the morning brings it to light: The woman he has made love to is Leah! The marriage is finalized and cannot be undone. Jacob does not ask that Rachel be given him instead of Leah. Nothing more is said about Leah, but Rachel is another matter. With an accusatory formula that points to a wrong suffered, he addresses Laban: "'What have you done to me? Did I not serve you for Rachel? Why have you betrayed me?'" (29:25).

Anyone who has been reading the ancestral narratives in order already knows that this is how men react when they have thought they were sleeping with the right woman and come to realize that they have been deceived. Pharaoh had reacted in the very same words plus two additional questions, asking for an accounting when he realized that he had taken

4. This notice (like 29:29) is very clearly inserted into the context; it links to ch. 30 (see Erhard Blum, *Die Komposition der Vätergeschichte*. WMANT 57 [Neukirchen-Vluyn: Neukirchener Verlag, 1984] 104–105, 131).

5. Stefan Zweig has, with unsurpassed ability to shock, incorporated into his legends the explanation in the Midrash, that Rachel helped her sister not to be recognized as Leah (see Stefan Zweig, "Rahel rechtet mit Gott," in idem, *Legenden* [3rd ed. Frankfurt: S. Fischer, 1979] 7–27).

someone else's wife (12:18-19). And just so had Abimelech accused Abraham (20:9) and Isaac (26:10). What then was done by the patriarchs to foreign rulers has now been done to one of their descendants within their own family! But this is not falling on an innocent: Jacob himself had stolen the blessing from his father by pretending to be his own brother. Now his father-in-law has repaid him like for like. As once the false brother went in (בוא אל, 27:18), so Laban has caused the false sister to go in (בוא אל). The text is silent on the matter, but here it was probably again the clothing that deceived the one who had once used his brother's clothing to deceive. The bridal dress made the woman a bride, even though she was not.

Jacob reacts differently from the betrayed rulers who desired a woman but had to give her back because she was married. Leah is not someone else's wife; she is his. Jacob does not want her, but after having consummated the marriage he cannot dismiss her. The man's powerful emotion, as in the narratives of abandonment, is contrasted with the woman's silence. Leah is the real victim, not Jacob! The narrator has been preparing a long time for what Laban will say in justification:

> "It is not done in this place, that one gives the younger before the firstborn! Complete the bridal week with her, and I will also give you the other for the service you will yet perform for me, another seven years!" (29:26-27)

Jacob had already come into conflict with the local customs on his arrival. The shepherds had special agreements to water the flocks together. When Laban invites all the men in the place to the marriage we expect other special customs that the stranger in Haran does not know about. And so it is. Laban appeals to the custom of the place that the firstborn must be married first, and he sweeps away his son-in-law's complaints. In Haran the right of the firstborn still counts for something—the right that Jacob had despised, purchased, and obtained through swindle.

Jacob had come to Haran so full of hope; he had met his Rachel right away and been received into the house of his mother's brother. Even seven years of labor did not bother him when served for love. Now his past catches up with him. He has to agree with his father-in-law's suggestion if he does not want to lose Rachel. Jacob complies. He completes the bridal week with Leah, and then Laban gives him his daughter Rachel as his wife (v. 28). He gives her, too, a slave woman, Bilhah, as a bridal gift.

So as not to enrage the deceived young man, Laban agrees that the bride-price can be paid off after the fact. Hence Jacob lives the first seven years of his marriage not as a free man, but as Laban's servant.[6] The injury done by the father-in-law to the three young people will become clear, in its full extent, in the course of the story. We begin to understand why, in

---

6. Hosea 12:13 regards this "servanthood" for the sake of a woman in a highly critical light!

Lev 18:18, the Torah forbids a polygynous marriage with two sisters: The tie between sisters is not to be ruptured by making them rivals.

Excursus: A Lesson in Marriage Law

Anyone who approaches the texts of the Jacob cycle equipped only with the dreams of our present Western society that lifelong marriage must be coupled with the lifelong love of two partners will come a cropper on the story of the God-contenders Leah and Rachel. People in the ancient Near East were more sensible. If love developed before or during a marriage, that was a happy accident. Not by a long shot does the First Testament say of every marriage it recounts that the man and woman loved each other. Marriage was a contract that gave the two partners their position in society, and it was secured and supported by children. Sons, in particular, raised the standing of both husband and wife.[7] This was due on the one hand to the patriarchal social order, which advantaged the male sex, but also to their concrete conditioning, for example in the social system or in legal rulings. Aged parents were cared for by their sons. Sons of one's youthful years provided security for fragile old age (cf. the commandment regarding parents in the Decalogue, Exod 20:12; Deut 5:16). Representation in conflict situations was also the job exclusively of male members of the family (cf. Ps 127:3-5). If a woman had no husband, brother, or father, she had no assurance of anyone to support her interests in a legal dispute. The childless widow was therefore under the special protection of YHWH, who was concerned for a just order among his people (cf. Exod 22:21-22; Deut 10:18, and frequently elsewhere). However, the Hebrew Bible is too realistic to pay homage without exception to patriarchy and its glorification of the male. In a crisis, a daughter-in-law can be of more value than seven sons (Ruth 4:15). In times of peril it is precisely the women who rescue their own house (Abigail) or even the whole people (Deborah, Esther, Judith).

In ancient Israel marriage was not—as it was for a long time in Christian Europe, where male and female servants had to remain single—a privilege of the propertied and the rich. Founding a family was the right even of unfree persons.[8] A man could have any number of wives. Polygyny was

7. As Athalya Brenner, "Female Social Behaviour: Two Descriptive Patterns within the 'Birth of the Hero' Paradigm," in eadem, ed., *A Feminist Companion to Genesis*. FCB 1/2 (Sheffield: Sheffield Academic Press, 1993) 204–21, at 212, shows, fertility in marriage was of far more value to women than, for example, romantic love. In the ancestral narratives there are very few stories that do not center on the theme of offspring. The blessing of children is a central interest of *both* genders (cf. Gen 15:1-6)!

8. Even marriage between free and unfree persons was possible; cf. Innocenzo Cardellini, *Die biblischen "Sklaven"-Gesetze im Lichte des keilschriftlichen Sklavenrechts*. BBB 5 (Königstein: Hanstein, 1981) 251ff., as well as Irmtraud Fischer, *Die Erzeltern Israels*. BZAW 22 (Berlin: Walter de Gruyter, 1994) 101–102.

a real possibility, even though from the OT evidence most marriages were monogamous. Legal texts about the ranking of wives in polygynous marriages have not come down to us. But certainly the wife who bore her husband his first son held prior rank in the family; it was through her child that the main line of the genealogy would continue. However, that wife certainly did not have to be the husband's best-loved. Two texts that give us insight into a polygynous marriage, Genesis 29 and 1 Samuel 1, talk of major tensions between the wives and the decided partiality of the husband for the barren wife. That is not to say that women were always unhappy in such multiple marriages. But the constellation was certainly problematic when the husband's love belonged exclusively to one wife.

3. The man's love, or many children

The injustice Laban has done to Jacob has to be paid for by the woman he had married against his will. Leah is her husband's detested one as Rachel is his beloved one (29:30-31). Laban's firstborn is a double victim: She is the actual victim of her father's betrayal, and she becomes the victim of her husband, who discovered with shock that it was she with whom he had spent his wedding night (29:25a). Jacob does not want to "know" this woman; he does not want to love her.

> When YHWH saw that Leah was hated, he opened her womb. But Rachel was barren. (29:31)

Wrong has been done to Leah. The result is that the defender of the afflicted takes her side. YHWH gives the rejected one fertility. For Rachel he does not act. She is and remains barren. YHWH evens out what the husband has so unjustly distributed!

What follows has caused the accusation to be made that the First Testament degrades women to "baby machines." In nearly every verse there is a son—the one daughter at the very end, as if Leah's declining fertility was only adequate to produce a daughter by then!

What is being narrated here is the beginning of Israel. Twelve tribes trace their origins to the wrestling with God (30:8) carried on by these two vital women. Leah and Rachel are the two people who together built up the house of Israel (Ruth 4:11). The story of the two women is Israel's national history! It is narrated in shattering scenes of struggle for the real happiness of marriage: the partner's love, and children. One wife has the one, the other has the other. Neither is happy. How Jacob's marriage is for him, we do not know. His feelings were central at the time of the wedding, and the narrator was silent about how it was for the women. Now it is the emotions of the two wives that draw all the attention. After the earlier story of the betrayal of the "lovers," Rachel and Jacob, the readers' sympathy goes out to them.

But if we read the text more closely we find that the narrator makes a distinction at a crucial point: Jacob loves Rachel. Nowhere is it said that Rachel loves Jacob. Leah loves Jacob, but he hates her. The man's love is returned by the unloved woman, while the beloved is so sure of his love that she can sell the man for a night (30:15-16). For Rachel, her husband's love is not the whole world; for her, it is the children she cannot bear! The product of Laban's betrayal is unfulfilled desires in marriage, for all three participants.

It is YHWH who cares for the weakest. The narrator positions himself at YHWH's side as he first concentrates all attention on Leah (vv. 31-35). His language, however, speaks volumes about the injured feelings of the rejected wife:

> And Leah became pregnant and bore a son. And she called his name "Reuben" (ראובן), for she said: "Truly, YHWH has seen (ראה) my affliction, for now my husband will love me!" (29:32)

Leah bears the firstborn son. As the mother of the principal heir she must be assured of an unassailable place within the family. But Jacob's relationship to his firstborn lies only in his wife's wishing! The narrator does not say that he went to her, nor does he say that Leah bore "for Jacob." He gives his attention only to the woman, who was pregnant and gave birth (alone). She gives her child a name of thanksgiving. YHWH has seen her affliction (v. 31). She ties her hope for her husband's love to this first birth, which she understands as the doing of God. But her second pregnancy is like her first:

> And she became pregnant and bore a son. And she said: "Truly, YHWH has heard (שמע) that I am hated, and so he gave me this one also!" And she called his name "Simeon" (שמעון). (29:33)

Leah explained her first child's name through YHWH's deed (v. 32); now she derives the second from his intervention (v. 33): Because she is the hated one he has listened to her and given her another son. She does not explicitly tie her hope for Jacob's affection to this son. He is her compensation for being hated.

> And she became pregnant again and bore a son. And she said: "Now, this time, my husband will join with me (ילוה), for I have borne him three sons!" Therefore his name was called "Levi" (לוי). (29:34)

It is disturbing that, of all people, the ancestor of the priestly tribe has no reference to YHWH in his name.[9] The name expresses only the hope of his

---

9. The grammatically masculine form of the giving of the name is here (as also in 25:25-26; 38:29) to be translated "they called him"; there are also textual variants that attest the feminine form. From the context we cannot assume that the father gives the name in any of these instances (on this see Fischer, *Erzeltern*, 67–70).

mother that now, after three sons, she will finally win the love of her husband. But again her hopes are dashed. The next son, like all the others before him, has no explicit relationship to his father:

> And she became pregnant again and bore a son. And she said: "This time I will thank (אודה) YHWH!" Therefore she called his name Judah (יהודה). And she ceased bearing. (29:35)

After three sons, and now another, Leah has been compensated for her injury. The name of this child directly expresses gratitude. Leah has apparently given up hoping for Jacob's love. But YHWH has not failed in care for her. He has given her sons and elevated her to the honored place of the mother of many children. With her proclamation of thanks to YHWH, Leah ceases bearing. Has YHWH now satisfied Leah? Or has Jacob stopped going in to Leah, something we have never explicitly heard anything about?[10] The birth of the next son of this couple seems to point to the latter conclusion.

4. Two women who wrestled with God

Leah's most urgent crisis is past. Now the narrator turns to Rachel. Her sister has named three of her children in terms of her longing for the love of her husband, but it appears that only Rachel has his love. Still, she is not happy either:

> When Rachel saw that she could not bear for Jacob, she was jealous of her sister. Then she said to Jacob: "Give me children, or I shall die!" Then Jacob's anger was kindled against Rachel, and he answered: "Am I in the place of God, who has withheld from you the fruit of your body?" (30:1-2)

Rachel, like Leah, longs for what she does not have, but her sister has in abundance. As Leah is jealous over the love of her husband, which belongs only to Rachel, so Rachel is jealous of Leah's abundance of children.

Impatient as her husband was before their marriage, she is not prepared to wait any longer (הבה, 29:21; 30:1). Rachel longs for children so much that she thinks she will die if her desire is not fulfilled. Her husband's love is not enough for her. Jacob is not worth more to her than children (cf. 1 Sam 1:8). With her longing, expressed in the tone of a command, she provokes a violent marital quarrel. Jacob flies into a rage, denies any responsibility for her barrenness, and defends himself from Rachel's attempt to put him in the place of God. He says God is responsible for the fact that his beloved cannot bear children.[11]

---

10. Thus also Annemarie Ohler, *Mutterschaft in der Bibel* (Würzburg: Echter, 1992) 131.

11. Mary Callaway, *Sing, O Barren One*. SBLDS 91 (Atlanta: Scholars, 1986) 28, who investigates the motif of barrenness in the Hebrew Bible, because of the constellation of the husband between two wives sees a parallel between the narratives in Genesis 16 and Gen 29:31–30:24.

Rachel does not collapse in suffering, nor does she persist in the conflict with her husband. She seeks a constructive solution:

> And she said: "Look, here is my maidservant Bilhah! Go in to her, and she shall bear on my knees, so that I, even I, may have a child through her!" (30:3)

What Rachel suggests to her husband here was already attempted by Sarah. Rachel gives Jacob her slave Bilhah to bear in her place. The formula of the "surrogate mother's" bearing "on the knees" of the wife is a vivid illustration of how Bilhah is to bear in Rachel's place. When Bilhah is called "Rachel's slave" (30:4), while Rachel presents her to Jacob as "my maidservant," this does not mean that in giving her to her husband she intends to change her social status. Bilhah remains Rachel's slave (שׁפחה). But within the family circle, as a result of her sexual congress with Jacob, she attains the rank of maidservant (אמה).[12] The arrangement that went awry between Sarah and Hagar, because the two women did not accept each other, succeeds for Rachel and Bilhah. Rachel does not see her slave merely as a problem-solver; she acknowledges her status within the family from the outset. She calls her by name and takes her seriously as a person.

When Jacob goes to Bilhah she immediately gets pregnant and bears him two sons. Rachel accepts these children as her own by giving them their names.

> Then Rachel said: "God has done justice for me (דנני) and has listened to my voice, for he has given me a son!" And she called his name "Dan" (דן). And she was pregnant again; and Bilhah, Rachel's slave, bore a second son for Jacob. Then Rachel said: "Wrestling with God (נפתולי אלהים) have I wrestled (נפתלתי) with my sister, yet I conquered!" And she called his name "Naphtali" (נפתלי). (30:6-8)

Rachel, like her sister, expresses her experience in the names of her children. God listened not only to Leah (29:33), but to Rachel's voice as well. Through her servant's son he has done her justice. Although the narrative passage says that Bilhah bore "for Jacob," Rachel relates the child exclusively to herself. To the second child Bilhah bears "for Jacob," Rachel gives a name that expresses her relationship to Leah, again not to her husband. Naphtali is the name that commemorates the divine wrestling Rachel has wrestled with her sister. God took Leah's part because she was rejected. He did not act for Rachel. So she remained barren. The firstborn son of her slave, born representatively for her, was her sign that God was now listening to her voice, too. With the second son she considers herself the victor in the struggle for God's affection. While Leah fought for the

---

12. For the positions of slave woman and maidservant see Fischer, *Erzeltern*, 91–97.

love of her husband, Rachel is fighting for God, so that God will give her fertility as well.

The two God-wrestlers,[13] Leah and Rachel, anticipate what is still in the future for their husband: At the Jabbok he will wrestle with a man, but he will neither conquer nor be conquered. Nevertheless, the wrestler will give him the name "Wrestler with God," because he has wrestled with God and men and prevailed (32:29). Jacob will do as his beloved Rachel has done; he will not let go of God until God blesses him![14]

The narrator's view is YHWH's view. First it was turned only on the disadvantaged Leah (29:31-35). Since Rachel, despite her husband's love, is not happy, the attention then turns to Rachel (30:1-8). At 30:9 it returns to Leah. In 29:35 the sequence of her bearings ended with the note that she had ceased to give birth. Now 30:9 takes up this point to begin a new narrative thread. Leah sees that children have been born to Rachel through a substitute, her slave Bilhah, and she does not want to be left behind in the domain of fertility that previously was hers alone. Leah, too, had received a slave as a wedding present from her father (29:24, 29). So now she, too, gives Zilpah to her husband for surrogate motherhood.

> And Zilpah, the slave of Leah, bore a son for Jacob. Then Leah said: "Good fortune!" (בגד). And she called his name Gad (גד). And Zilpah, the slave of Leah, bore a second son for Jacob. Then Leah said: "For my happiness (באשרי). For the daughters will call me happy!" (אשרוני). And she called his name Asher (אשר). (30:10-12)

It appears that with the thanksgiving-name Judah a change has come over Leah. These two children, also, borne for her by her slave, receive names that no longer express a desire for her husband's affection. She gives both sons names connected with happiness. Gad is not otherwise explained; Asher apparently has in view a dignity within female society: A mother with six sons is called happy by the other women. If the names of the first three sons were motivated by a struggle for her husband's love, the next three show that Leah has grown happy even without a return of love. From her sister's jealousy (30:1) she can see that YHWH has given her a lovely, indeed a fulfilling portion of life's happiness. In spite of Jacob's undivided love, Rachel is dissatisfied. The two sons borne by Bilhah as her surrogate

---

13. Jürgen Ebach, "Liebe und solidarisches Leben—über biblische Paare," in idem, *Biblische Erinnerungen: Theologische Reden zur Zeit* (Bochum: SWI-Verlag, 1993) 164–84, at 181, plays down the women's struggle with God in contrast to Jacob's wrestling with God as "trivial fighting" and a survival struggle between women for Jacob's love. Eva Renate Schmidt, "1. Mose 29–31: Vom Schwesternstreit zur Frauensolidarität," in eadem, et al., eds., *Feministisch gelesen 2* (Stuttgart: Kreuz-Verlag, 1989) 29–39, at 33, on the other hand, contrasts the "strife between the sisters" with the "rooster fights of three generations of men."

14. Frank Crüsemann, "Die Gotteskämpferin," in Dorothee Sölle, ed., *Für Gerechtigkeit streiten. FS Luise Schottroff* (Gütersloh: Kaiser, 1994) 41–45, draws the same parallel.

can only change that temporarily. The names Rachel gives them have to do with strife and mediation. In contrast to the happy names[15] given by her sister, these seem instead to reflect getting even. The desire for her own physical offspring remains unappeased.

5. Love potions, homeopathy, and male sexuality for sale

The scales are again in balance: The older sister is fertile, the younger beloved; each has two sons through her slave woman. Whereas the narrator has allowed the women to act individually up to this point, now he brings them together. Their relationship and interaction is shaped by their rivalry.

> In the days of the wheat harvest Reuben went out and found mandrakes in the field. And he brought them to Leah, his mother. Then Rachel said to Leah: "Give me some of your son's mandrakes!" And she answered her: "Is it not enough that you have taken my husband from me? Must you take my son's mandrakes, too?" Then Rachel said: "Tonight he will lie with you, in exchange for your son's mandrakes!" (30:14-15)

After the "birthing contest" the two sisters conducted individually, we now have the first dialogue between them. The occasion is the mandrakes that the firstborn, Reuben, has found at a time of obvious fertility, the days of the grain harvest. The mandrake, a plant whose roots have a human shape, were thought in the ancient Near East to have an aphrodisiac effect. It is impossible to say for certain whether ancient cultures applied them for homeopathic or magical purposes.[16] Rachel wants to use them for fertility; she is already certain of her husband's love. For Leah the mandrakes offer the possibility of a love potion that could finally bring Jacob to her. In this episode, again, possession and desire are distributed in such a way that each woman seeks what she does not have. Leah has the firstborn, Reuben. He brings the love-plants home to his mother. It is *his* mandrakes that are the subject of the subsequent quarrel. Rachel recognizes what her sister has. She begins the dialogue. She asks Leah for *her* son's mandrakes. Her sister answers with an accusation that confirms Rachel's all-encompassing greed. Rachel has taken her husband; now she wants *her* son's mandrakes, too![17] Her speech throws light on the double notice about her bearing hav-

15. It is possible that the names Gad and Asher echo the names of deities. Gad was a god of happiness (cf. Isa 65:11), and Asher could be connected to the goddess Asherah. (On this see Claus Westermann, *Genesis.* BK I/2 [Neukirchen-Vluyn: Neukirchener Verlag, 1981] 579).

16. On this see Kate Bosse-Griffiths, "The Fruit of the Mandrakes," in Manfred Görg, ed., *Fontes atque pontes. FS Hellmut Brunner.* ÄAT 5 (Wiesbaden: Harrassowitz, 1983) 62–74.

17. Klara Butting, *Die Buchstaben werden sich noch wundern.* Alektor Hochschulschriften (Berlin: Alektor-Verlag, 1993) 35–37, connects the two women's birthing competition and the mandrake episode through linguistic parallels with Jacob's contest with Esau over the birthright and the blessing.

ing ceased (29:35b; 30:9a): Leah did not suddenly become infertile. She could no longer count on sleeping with her husband, because in general he only goes to Rachel. The sister knows it, and she offers to exchange the mandrakes for a night with Jacob. Rachel controls her husband's sexuality; she offers it for sale!

> When Jacob came from the field that evening, Leah went to meet him and said to him: "You are coming to me! Because I have obtained your services as a wage (שָׂכֹר שְׂכַרְתִּיךָ) for my son's mandrakes!" And he slept with her that night. (30:16)

That is how the inner life of a polygynous marriage looks. The man with many wives permits, without objection, that he can be "sold off" for a night! He, who did not want Leah as his wages (שׂכר, 29:15), has become Leah's wage (שׂכר, 30:16).[18] As if in triumph, Leah approaches him in the early evening to demand a night with him. What she could no longer count on, she has bought for herself. Her son has helped her get this by bringing her the mandrakes.

> And God listened to Leah, and she became pregnant and bore Jacob a fifth son. Then Leah said: "God has given me my wages (שְׂכָרִי) because I gave my slave woman to my husband!" And she called his name "Issachar" (יִשָּׂשׂכָר). And she became pregnant and bore a sixth son for Jacob. Then Leah said: God has given me a good gift! This time my husband remained and dwelt (יִזְבְּלֵנִי) with me, for I have borne him six sons!" And she called his name Zebulon (זְבֻלוּן). After that she bore a daughter. And she called her name "Dinah." (30:17-21)

Leah gets pregnant even without the mandrakes; for Rachel, even these do not help her achieve fertility. So Leah has purchased the better part, for she bears a son even though she gave away the love-plants. However, she does not trace the child's name to her business with the mandrakes; she gives the credit to God. God has given her these wages. It is true that the key-word association alludes to the story about wages in v. 16, but Leah explains the name in terms of her "deserving," for having given Jacob her slave. This misalignment makes it clear that a number of hands have worked on the birth stories of the twelve sons.[19] However, in the final text a context of meaning is created in that Jacob is again taking his marital duties toward Leah seriously. She does not see the next son she bears as a wage from God, but as a gift. Still, for the first time since Levi she again

---

18. Butting, "Rachel und Lea," 49, points to this correspondence.

19. The little story of the mandrakes appears to be an insertion, enabled by key-words, into the birth-notice-like accounts of bearing for Jacob (30:1-13, 17-21). "Elohim" is used as the divine name, while the births of the first four sons (29:31-35) are attributed to fertility bestowed by YHWH, and the notices about bearing for the father are missing.

grounds the name of the son in the attitude of her husband. The imperfect should not be translated as future in this context. She does not hope that her husband will continue dwelling with her; it is Jacob's remaining that is the reason for the new birth and so for the name of the sixth son.

The birth of Leah's only daughter is mentioned merely in passing. Here is neither a notice of pregnancy nor a reason for her name. In the final text this reads like a depreciation of the birth of a female child.[20] Probably this note is a later insertion meant to anchor the tradition in Genesis 34 back in the birth narratives.[21] Dinah is the last to be born, and yet at the time of the return to the Land she is already past puberty?

The mandrakes were of no use to Rachel. She remained barren, while Leah bore three more children. Not by magic, not with homeopathy, but through God's merciful intervention, Rachel finally becomes pregnant:

> Then God remembered Rachel and God listened to her and opened her womb. And she became pregnant and bore a son. And she said: "God has withdrawn (אָסַף) my shame!" And she called his name "Joseph" (יוֹסֵף), for she said: "May Yʜᴡʜ add (יֹסֵף) to me yet another son!" (30:22-24)

The equality between the sisters had sensibly shifted, since Jacob was no longer avoiding Leah. So God listened to Rachel and gave her fertility, too. In their quarrel, Jacob had thrown it at her that God denied her the fruit of her body (30:2). Therefore she interprets the birth of her own child as a removal of the shame that had been laid upon her. The name of her firstborn expresses her hope that she would have another child. The woman who thought she would die of her childlessness is still unsatisfied even after she has achieved the desired goal. In answer to her despairing cry: "Give me children!" (30:1), *one* son is too little. The tragedy of this woman will lie in this: that she, who longs so much for children of her own, will die in fulfilling her wish (35:16-20).

6. The family sticks together for the first time: *Yʜᴡʜ calls them to return home*

Now that Rachel has given birth, Jacob begins to think about his own household. During the first seven years of his marriage he was in a status of servant to his father-in-law, since he still had to pay off the bride price for Rachel. Now he wants to return to his homeland. Jacob asks for the of-

---

20. For the lack of interest in daughters in Genesis see Ilona N. Rashkow, "Daughters and Fathers in Genesis . . . or, What is Wrong with this Picture?" in Athalya Brenner, ed., *A Feminist Companion to Exodus to Deuteronomy.* FCB 1/6 (Sheffield: Sheffield Academic Press, 1994) 22–36. Of course, the daughters are missing only from the line of the promise!

21. Cf. Blum, *Komposition,* 110–11.

ficial surrender of his own family, won and created during fourteen years of service (30:26). In ancient Israel, marriage was patrilocal. That means that the woman married into her husband's household, and not the other way around. Jacob had come to Laban's house as a fugitive. He has lived his marriage in the household of his wives. That Laban, as a patriarchal father, makes decisions for his daughters as he sees fit had already been made clear on the wedding night. As long as the daughters are in his house, their father has the duty to protect them, and even after their marriage he has a claim to participate in decisions within the young family. He does not want to let Jacob go, since this man has obviously bestowed a blessing on him and the flocks have abundantly increased under his care (30:25-30). Jacob stands there, with his wife and children, penniless. So the two men make a further agreement for service with no set time limit. Jacob receives a share in Laban's flock and can breed animals for himself. He is so successful at this that he brings the envy and mistrust of Laban's sons and heirs on himself. Laban also visibly distrusts him.

> Then YHWH spoke to Jacob: "Go back to the land of your fathers and to your kinfolk. I will be with you!" Then Jacob sent and called Rachel and Leah into the field to his flocks. (31:3-4)

It is not Rebecca who, as they had agreed, calls Jacob back, but YHWH, who renews his promise of being with Jacob (cf. 28:15). The husband wants to discuss the change in his life with his wives alone, so he calls them to him in the fields. The words he says to them serve as a description of the situation and a justification that traces the conflict between him and Laban exclusively to their father. The fact that he is now a rich man is not a well-earned wage for his work, but is due to God's support, which prevented his father-in-law from doing him harm. Jacob attributes the magic practices he has used in his animal breeding to a dream in which an angel appeared to him and told him what to do (31:5-12). But the end and goal of Jacob's speech is the divine word in v. 13:

> "I am the God of Bethel, where you anointed a stone pillar, there where you swore me a vow. But now get up, go forth from this land and go back to the land of your kinfolk!"

The revelatory discourse rounds off the circle to the first station of his flight. Jacob has acknowledged before his wives that the conditions of the vow have been fulfilled: The God who showed himself to him at Bethel has been with him in everything. Now the time to return—and the time of the fulfillment of the vow—has come.

> Then Rachel and Leah answered and said to him: "Do we not also have a share and an inheritance in our father's house? Does he not regard us like

strangers? For he has sold us and used up, yes, used up our money. For the whole property that God has withdrawn from our father belongs to us and our children! But now: Do everything God has said to you!" (31:14-16)

Jacob's marriages were not made, like Rebecca's with Isaac, on condition that the women would be prepared to leave their land. Jacob had to obtain the agreement of his wives, to learn whether they were prepared to depart with him. Although the relationship between the sisters has always been marked by rivalry and dislike, they now speak as if with one voice. They are united in rejecting any solidarity with their father.[22] For the first time we get a glimpse of what the women think of the betrayal on the wedding night: Their father sold them both; they are worth no more to him than foreigners, and he has held back the portion of the bride price[23] that rightly belonged to them. Their accusations against Laban are not less bitter than those Jacob has to bring against him. The women self-assuredly describe the wealth that Jacob, with God's help, has developed out of Laban's property as their own. It is the reparation for all the wrong for which they reproach their father. The women agree with one accord to the departure of the whole family. Calling into question their share and inheritance in a community is equal to expressing a definitive will to separate (cf. 1 Kings 12:16).

The departure is swift and secret, resembling flight. Without saying goodbye to Laban, the daughters and the son-in-law leave Haran. Rachel exacts revenge before she goes:

> But Laban was at the sheep-shearing. Then Rachel stole the teraphim that belonged to her father. And Jacob stole the heart of Laban the Aramean, because he did not tell him that he was going to flee. But he fled with everything that belonged to him, he arose, crossed the river, and set out in the direction of Gilead. (31:19-21)

Rachel makes use of her father's absence to collect the household gods. The teraphim are probably statues of the gods[24] (cf. 1 Sam 19:13-16, where Michal lays the teraphim in David's bed to deceive Saul's messengers). By stealing the household gods Rachel steals her family's legitimacy. It is no accident that after this theft none of the sons of the lines of the promise ever goes to Haran again to obtain a wife. Rachel has carried the legitimacy of the clan with her into the Land! However, as Ktziah

---

22. On this see previously Schmidt, "Schwesternstreit," 20, 36.

23. For the modalities of payment of the bride price see Fischer, *Erzeltern,* 82.

24. On this see Klaus Seybold, "תרפים, Idol(e)," *THAT* 2:1058–60. If the teraphim were ancestral gods (cf. Susan Niditch, "Genesis," in Carol A. Newsom and Sharon H. Ringe, eds., *The Women's Bible Commentary* [Louisville: Westminster John Knox, 1992] 21), the interpretation given in what follows would be still more revealing.

Spanier has shown, Rachel is not acting for Jacob or the whole family, but only for herself: *Her* genealogical line, with Joseph, is to have the primary status, not that of Leah.[25]

Jacob matches the thievery of his favorite wife: He steals Laban's heart. It is not clear what is meant by this statement. In 2 Sam 15:6 Absalom steals the hearts of the Israelites from his father David. This is a description of the shift in their sympathy from father to son. The double theft could be understood to mean that Rachel steals the teraphim and Jacob makes off with everything, including the woman who has the teraphim. Laban himself uses this expression in his reproach that Jacob has stolen not only his heart, but his daughters, and is carrying them off like prisoners of war (31:26). Are the daughters, who say of themselves that their father treats them like foreigners (31:15), now regarded by the father as "his heart," so that Jacob has stolen from him what he loves best? That would fit the character of Laban, who is portrayed as conflicted in the extreme.

Three days after the flight, Laban is told about it. He pursues Jacob with his troop and catches up with him at Mount Gilead. Warned by God in a dream by night not to say a word to Jacob, good or bad (v. 24), he nevertheless rains reproaches on him: Jacob has stolen away his daughters, robbed him, and thus denied him the opportunity to give a farewell banquet and to kiss his sons and daughters before they departed (v. 28). If Jacob was so homesick for his father's house that he had to return there, why has he stolen Laban's gods (v. 30)? This accusation sheds light on Rachel's theft: The teraphim—Laban calls them "my Elohim (my gods)"—are going to move from one paternal house (v. 19) to another![26]

Jacob is innocent of the theft of the teraphim. He does not know that Rachel had stolen them. He offers to allow all his possessions to be searched, and says of the one in whose possession they are found: "That one shall not live!" (31:32). Laban then searches Jacob's tent, Leah's tent, and the tent of the two maidservants, but he finds nothing. Only then does Laban go from Leah's tent to Rachel's. The narrator uses this sequence to increase the tension. As the father is in the process of turning her tent upside down, the readers are told where the teraphim are: Rachel has put them under the camel's saddle and is sitting on it. She acts on the principle that a good offense is the best defense, and speaks to her father, asking that he not be angry with her, but she cannot get up, since it is with her according to the way of women. This lie rescues Rachel immediately from the punishment Jacob has proposed.

---

25. Ktziah Spanier, "Rachel's Theft of the Teraphim: Her Struggle for Family Primacy," *VT* 42 (1992) 404–12. Teraphim appear in the Hebrew Bible only in the context of the Northern Kingdom, in the territory of the tribes descended from Rachel (see ibid., 406).

26. Annemarie Ohler, *Frauengestalten der Bibel* (Würzburg: Echter, 1987) 36–37, connects the episode of the teraphim with Josh 24:2 ("your fathers dwelt beyond the river and served other gods").

A little later in the journey two members of the family will die: in Bethel, Rebecca's nurse, Deborah (35:8), and in Ephrata, Rachel herself (35:16-20). The news of the death of her son Joseph (37:32-35) is a bald-faced lie, but Jacob believes it—it would be the third death from Rachel's tent. The protecting gods of her father can no longer "shield" Rachel and those belonging to her. They are among the foreign gods that are buried under the oak at Shechem before the party journeys on to Bethel (35:2-4). Nevertheless, it is Rachel's line alone that enables all Israel to survive and will thus achieve a higher degree of legitimacy: Joseph, believed dead, lives in Egypt and saves the house of Jacob from famine and death.

Jacob has fled from Laban without saying goodbye. He defends himself against this accusation by speaking of his fear that his father-in-law might take his daughters from him (31:31). He thus justifies himself in words very similar to those his father Isaac used in answering Abimelech's accusations (26:9: כִּי אָמַרְתִּי פֶּן־). There, too, it was a matter of demanding an accounting for behavior that offended against custom and decency. The formula Jacob uses ("your daughters") indicates Laban's patriarchal claims. Jacob's wives are still Laban's daughters; he has not released them from his guardianship. In the quarrel that follows his fruitless search of Jacob's possessions, Laban even has the gall to lay claim to Jacob's whole family as his own:

> Then Laban answered and said to Jacob: The daughters are my daughters and the sons are my sons and the flocks are my flocks! Everything you see here belongs to me! And my daughters, what can I do about them today— or about the children they have borne?" (31:43)

The man who had bargained away both his daughters[27] portrays himself as a faithful and caring father. He denies every claim that Jacob might have and thus degrades his twenty years of work (v. 41) into the service of a slave. In the course of Genesis 31, Laban is painted as a despot with Pharaonic features. He hunts down (רדף, 31:23; Exod 14:4, 8-9) the fleeing (ברח, 31:20-27; Exod 14:5) family of "Israel"; he has ten times changed Jacob's wages, as later Pharaoh will ten times change the conditions under which he will allow Israel to depart (31:7, 41; Exodus 7–14). What Jacob has experienced with him is oppression (ענה, 31:42; Exod 3:7) and slavery (עבד, 31:41; Exodus 1), and it is thanks only to the God of the ancestors that "Israel" came away safely (31:42; Exod 3:6).

Laban knows that God is on Jacob's side (31:34), and at length he offers to make a covenant. The clause he imposes on Jacob is for the protection of his daughters. Jacob may not mistreat his daughters and may not

---

27. Niditch, "Genesis," 20, points out that nowhere in the First Testament apart from the two women's accusation against their father (31:15) is anything said about "selling" a woman.

marry any other wives (31:50). Ordinarily such conditions would probably be formulated on the occasion of the marriage. Since Jacob remained in his father-in-law's house, it is consistent that they are stated at the time of his departure. That, of all people, the despotic father who had initiated the oppressive triangular relationship and made himself responsible for Jacob's polygynous marriage should formulate such a protective clause sounds cynical. He forbids Jacob to do what he himself has already done. With kisses and blessings, Laban takes leave of his daughters and his grandsons (32:1).

Jacob had set up a stone before beginning his journey to Haran (28:18). The stone over the mouth of the well at Haran had for the first time brought him into conflict with the special customs of the place. By moving away that stone he had first watered the flocks of Laban (29:2-10). Now a stone becomes the sign of enduring separation from the family of Laban (31:45-46). This stone, set up on the threshold of the promised land, sets a seal on Jacob's history in the foreign country.

7. Again the danger of losing everything

Jacob has escaped his father-in-law, who pursued him as he fled. He has been able to close this part of his history with a contract. Now, as he moves farther into the Land, he has to come to terms with his previous past. He, the blessed one to whom the full inheritance had been promised, has lived half his life outside the Land, far from his parental household. Since there has been no news from his mother, Jacob does not know whether Esau's wrath has burned out (cf. 27:43-45). He sends messengers to Esau to announce his coming:

> He commanded them as follows: "So shall you speak to my Lord, to Esau: 'Thus says your servant Jacob: I have dwelt as a stranger with Laban until now. I have ox, ass, and sheep, manservant and maidservant. Now I am sending to you to announce this to my Lord, that I may find favor in your sight!'" (32:5-6)

Jacob, who by a betrayal had been made lord over his brother (27:29), addresses Esau as his lord and describes himself as Esau's servant. It is true that such designations were regarded in ancient Israel as polite expressions, but in relation to Esau they have a different echo. Jacob knows that he is the blessed one. He does not want to open up the old wounds all over again. Since he is returning a wealthy man, he does not need his brother's property. Jacob speaks of his own property in the singular, as an expression of modesty. The real extent of his wealth is indicated by the gifts he will send forward to his brother, divided into caravans, as appeasement presents (32:14-22).

The word the messengers bring back is ominous: Esau is already on the way to meet him; four hundred men are with him (32:7)! When Jacob hears this, for the first time in his life the betrayer feels fear and anxiety (v. 8). He has to reckon with his brother's attack on his defenseless baggage train. So he divides everything he has into two camps in order that at least half will have a chance to escape. Even in this dangerous situation, Jacob's slyness and cunning do not desert him!

The prayer Jacob sends up to heaven in his crisis is imbued with fear and is a simple appeal to his God. This is the God of his fathers, who has commanded him to return, and has promised to do good to him. He sets before God's eyes also the combined promises transferred to him before he left the Land (28:3-4), in order to beg God's help. How can the promise of numerous offspring be fulfilled if Esau kills both the mothers and their children? Jacob's speech is a psalm[28] in crisis. The God who was revealed to him is now distant. There is no divine appearance, no answer to his urgent, pressured cries!

But a sign had already been given to Jacob in advance: Even before he sent to Esau, he had come across the camp of God's host (32:2-3). He called it Mahanaim, "double camp." The idea of dividing his possessions into two parts seems to have been sparked by that. With the camp of God at his back, the betrayer hopes that he can survive the encounter with his betrayed brother in good shape.

8. The man who wrestled with God

With the ominous meeting with Esau in view, Jacob has his whole family, wives, slave women, and the twelve children, cross the Jabbok in the middle of the night. He alone remains on the other bank (32:23-25a). In times of danger on a journey, normally people draw closer together because they are stronger as a group. But in this situation Jacob separates himself from his whole family and property. He abandons his whole caravan by sending them across the river in the direction of Esau, protecting only himself from a nocturnal attack by his brother.

Suddenly a man appears and fights with him until dawn is breaking. Because Jacob cannot be overcome, the man wounds his hip in order to get away from him. But Jacob will not let him go; he wants the warrior's blessing.

---

28. This prayer presumes most of the Jacob texts and is to be seen as part of the layer that introduces a concentration on endogamous marriage. The insertion of prayers into narratives is a sign of a late period of origin (cf. Gen 24:12-14, 27).

Then he said to him: "What is your name?" He answered: "Jacob!" And he
said: "Let Jacob be your name no longer, but Israel (יִשְׂרָאֵל)! Because you
fight (כִּי־שָׂרִיתָ) with God and men and conquer! (32:28-29)

The man answers the question about his name with a blessing (v. 30). The
struggle with the brother of whom Jacob is so afraid is symbolically decided
ahead of time by this fight with a much stronger one. Jacob calls the place
Penuel, "face of God." He knows that he has fought with God, and God has
not conquered him; so Esau, too, will not be able to conquer him. He will
meet the one robbed of his blessing as a newly-blessed man. But Jacob goes
away from this encounter a marked man. He limps from his wound and cannot encounter his brother in the full strength of his manhood. He can no
longer count on his own strength; he must trust in God's blessing!

9. Reunion with Esau: Rachel receives the greatest protection

Immediately after this fight with God, Esau arrives. Jacob divides his
children among the women and places them according to his estimation of
their value. The slave women are in front, behind them Leah, even though
she has the firstborn with her. In the most sheltered place, farthest removed
from Esau, is his beloved Rachel with Joseph.[29] He is the only son who is
explicitly named; he is the beloved son (cf. Genesis 37). Purified by the
struggle with God, he no longer uses his family as protection for himself,
but sets himself in front of his wives and children.

Jacob goes to meet Esau, bowing to the ground seven times. But Esau
does not come with evil intent. He comes to meet his brother, kisses and
embraces him. The fight Jacob had feared so much does not take place.
Esau's wrath has burned itself out. His question about the great many
people accompanying Jacob raises the level of tension again. But Jacob
turns the presentation into a ceremony. One after another the women and
their children bow down before Esau: first the slave women, then Leah,
and last of all Joseph and Rachel.

Jacob's fear was groundless. Esau even refuses the gifts that Jacob had
sent ahead to him. Jacob has to press him to accept them—another way of
sealing a peace. Jacob draws a parallel between his encounter with his
brother and his fight with God in the night just past: As he beheld the face
of God and remained the victor, yet came away from the battle with God
a wounded man, so he now sees the face of his brother (v. 10). In this encounter, too, he receives undeserved favor. The betrayer Jacob experiences
this reunion as a changed man, the marked man Israel. And the redeeming
address, "my brother!" comes to him like a gift (33:9).

29. Ohler, *Frauengestalten,* 40, sees this positioning of Rachel as giving her the best chance
of escaping.

Jacob refuses to let Esau accompany him, with the excuse that his baggage train, with children and nursing animals, cannot be overtired. He also refuses the protection of some of Esau's men. His terror of the meeting was too great, and the peace is too fragile.

Jacob enters *the* Land alone. His stations are Succoth and finally Shechem. Like his ancestor Abraham before him (12:7), he builds there an altar to his God (33:20), whom he now calls "the God of Israel." He builds the altar to the God of the one who wrestled with God. Israel's wives, Rachel and Leah, have fought their own battles with God for their offspring. Jacob/Israel, the God-battler, has withstood his battle as he passed over into the promised Land and the contest with his rival for the inheritance of the promise. The family of the female and male God-wrestlers have, through their engagement, won the goods of the promise, offspring and land. Israel had to acquire through struggle the inheritance first craftily obtained through betrayal. His God, who appeared to him at Bethel, has remained true to his promise to remain with him. Jacob, in turn, will fulfill his vow in Bethel (35:1-15).

10. The desire for children, and death

On the journey southward from Bethel, Rachel's labor pains begin. From the course of the narrative it appears as if she has had to make this toilsome journey in an advanced state of pregnancy. The narrator emphasizes twice that it was a difficult birth (35:16b, 17a). The midwife who is with her wants to encourage and strengthen the laboring woman and promises her, in the form of a salvation oracle, that she will have a son again. "Fear not!" should not be misinterpreted to mean that Rachel would have to be afraid if it were a daughter. It is true that in a patriarchal society sons count for more than daughters. Leah already has six sons and a daughter. Her fertility made her sister jealous (30:1). With the birth of another son, Rachel gains in prestige. Her plea, associated with the giving of a name to her first son (30:24), is answered: this time again it is a son. Rachel, who thought that without children she would die (30:1), dies in fulfilling her life's wish. She does not die because she is childless, but because she now has child*ren* (plural in 30:1).

Death in childbirth or soon afterward was a much more present danger for women in the ancient Near East than it is now, in our Western culture. The countless amulets and invocation rituals we know of from Israel's environment give an impressive witness to this.[30]

---

30. Cf. the chapter "Familienzuwuchs," in Emma Brunner-Traut, *Die Alten Ägypter* (4th ed. Stuttgart: Kohlhammer, 1987) 50–67.

And it happened that her breath was leaving her, for she was dying. Then she called his name Ben-oni (בֶּן־אוֹנִי). But his father called him Benjamin (בִּנְיָמִין). (35:18)

Before Rachel dies, she names her child. Ben-oni is usually interpreted as a cursing name, "son of my sorrow," but Stefanie Schäfer-Bossert has argued persuasively for a translation as "son of my life-force" (cf. Gen 49:3, where Reuben is called "first-fruits of my life-force, כֹּחִי וְרֵאשִׁית אוֹנִי).[31] In that case Ben-oni is not the child who brings Rachel her death, but the son in whom she has laid the whole power of her life. Still, even with this interpretation the name is ambivalent. Rachel's pains and sorrow are not obliterated, since the son takes her life-force.[32] But he bears them in turn; her strength lives in him.

Even before Rachel dies, Jacob gives the son a different name, taking up the sound of the first. He calls him "son of the right hand" or "son of happiness." Renamings happen frequently in the ancestral narratives. But it is always God or a messenger from God who gives the new name. So Abram and Sarai are renamed Abraham and Sarah in Genesis 17, and Jacob becomes Israel in Genesis 32. There is no contrast between the content of the first and second names, but they add a dimension that is connected with the life of the name-bearer. While Abraham and Sarah are consistently called by their new names after the renaming, we still hear of Jacob after he has been given his new name. As for Benjamin, only the name his father gives him is attested later. That here, as with Ishmael and Isaac, the mother's original giving of a name is later augmented or replaced by a name-giving by the father appears to me improbable, since the birth narrative is a literary unit. Thus the renaming of the child in the presence of his dying mother is a last proof of Jacob's love for his darling Rachel.[33] The child will go through life with a memorial name recalling the beloved wife. Benjamin, the son of the right wife, is the only one of the twelve sons who is born in the right Land.

Rachel is buried where she dies. Jacob marks her grave at the side of the road with a stone pillar (35:19), known "even to today." Rachel's grave is firmly fixed in biblical tradition (Gen 48:7; 1 Sam 10:2; Jer 31:15-17; cf. also Matt 2:17-18). The cult at her grave was not only practiced in Old Testament times, but endures in Israel today. In particular, women who want to have children come to her tomb to pray for fertility and an easy

---

31. Stefanie Schäfer-Bossert, "Den Männern die Macht und der Frau die Trauer?" in Hedwig Jahnow et al., *Feministische Hermeneutik und Erstes Testament* (Stuttgart: Kohlhammer, 1994) 106–25.

32. Ibid. 122.

33. I maintain this position in spite of the critique of Schäfer-Bossert, ibid. 122.

labor.[34] It is a peculiar feature of the First Testament that has been little noticed thus far that tomb traditions, which are relatively few, are mainly those of women. The burial place of the ancestral couple in the cave at Machpelah near Hebron, which in terms of tradition is much newer than that of Rachel's tomb, was purchased for a woman. Sarah was the first to be buried there (Genesis 23). Likewise, the sole tomb tradition within the narratives of the Exodus and the acquisition of the Land is related to a woman: Miriam, according to Num 20:1, was buried in Kadesh. No traditions have been handed down about the locations of the burials of her later much more prominent fellow-fighters for the exodus from Egypt, Moses and Aaron.

Jacob's story apart from his parents began with the erection of a *mazzebe,* a stone pillar (Gen 28:18, 22). With the erecting of a *mazzebe,* it ends. Jacob's next station is Mamre. There, together with Esau, he will bury his father Isaac (35:27-29).

---

34. For women's rituals at Rachel's tomb in present-day Israel see Susan Starr Sered, "Rachel's Tomb and the Milk Grotto of the Virgin Mary: Two Women's Shrines in Bethlehem," *JFSR* 2 (1986) 7–22.

❧ Chapter Five ❧

Dark Sides of the Family Chronicle

1. The rape of Dinah—An insult to male honor?

Dinah, the daughter of Leah and Jacob, was mentioned in the listing of births in Gen 30:21 under "afterwards." This daughter is absent from the register of generations in Gen 35:23-26, where only the twelve sons are listed. The account of the migration of Jacob/Israel to Egypt includes her name as an example of Leah's daughters, in addition to the summary formula.[1] Here again, Dinah has a special place. It is possible to account for this in terms of disdain for female progeny, but this is not satisfactory within the ancestral narratives, where the female line is not consistently discriminated against. In the branch of the family that remained in the East it is precisely the women who are at the forefront, because they will ultimately be the mothers of Israel. Nevertheless, in the line of promise the daughters are strikingly neglected. That in the many births within the four generations of the ancestors only a single daughter would have been born is improbable even from a purely demographic point of view. The daughters are marginalized because they could not continue a genealogical line of their own within a patrilocally-structured society.

Dinah's special position can probably be explained by tradition criticism. Genesis 34, like Gen 35:21-22 and Genesis 38, is closely related to the tribal blessings in Genesis 49.[2] The dominant place given to the tribe of Judah is facilitated by the successive disinheriting of his three older brothers, Reuben, Simeon, and Levi.

Dinah's story is introduced by the notice of settlement in Gen 33:18-20. Jacob's family sets up its camp before the gates of Shechem. An additional

---

1. On this see Chapter Six, section 1.
2. Cf. Erhard Blum, *Die Komposition der Vätergeschichte.* WMANT 57 (Neukirchen-Vluyn: Neukirchener Verlag, 1984) 228–29.

note mentions the purchase of a piece of land from "the sons of Hamor, Shechem's father." Here the family pitches its tent.[3]

> And Dinah, the daughter of Leah, whom she bore to Jacob, went out to visit the daughters of the land. But Shechem, *the son of Hamor the Hivite,* the prince of the land, saw her. And he took her, lay with her, and raped her. Then his soul clung to Dinah, Jacob's daughter, and he loved the girl and spoke to the girl's heart. (34:1-3)

The birth notice for Dinah was missing from Gen 30:21, but it is introduced here. We get the impression that this woman is being presented here for the first time. Dinah goes outside the camp[4] to see (ראה) about female companionship. The narrator's description of her motivation is not merely an aside, because it turns out differently from what Dinah had intended. She is seen (ראה), not by the women of the place, but by Shechem, the local prince.[5] He seizes and rapes her. If Dinah was seeking the company of women, she finds herself instead in the brutal company of a powerful man. The violent act against the woman is given a threefold emphasis. But after his deed the man's attitude changes. The rapist is moved by the girl at the depth of his being; he falls in love with her and seeks to win her love in return.

Although the narrative reports the deep emotions of the man immediately after the violent act, it passes over Dinah's feelings. In the ancestral narratives this kind of silence manifests the role of the woman as victim. In such situations women are not only described as passive; there is not even a cry of lament from the victim.

Excursus: A Lesson in Penal Law

The crime reported here is treated in the Hebrew Bible within the case law applying to the rape of a virgin. Two different legal codes offer different ways to obtain satisfaction.[6]

---

3. In my opinion it is questionable whether the notices about the purchase of land and building of an altar at Shechem belong to the same layer as the basic narrative of Genesis 34.

4. Dinah's going out was already regarded, at a very early stage in the history of exegesis, as inappropriate behavior for a woman. If a daughter goes into a city alone, it is her own fault if she is raped! On these kinds of interpretations and notions of what was fitting behavior for the daughters of Israel see Naomi Graetz, "Dinah the Daughter," in Athalya Brenner, ed., *A Feminist Companion to Genesis.* FCB 1/2 (Sheffield: Sheffield Academic Press, 1993) 306–17, especially 313.

5. In the basic narrative (see n. 11 below) Shechem is not the son of the ruler, but is himself the ruler of the city; "the son of Hamor the Hivite" should be regarded as an expansion by the redaction.

6. On this see Irmtraud Fischer, *Die Erzeltern Israels.* BZAW 22 (Berlin: Walter de Gruyter, 1994) 85–88.

The Book of the Covenant, in Exod 22:15-16, treats the case of intercourse with a virgin who is not yet betrothed. The choice of language[7] does not clearly indicate rape, but rather the seduction of an inexperienced girl. As recompense for the crime, the man must in every case pay the bride-price. It is no longer his choice whether to make the girl his wife. He must marry her unless the girl's father refuses to permit it. Even then, he has to pay the bride price. The Book of the Covenant regards the crime as "property damage" inflicted on a man.[8] If his daughter is deflowered he can no longer demand the full bride-price from her bridegroom. Hence the seducer has to pay it. The clause permitting the paternal veto has a mixed effect. On the one hand it offers a raped woman at least the possibility of influencing her father not to hand her over for a lifetime to a brutal husband. If the girl has been seduced, she has a guarantee of being married. On the other hand, the rule hands the decision over to the father, who can deal with his daughter however he pleases. He can pocket the bride-price and keep the woman in his house as a laborer.[9]

Deuteronomy solves the case differently. Deuteronomy 22:23-29 distinguishes according to the place of the deed and the status of the young woman. The first case treated is one of intercourse with a betrothed girl in an inhabited place (vv. 23-24). The punishment prescribed for both man and woman is that for adulterers: stoning. With her betrothal the girl undertakes the wifely obligation of fidelity. Another man's intercourse with her is therefore always adultery (cf. the connection with v. 22). The legal text proceeds on the assumption that the girl, if she was being raped, could have called for help and obtained it. The false assumption on the part of the lawgivers here is vividly illustrated by events in David's household. Tamar defends herself vigorously against rape by her brother Amnon. He had previously sent all the servants out of the house in order to be undisturbed (2 Sam 13:9-10). His father David had Bathsheba brought to him even though he had been expressly told that she was someone's wife (2 Sam 11:3-4). Those closest to the king knew what he meant to do with the woman. But if the woman were to cry for help, no one would dare force his or her way into the royal chambers to rescue the woman from the hands of her rapist! Thus the distinction established in the Deuteronomic

---

7. For a comparison of the two laws, in the Book of the Covenant and in Deuteronomy, see Carolyn Pressler, *The View of Women Found in the Deuteronomic Family Laws*. BZAW 216 (Berlin: Walter de Gruyter, 1993) 37–41. She points out (p. 37) that the girl's agreement or refusal does not define the legal situation.

8. On this see Ludger Schwienhorst-Schönberger, *Das Bundesbuch (Ex 20,22–23,33)*. BZAW 188 (Berlin: Walter de Gruyter, 1990) 211–12.

9. Thus Eckart Otto, "Zur Stellung der Frau in den ältesten Rechtstexten des Alten Testaments (Ex 20,14; 22,15f.)—wider die hermeneutische Naivität im Umgang mit den Alten Testament," *ZEE* 26 (1982) 279–305, at 288.

law code only protected the rights of a future husband in case the girl should willingly sleep with another man. It offered no protection for the woman. If the rapist was in a position of authority over those who heard her cries for help, the woman was without protection. This is generally the case with intra-familial sexual assault even today.

The second case treated by Deut 22:25-27 is rape in the open field. This text establishes a presumption of innocence for the woman, since her cries would not be heard in an uninhabited place. In this case only the rapist is to be punished as an adulterer; the betrothed woman is to be acquitted.

The third case, Deut 22:28-29, treats sexual assault on an unbetrothed girl. The solution is different from that in the Book of the Covenant. No distinction of place is made. The rapist has to pay a bride-price of fifty pieces of silver to the father of the woman and must marry her.[10] In such a marriage the husband has no right to divorce his wife. This rule is extremely dubious for the woman. On the one hand, the prohibition on divorce guarantees her that her husband will not be able to treat her as he pleases yet again. On the other hand, here the woman can be bound for life to a brutal husband, without her father being able to intervene. This legal text does not, as does the Book of the Covenant, speak of the possibility of seduction, but expressly of rape. Thus the man's obligation to marry the woman does not serve her as security in case she has allowed herself to be persuaded. It only relieves the father of the need to seek a husband for his daughter who will take her in spite of her no longer being a virgin.

Ancient Israel—unlike Christianity—placed no value on virginity as such. The intactness of a young woman was of vital interest only to her husband at the time of marriage. He is thus assured that the children his wife bears, who will continue his patrilinear genealogy, are his own.

All four legal texts that establish punishment for rape assume an intact girl as the victim. The agents of the law did not imagine the rape of a married woman. However, the narrative texts of the Hebrew Bible speak a different language. Again and again there are reports of sexual violence against women (cf. Judges 19 and the narratives of abandonment; Gen 35:22 and 2 Samuel 11 seem at least to presume sexual force). The divergence between codified law and stories told from life lays open the whole problem of the lack of protection for women. The law was written by men in a patriarchal society. That such vital interests as protection of the personal and bodily integrity of women are not anchored in law is a fatal consequence of the legal system of an androcentrically ordered society. However, our present Euro-American culture has no legitimate reason to

10. The rule that rape is not simply rape, but the severity of the offense is measured by the status of the woman, clearly reveals the lawgiver's androcentric point of view. It is not the woman who, in principle, is being protected from assaults, but the husband's rights over female sexuality (on this see Pressler, *Women,* 37).

condemn the First Testament for having laws that are inhumane toward women. Rape is still regarded as a trivial offense, and it is frequently the case that women have to supply the proof of the deed. If some countries have changed their laws in this regard in very recent times, this is only because the women's movement has brought pressure on this particular point.

2. Don't trust anybody about marriage!

After Shechem has raped the young woman, his uncontrolled lust changes to a desire to possess her for life. When v. 3 says that he loved the girl, it reflects the male view of reality. In any case, he tries everything in order to obtain Dinah as his wife.

The narrative about the marriage negotiations that follows is probably not all from the same source. A basic narrative was later expanded by a redactor.[11] The older version has Shechem, the ruler of the city, appear on his own behalf to seek the woman as his bride. When the man goes out to Jacob to negotiate, the latter's sons are just coming from the field and hear what has happened. They react with shock and wrath. What Shechem has done is shameful in Israel. Rape is one of the things that are not done (v. 7).[12]

> Then Shechem spoke to her father and brothers: "If I find favor in your eyes, tell me what I must give! Make the bride-price and bride-gift as high as you will, I will give what you ask of me. But give me the girl as my wife!" (34:11-12)

Shechem knows that he is in a very weak negotiating position. He makes a formal petition for the woman. The amount of the bride-price and the morning gift play no part for him. He is ready for anything, if he can only have Dinah as his wife. But the brothers respond deceptively by presenting circumcision as the *sine qua non*. They negotiate, as a precondition for the marriage, the collective circumcision of the male inhabitants of the city of Shechem (vv. 14-15). If the condition is not fulfilled, they will take their sister and go (v. 17). Shechem does not hesitate to fulfill even this

---

11. The idea of a basic narrative expanded by a redaction was proposed by Martin Noth, *Überlieferungsgeschichte des Pentateuch* (3rd ed. Stuttgart: Kohlhammer, 1948) 31. Blum, *Komposition*, 215, has slightly modified the thesis. According to him the redaction includes vv. 4, 6, 8-10, (15-17*?), 20-23, and the allusions to Hamor in vv. 13, 18, 24, 26. Following these suggestions (and Claus Westermann, *Genesis*. BK I/2 [Neukirchen-Vluyn: Neukirchener Verlag, 1981] 652–53), I define the basic layer as follows: vv. 1-3, 5*-7, 11-13*, 14-15*, 17-18*, 19a*, 24*-26*, 30a*, 31; * indicates the references to Hamor, attributable to the redaction, as well as the view of the rape of Dinah as "pollution" (טמא, vv. 5a, 13a, 27b).

12. This formulation is also found in Abimelech's demand for accounting in 20:9; it refers to deeds that offend against propriety, custom, and law.

condition, and he successfully persuades his subjects (vv. 19a*, 24). But when the men are feverish after the surgery, Dinah's full brothers, Simeon and Levi, attack the defenseless city, force their way into Shechem's chamber, kill him, and remove Dinah from the house. When Jacob rebukes them, saying that they have ruined his reputation among the inhabitants of the land, Simeon and Levi justify themselves: "Can they treat our sister like a whore?" (34:31).

Even though all the events center on Dinah, her fate is completely obliterated. The woman's will counts for nothing, neither for Shechem, who wants to marry her at all costs, nor for her brothers, who exact revenge for her.[13] Dinah's mother, Leah, never appears in the story at all. Considering all that has already been said about the mothers' intervention on behalf of their *sons* in Genesis, the absence of the mother when her *daughter* is threatened is doubly noticeable. Dinah herself says not a word. The center of interest is the rapist, who is betrayed and becomes a victim of the brothers. The demand of the sons of Jacob for circumcision turns out to be a ruse. It serves to neutralize the armed men and enable them to approach the defenseless ruler of the city without danger. The brothers carry out what Deuteronomy envisions for the rape of a virgin in the open field: the death of the perpetrator.

Only in the course of the narrative does it become clear that Shechem had taken the girl into his house. Whether she is held there against her will or whether this is the result of his "speaking to her heart" remains open.[14] After Simeon and Levi have killed the man, they take their sister away from the foreign ruler's house.

The story told here is, from several points of view, a variation on the three abandonment stories (Gen 12:10-20; 20; 26:1-11).[15] Shechem confirms the ancient prejudice of the ancestors, that the people of the foreign cities are sexually unbridled. He takes the woman by force, although without endangering the men. A woman from the family in the line of the promise is desired by the ruler of a city and taken into his house. He wants to have her as his wife and in this matter he is deceived. The woman, as in

13. "If the same assumptions are operating in the Deuteronomic laws and in the Dinah story, then the offence in the story is not that Shechem had sexual intercourse with Dinah without her consent. It is that Shechem had sexual intercourse with Dinah without her father's or brothers' consent. They control her sexuality. Their rights are violated." (Carolyn Pressler, "Sexual Violence and Deuteronomic Law," in Athalya Brenner, ed., *A Feminist Companion to Exodus to Deuteronomy*. FCB 1/6 [Sheffield: Sheffield Academic Press, 1994] 102–12, at 111).

14. Danna Nolan Fewell and David M. Gunn, "Tipping the Balance: Sternberg's Reader and the Rape of Dinah," *JBL* 100 (1991) 193–211, at 196 and 200, argue that Shechem's "speaking to Dinah's heart" caused Dinah to remain willingly in Shechem's house. But because of the offended honor of the family, her brothers refuse the marriage, which would have been the best solution for Dinah (cf. Tamar's speech in 2 Samuel 13) (ibid. 210–11).

15. On this see Fischer, *Erzeltern*, 231–33.

the abandonment stories, is omnipresent, but never has anything to say. The narrator leaves her in her silent role as victim.

The sign that marked the covenant for Israel in the post-exilic period, circumcision (cf. Genesis 17), is here regarded as a mark of belonging to the people, without any religious context. Shechem is prepared to adopt it. But the brothers take vengeance on him *after* he has allowed himself to be circumcised. Circumcision proves to be a means to the end of blood-vengeance. The brothers are explicitly shown to be breaking their word. What they propose will happen if Shechem refuses is carried out even though Shechem accepted their condition: They take their sister and go (vv. 17b, 26b). In marriage negotiations the patriarchs should not be trusted. As Abraham and Isaac betrayed foreign rulers by declaring their wives to be their sisters, so Jacob was betrayed by Laban through the breaking of a previously established agreement (29:18, 23-30). His sons continue the betrayal by pretending to the potential bridegroom that they are negotiating in all seriousness. Shechem pays for trusting Dinah's family with his life. Yнwн is absent. *His* "vengeance" was never deadly for the men, even though it was saving for the *woman*!

3. The escalation of vengeance

The later redaction altered the basic narrative in a number of ways. Shechem becomes the son of the local prince Hamor. Now, since the two fathers, Jacob and Hamor, are present to deal with each other, there is a negotiation about the intermarriage of the two groups. Through marriage the two will become "one people" (vv. 16, 22). In this way the demand for collective circumcision becomes a condition for peaceful dwelling together with mutual exchanges. Hamor, who now also enters into consultation with his subjects, succeeds in Shechem by promising them a share in Jacob's wealth. On the third day, when all the male inhabitants of Shechem are fevered and in pain, Jacob's sons attack the defenseless city and kill not only the rapist, but all the male inhabitants, take the women and children prisoners, and plunder the city. Because Jacob fears the collective vengeance of the inhabitants of the land, he leaves the area and journeys farther, to Bethel.

The changes made by the redaction are disadvantageous to all the participants. Shechem's father is portrayed as greedy; Jacob's sons escalate vengeance. The two young people who are the ones really involved are both victims. Not only Dinah, but Shechem too is shoved out of the center of interest in favor of a concentration on the two peoples. Although cultic evaluations that declare the assault on Dinah to be "pollution"[16] enter

---

16. This qualification of a rape as "pollution" is apparently unique in the OT (on this see F. Maas, טמא, be impure, *THAT* 1:664–67).

into the narrative, the demand for circumcision does not acquire a religious dimension. The critique of the behavior of the two sons, Simeon and Levi, is retained, and indeed is strengthened by the expansion of their revenge beyond all bounds.

4. The story of Dinah in its canonical context

There is an echo of the narrative in Genesis 34 in the words spoken of the tribes of Simeon and Levi in Gen 49:5-7. The two brothers are taken together, and both of them are condemned for their violent acts. Instead of a blessing, these two sons receive a curse (v. 7a) and lose their independence as tribes. Their peculiar existence as companion peoples of common origin who live scattered within Israel is explained by their brutality. Leah's second and third sons have disqualified themselves for the inheritance succession. The firstborn will do so as well. Thus the right of the firstborn in Israel is inherited by Leah's fourth son, Judah. He is endowed with the insignia of rule that point forward to the royal line of David, which will emerge from his tribe (49:8-12).

The narrative acquires a further dimension of meaning in the end-text of the Torah. It becomes an example story for the carrying out of the directions in Exod 34:12-16 and Deut 7:1-4,[17] which forbid intermarriage with the people of the land in order to preserve the exclusive worship of YHWH. The imposition of the ban is expressly demanded (Deut 7:2), and it is forbidden that a covenant be made. The brothers who escalate revenge carry out precisely these regulations in the context of the Torah. In this interpretation two groups confront each other:[18] Jacob, in his inaction (v. 5) and his scolding (v. 30), stands for the position that argues for both exogamous marriages and economic cooperation with foreign peoples. But the brothers act against mixing—militantly, to the point of dedicating the others to destruction.[19]

In the context of the First Testament the story of Dinah receives its exposition in Judith's prayer (Jdt 9:2-4). The raped Dinah stands here for defiled daughter Zion, indeed, for the polluted sanctuary (9:8). But the brothers, who are praised for their zeal, could not protect Dinah from

17. On this see Westermann, *Genesis,* 663–64.

18. This point of view is represented by Lyn M. Bechtel, "What if Dinah is not Raped? (Genesis 34)," *JSOT* 62 (1994) 19–36. The text, she says, does not speak of a rape of Dinah, but she, too, is on the side of those who argue for exogamous marriages.

19. It may be the intention of the redaction to shape Genesis 34 as a midrash on Exod 34:12-16 and Deut 7:1-6. YHWH's exclusive claim is expressed in the frame of Genesis 34: Immediately on their arrival at Shechem an altar is set up for the God of Israel (33:20), and after their flight, before the move to Bethel, the foreign gods are removed from the midst of Israel and buried (35:2-4).

being shamed. Judith, the God-fearing widow, will succeed by killing the violent and powerful man before he can lay a hand on her.

5. Reuben breaks the taboo

Immediately after the narrative of Rachel's death there is an inconspicuous notice regarding her slave Bilhah:

> And Israel journeyed on and pitched his tent beyond Migdal-Eder. And it came to pass, as Israel was dwelling in this land, that Reuben went and lay with Bilhah, his father's concubine. And Israel heard of it. (35:21-22)

Here, told in a single verse, are three capital crimes at once: Reuben, Jacob's firstborn, not only commits adultery, but sleeps with his father's wife. He thus offends against the incest taboo. He uncovers the nakedness of his father and at the same time sins against his half-brothers, Bilhah's sons (cf. Lev 18:8). Since nothing is said about Bilhah's agreeing to this, we must reckon at least with the possibility of sexual compulsion, if not rape. The formula "lie with" (את שכב) primarily refers to irregular intercourse, in most cases forced upon the woman (cf., for example, Gen 26:10; 34:2; 1 Sam 2:22; 2 Sam 13:14).[20] Bilhah is represented as having a changed social status. Either she became Jacob's concubine after the death of her mistress, or else the narrator uses the term "concubine" (פילגש) to designate the magnitude of Reuben's sin. The second interpretation is more likely. To refer to Bilhah as Rachel's slave, who had been given to the father to bear in her place, would lighten the guilt. Sleeping with the father's wife means putting oneself in his place. The rupture the son brings about by such a deed is final (cf. 2 Sam 16:21-22).

Israel's reaction—as before, when Dinah was raped (34:5)—is unusually lame: He hears about it, but does not call his son to account. Only in the great tribal blessing in Gen 49:3-4 is the consequence of the deed drawn:

> "Reuben, you are my firstborn, my might,
>   the firstfruits of my vigor!
> Superior in rank and superior in power!
> He foamed over like water—
>   you will not have the superior rank,
>   for you went up into your father's camp;
>   then you defiled my bed—
>   he has gone up!"

---

20. שכב in narratives very seldom (Gen 30:15, 16; 2 Sam 11:11; 12:24) describes legal sexual relations (on this see Wim Beuken, שכב, *ThWAT* 7:1306–18, at 1309).

Reuben is disinherited because he could not control his upwelling strength. The strength of the father that is manifested in the firstborn has turned against him. Nevertheless, the father retains his power by depriving the heir of his right of primacy.

The woman who was the victim of this unbridled strength is not mentioned in the tribal blessing. Reuben alone was active. As in the narratives about the abandonment of the ancestral mother and the rape of Dinah, the woman remains entirely passive. Through her silence and his silence about her feelings the narrator emphasizes the victimized role of all these women. While in the abandonment narratives the fear of the men that their wives would be desired and they might suffer for it was unjustified, Dinah's rape justifies the prejudice that foreign men are sexually promiscuous. But Reuben's act shows that women are not even safe from members of their own family. In having intercourse with Bilhah, Reuben not only injures the woman's integrity. He tears the social net that holds the family together.

6. Kidnapping in the house of Jacob

The book of Genesis is divided into three major sections: The so-called "primeval history," presented as a general history of humankind before the beginnings of Israel's history and linked to it by genealogical lists, the ancestral narratives, and the Joseph story, Genesis 37–50. In this last section of Genesis the narrative proceeds on two levels: one continues the story of Jacob and his sons, while the other narrates events in the life of the son who was violently separated from the family and later, in Egypt, was able to rescue all of Israel from death by famine. In the canonical final text the Joseph story constitutes the narrative bridge between the ancestors and the story of the people in Egypt.[21]

Genesis 37 traces the prehistory of the two narrative threads that will run parallel from Genesis 38 through 41 and are successively interwoven from Genesis 42 onward. The introduction, Gen 37:1, establishes a loose link to the Jacob narratives, reporting that Jacob settled in the land of Canaan. He comes to live in the land where his fathers dwelt as foreigners (37:1; cf. 35:27; 23:4). The *toledot* formula in v. 2 indicates that the story will continue from Jacob to his sons.[22] The introduction, with the note that Joseph was tending sheep, assisting the sons of Bilhah and Zilpah, is not continued in the narrative itself. The two brothers who emerge from the crowd in what follows are both sons of Leah (37:21-24, 26-30).

---

21. For the links between the two narrative complexes, see below, chapter 6, section 1.

22. The formula "this is the history (of the generations) of X" is always placed at the transition from one generation to the next. On this see Fischer, *Erzeltern,* 40–45.

Joseph, firstborn of the favorite wife Rachel, is not endowed with many sympathetic features. He busies himself with carrying bad reports about his brothers (v. 2b), he is preferred by his father, who shows partiality toward him, and he receives from his father a special garment that sets him apart from his siblings. And Joseph is a dreamer. He dreams dreams whose symbolism expresses his exaltation over the whole family. His brothers react to his frank description of these dreams with hatred; his father corrects him, but keeps the words in mind. The interpretation the old man rejects as presumptuous will later be fulfilled: In fact, the whole family will come (cf. Genesis 46) and bow down before Joseph (37:10; cf. 42:6; 43:26).

While Gen 37:2b-11 points a few spotlights at aspects of the family situation, from v. 12 onward this is a story of action. The brothers go to pasture their father's flocks near Shechem. The pampered Joseph at first remains with his father, but later the father sends him to his brothers to see if everything is well with them. Joseph is then supposed to return to his father with the news (v. 14). Joseph obediently leaves Hebron and goes to Shechem. The fact that the brothers are pasturing the flocks in, of all places, the locale where some of these sons had already brought trouble on their father does not portend good things. But Joseph does not find his brothers there. He follows the directions of a man he meets in the fields, and finally locates his brothers in Dothan (vv. 15-17).

At the encounter, the narrator shifts the point of view from that of Joseph to his brothers. They see him approaching in the distance. Even before he gets near them they decide that he should fall victim to their plot and die (v. 18). They make fun of their brother and mock him as "the little dreamer." They decide to kill him, throw him into a cistern, and say that a wild beast has eaten him. Then everybody can see what all his dreaming was for (vv. 15-17).

In the next scene the narrator focuses his interest on one of the brothers. Reuben, Jacob's firstborn, wants to rescue Joseph and bring him back to his father (v. 22; cf. v. 14a). He has already played his part in the inglorious sides of the family chronicle. Now he tries to restrain his brothers from their murderous deed. But Reuben does not take on his brothers face to face. He does not reject their whole plan, but only tries to stop the bloody deed. They can throw him into the cistern, and then he will rescue him secretly.

The spotlight shifts back to Joseph, who has now reached his brothers (v. 23). Immediately they attack him, strip him, and rob him of the sign of his father's obvious favor, the garment with which he has distinguished his favorite son (vv. 3, 23). Then they take Reuben's advice to heart. They do not kill him, but throw him into the cistern that contains no water. The brothers' cold-bloodedness reaches its high point here as they sit down, after their violent deed, and share a meal.

While they are still eating it happens that a caravan of Ishmaelite traders approaches on its way to Egypt. The precious cargo the merchants are carrying gives Judah the idea that such people must surely deal in slaves also, and the brothers could sell Joseph to them.[23] Judah argues in his speech—as Reuben had before him (v. 22)—that they ought to avoid the blood guilt that would be incurred within the family, between brothers.

What he suggests is trafficking in human life. Both the Book of the Covenant and the deuteronomistic legal code see such actions, which are described in the words of the commandment against stealing in the Decalogue (Exod 21:16; Deut 24:7; cf. 20:15; Deut 5:19: גנב, steal) as a crime deserving death. Thus depriving someone of freedom is assigned the same punishment as murder. It is true that Joseph survives the sale with his life intact, but he loses his freedom. The next chapters, Genesis 39–40, describe the meaning of that in detail. The brothers act together. They sell Joseph, and so make themselves in common guilty of the crime of trafficking in human life. The sale value of a seventeen-year-old (cf. v. 2) is established, in accord with Lev 27:5, as twenty pieces of silver.

One of the brothers did not take part. Reuben, who had suggested throwing his brother alive into the cistern, returns and discovers that Joseph is no longer there (v. 29). It appears that Reuben went to the well intending to bring his brother back to their father. He realizes that he has come too late to rescue Joseph from his brothers' hands. As an external sign of his deep distress he tears his clothes and begins to lament before his brothers: "The boy is gone; and I, where can I turn?" (Gen 37:30).

Reuben, as the oldest, feels responsible for his father's son. It remains unclear whether the brothers tell him what they have done. But after Reuben's speech they realize that they have to think of their father. As they had discussed in their initial plan, while Joseph was approaching (v. 20), they pretend that the boy has been killed by a wild beast. They take the robe their father had given his favorite son, dip it in the blood of a slaughtered animal, and send it to their father with the message that they found the robe in this condition. The father is supposed to guess for himself what it means. Jacob recognizes the robe, tears his garments, and begins an unconsolable mourning for his beloved son.

7. The betrayer grows old: The resumé of his life

Genesis 37 reads like a summary of the dark sides of Jacob's life. In his youth he betrayed his father by using clothes to pretend to be someone he

---

23. Sharon Pace Jeansonne, *The Women of Genesis* (Minneapolis: Fortress, 1990) 99–100, sees Judah's corrupt attitude toward Joseph as an introduction to his inglorious history in Genesis 38.

was not (27:15); so now his own sons fool him with a garment. What his father Isaac had once suspiciously tested (27:20-27), the old betrayer accepts without suspicion: "It is my son's robe!" (37:33a). Although Jacob is still in possession of all his senses, he does not entertain any mistrust against his sons. He utters the interpretation they are suggesting to him but do not dare to speak to his face. He himself had not only fooled his father with his robe, but had to speak the lie that he was the son Isaac wanted.

The constellation of partiality shown to one son, as initiated by Rebecca and Isaac, is repeated in the next generation. Jacob was his mother's favorite son; she helped him to obtain the blessing from his father. Rachel is already dead. She cannot protect her son any longer. So the father does it, in memory of his favorite wife. Jacob gives preference to Joseph among his sons in such a way that the others begin to hate him. Joseph himself nourishes these negative feelings by gossiping and arrogance (37:4, 5, 8). The brothers' mounting rejection reads in Hebrew like an additional etymology of Joseph's name (יוֹסֵף): "and they increased (וַיּוֹסִפוּ) their hatred toward him even more . . . (37:5b, 8b)."

Esau's rage and intent to kill Jacob resulted from betrayal (27:41); so now hatred grows among the brothers, and their plot to kill Joseph is the result (37:18-20). Rebecca's sensitivity about her two sons prevented catastrophe for Jacob. She sent him away to save his life. Joseph no longer has a mother to protect him. The father has no sense about his sons. He sends the endangered Joseph into the hands of his murderous brothers (v. 13).

Joseph survives his brothers' assault and even slavery through God's providence. His ability to understand God's plans through dreams links him to his father (cf. 28:11-22) and allows him to foresee not only events within the family, but political relationships in Egypt as well. This ability ultimately rescues the young slave from death and brings him to high position.

When he is reunited with his brothers, Joseph, like Esau before him, will experience the dissipation of his rage over the wrong done to him. Joseph can understand his life history as God's (45:5-8). In order to keep a great nation alive, God has reshaped the evil the brothers planned against Joseph into good (50:19-20).

8. Judah in the tradition of the line of promise

The story of the royal era is a story of the divided house of Israel. The house of Joseph and the house of Judah stand as symbols for the Northern Kingdom and the Southern Kingdom (cf. Ezek 37:16). Reflecting the political relationships of that era, in Genesis 37–50 the ancestors of these two kingdoms in Israel are selected out from the whole group of brothers. Embedded in the Joseph story is a narrative about the beginnings of the genealogical line of Judah.

The canonical final text, after the narrative of the sale of Joseph into Egypt and Jacob's mourning for his son, turns from the whole group of brothers and focuses on one of them. The bit of Judah's life story told in Genesis 38[24] is introduced by a statement that he moved away from his brothers (38:1) and joined a man from Adullam named Hirah. For the moment the narrator simply introduces Hirah, who plays no immediate part in the story that follows. Only when the narrated time has moved forward an entire generation will it emerge that Judah and this man have become fast friends. It is in his circle that Judah first meets his wife. Her name is not mentioned. The reasons for this, too, become clear only much later: The genealogical line will not continue through her sons. Thus it is no accident that the first attempt to establish the house of Judah takes place in Chezib, the city of betrayal. Of Judah's wife, we learn only her origins. She is a Canaanite and the daughter of Shua.

> And she conceived and bore a son. And they called his name "Er." And she conceived again and bore a son. And she called his name "Onan." And yet again she bore a son. And she called his name "Shelah." She was in Chezib when she bore him. (Gen 38:3-5)

The daughter of Shua is comparable to Leah in her fertility. The succession of pregnancy, birth, and naming inevitably reminds us of Gen 29:32-35. Nothing is missing except the speeches that explain the children's names. It is true that the three sons born here are not to be compared to Leah's sons in importance. In the case of Judah's firstborn, as in that of Levi (29:34), the naming is in masculine form. Many Hebrew manuscripts as well as the Samaritan Pentateuch have the grammatically feminine form. Since it can be shown that in the ancestral narratives naming usually follows immediately after birth, naming by the mother or the women present at the birth is the general rule. When the passages from the Priestly document later transfer the act of naming to the father, this does not indicate a change in an ancient custom,[25] but rather the intense interest in the agnatic family trees in the Priestly document.

---

24. For the structure of this chapter as a ring composition see Fokkelien van Dijk-Hemmes, "Tamar and the Limits of Patriarchy: Between Rape and Seduction," in Mieke Bal, ed., *Anti-Covenant. Counter-Reading Women's Lives in the Hebrew Bible.* JSOTSup 81 (Decatur, GA: Almond Press, 1989) 135–56, at 138.

25. This is, for example, Hermann Gunkel's interpretation of the state of the texts (*Genesis* [8th ed. Göttingen: Vandenhoeck & Ruprecht, 1969] 42). For the naming of children see Fischer, *Erzeltern,* 65–70.

9. *Tamar is to remain a widow for life*

After the birth of the three sons the narrator skips a whole generation and tells the story of the adult sons: "And Judah took a wife for Er, his firstborn. Her name was Tamar" (38:6). Judah had found his own wife, but he chooses a wife for his firstborn. There is no description of her origins, but she has a name. The narrator links the story of Tamar with Judah from the outset, for the arrangement of the sentence first names the woman, and only afterward the one to whom she is given. That *Judah takes* the woman will be repeated in the course of the narrative.

But Judah's son Er dies. It is said that he was evil in the sight of YHWH, who therefore caused him to die. Nothing more is said about his misdeed, only his name. Er (עֵר) could already hint at evil (רַע).[26] Biblical narrators love to play with revealing names (cf. the book of Ruth).

After the death of his son, Judah again takes the initiative. He initiates a levirate marriage for Tamar with his second son. The legal institution of marriage with a sister-in-law envisions, in the case where a childless husband dies, that his wife may remain in the family. The brother is supposed to beget a son with the widow in order to preserve the husband's name (cf. Deut 25:5-10). The firstborn of this union is not counted as the son of his physical father, but as belonging to the dead man. For the woman, levirate marriage means that she is spared the fate of the childless widow, with no one to defend her rights or care for her in her old age, and that she is again integrated into the family with full rights. However, levirate marriage cannot be demanded. The woman has no legal claim, but she does have a moral right to such a marriage. If the brother refuses to carry out the levirate marriage, the woman can appeal to the elders at the city gate. The one who refuses her must answer to the local authorities, and has to expect a social condemnation carried out publicly by the woman. Although the begetting of offspring for the deceased is given as the purpose of marriage with a sister-in-law,[27] in the narrative texts the law is regarded as a protection for the widow. All the narratives in the Hebrew Bible that speak of levirate marriage testify to the primary interest of the woman in this institution (cf. Ruth).

Judah's direct address to his second son is formulated as a command. The woman is again (as in v. 6) in first place; the levirate marriage is to be performed with her. Only in the second place does Judah formulate the purpose, namely, raising up offspring for the dead brother (38:8). Onan knows that the child to be begotten will not be his, so, while he does not

---

26. Benno Jacob, *Das Erste Buch der Tora. Genesis* (Berlin: Schocken, 1934) 712, refers to this wordplay.

27. On the levirate law in Deuteronomy and its interest in the preservation of the patriarchal family see Pressler, "Women," 63–74.

refuse to sleep with Tamar, he prevents her from conceiving. Onan has, wrongly, given his name to another sexual practice.[28] What he does is not onanism, but *coitus interruptus*. He makes use of the woman's sexuality but refuses her offspring, the only thing that can help her gain the position in the family that is rightly hers.[29] Tamar is supposed to be the mother of the firstborn of Judah's oldest son. Judah's genealogical line is supposed to be continued through her son. Onan refuses her this because he wants to be the heir himself. Yнwн is displeased with what Onan does, and he causes him to die, like his brother.

Tamar is again a widow; another marriage is over and she still has no offspring. Judah once again takes the initiative:

> Then Judah said to Tamar, his daughter-in-law: "Remain a widow in your
> father's house until my son Shelah grows up!" For he said to himself: "So
> that he, too, will not die like his brothers!" And Tamar went and stayed in
> her father's house. (Gen 38:11)

Tamar is still Judah's daughter-in-law, the narrator maintains. But he sends her, a widow, like a divorced woman back to her father's house without provision. He offers her hope that the one remaining son, Shelah, will carry out the levirate marriage, but he conceals the real reason why he wants her out of the house: He accuses the woman for the deaths of her two husbands. He doesn't want to lose his third son as well.[30] Judah can give an elegant excuse for his action, since Shelah is not grown up yet. The levirate marriage has to be delayed in any case. But that Tamar may not wait in Judah's house is a flat injustice. As a widow in her father's house, Tamar would have the right to enter into a new marriage with another man. Judah denies her that opportunity because he does not release her from the levirate obligation. Refusal of marriage with a sister-in-law would be merely an offense against the obligation of family solidarity. But maintaining the levirate condition while at the same time refusing the obligation of support is an offense against the fundamental right of the woman to a family and offspring, and thus to social position. Judah denies his

---

28. The intention of the text is not to condemn a particular sexual act but to reprove asocial, unsolidary action (on this cf. Jürgen Ebach, "Liebe und solidarisches Leben—über biblische Paare," in idem, *Biblische Erinnerungen: Theologische Reden zur Zeit* [Bochum: SWI-Verlag, 1993] 172–74).

29. Cf. Jeansonne, *Women*, 102.

30. Elke Rüegger-Haller, "Tamar," in Karin Walter, ed., *Zwischen Ohnmacht und Befreiung.* frauenforum (Freiburg: Herder, 1988) 32–43, at 34, emphasizes that Judah, fearing that his third son might also die, is thinking of the possibility that he himself could be childless. Annemarie Ohler, *Frauengestalten der Bibel* (Würzburg: Echter, 1987) 50, points to the narrative redaction of the motif of the "dangerous woman" in Tob 3:7-9. There a demon kills all the husbands who approach the beautiful Sarah on their wedding night.

daughter-in-law Tamar a fulfilled life by abandoning her to the fate of a childless widow while at the same time denying her the advantages of widowhood.

10. The prostitute at the gate

Time passes, and Judah himself becomes a widower. Shua's daughter dies (38:12), and Judah mourns as prescribed. That his sorrow is not excessive is shown by his next actions, narrated in the same half-verse. Judah goes with his friend Hirah the Adullamite to Timnah to shear his sheep. Sheep-shearing was men's work and was always associated with a feast (cf. 1 Sam 25:7-12; 2 Sam 13:23-29).

But the narrator dissolves from Judah to Tamar, who has now been living for quite a while as a widow in her father's house:

> And they told Tamar as follows: "See, your father-in-law is going up to Timnah to shear his sheep!" Then she put off the garments of her widowhood, covered herself with a veil and wrapped herself up, and she sat down in front of the gate of Enaim, which is on the road to Timnah. For she saw that Shelah had grown up, but she had not been given to him as his wife. (Gen 38:13-14)

The news given to Tamar, that Judah was going to the sheep-shearing, was apparently the usual village gossip. But Tamar acts immediately. She changes the clothes that show she is a widow, puts herself in order and veils herself so she will not be recognized. Then she goes part of the way toward Timnah and sits down at the gate where she can expect her father-in-law to pass by. What she has in mind is not stated, but her motivation is given: Shelah has grown up in the meantime, and she, still waiting in her widowed condition for the levirate marriage, has not been given to him in marriage (cf. v. 11). We would expect that Tamar would publicly challenge Shelah to take on the levirate obligation at this point. But she takes a different route, one that touches the promise-breaker himself:

> And Judah saw her and thought she was a prostitute, because she had covered her face. Then he bent down to her at the roadside and said: "Come on, let me come in to you!" For he did not recognize her as his daughter-in-law. And she responded: "What will you give me if you come in to me?" And he answered: "I will send you a kid from the flock." But she answered: "Only if you give me a token to keep until you send it!" And he said: "What can I give you as a pledge?" She answered: "Your seal, your cord, and the staff in your hand!" And he gave them to her and went in to her and she became pregnant by him. Then she got up and went away, took off her veil and resumed her widow's clothing. (Gen 38:15-19)

In the ancient Near East it was a punishable offense for a prostitute to veil herself.[31] Nor did it make any sense to cover oneself if one wanted to sell one's body. Thus Judah cannot recognize Tamar as a whore by her clothing. The veil is not a mark of her profession, but a means of concealing her identity. So how does it occur to Judah to address her as a prostitute? It must be the place where he finds her. It is in the gate that the men gather, and through the gate that all the people go in and out. For a single woman to sit and wait at the gate must have seemed like a signal to him. The clothing that conceals from him who the woman really is deceives Judah, just as he and his brothers deceived their father by sending him the garment of Joseph, whom they had sold. Betrayal through clothing continues into the third generation.

Judah's action is not evaluated in moral categories. Only the notice of his wife's death immediately before this could be regarded as an "excuse" for his having gone to a prostitute. Prostitution is a phenomenon of patriarchal society. Since wives and daughters are required to be absolutely faithful, in this view of order there is no opportunity to exercise sexuality outside marriage. An honorable woman would not allow it. But since men do not impose the same standards on themselves, there is a "market niche" that is filled by women who sell their sexuality. Judah has just become a widower and has not yet remarried. Tamar can apparently assume, and rightly, that he will approach her: a drastically realistic assessment of her father-in-law! It is not only his son who exploited a woman's sexuality; he does the same thing, although in this case he pays.

Impatiently (הבה, v. 16a; cf. 29:21), he urges the unknown woman. The narrator here specifically emphasizes that Judah did not know who he was dealing with, but he gives a lot of space to the haggling over the prostitute's wages, devoting to it the first long conversation in this narrative. Here a little piece of everyday life among those whom religious groups like to dismiss as a subculture makes its appearance in the Bible. However, the narrator's interest is concentrated on Tamar's skill in negotiation. It has to be a wage that makes a token necessary. Judah himself offers such a payment, since he does not have the kid with him. Tamar chooses as his pledge the most personal objects an ancient Near Eastern man possessed: The seal, which was the equivalent of an identity card, the cord, probably a beaded one like those worn by men in the Near East even today, and the staff, the sign of a respected man's dignity. Judah's lust is so great that he agrees to this demand for pledges that take from him all the external signs of his identity.

---

31. Cf. §40 of the Middle Assyrian book of laws; I here revise my assumption (*Erzeltern*, 32–33) that Judah could see from the veil that she was for sale.

Judah sleeps with Tamar and she conceives.[32] Immediately she gets up, goes home, removes her veils, and resumes her widow's garments. This prompt sequence of actions leaves us in no doubt about the woman's motives. She has achieved what she wanted. She did not sit down at the gate to be a prostitute, but to remind Judah of his levirate promise.

Beginning at v. 20, the narrator dissolves to the other partner in the intercourse. Through his friend Hirah the Adullamite, who here at last has a function after being named twice before, Judah sends the promised kid. But Hirah is not sent merely to deliver the wages; he is supposed to retrieve the pledge. He cannot find the woman. When he inquires closely of the *men* in the place about the prostitute, they tell him there is no such person in Enaim. On his return Hirah gives the same message to Judah, again in direct discourse: "Then Judah said: 'Let her keep them! Just so there is no scandal! You see, I sent the kid, but you didn't find her'" (Gen 38:23).

Judah is worried about scandal. Whether it is about his having withheld the agreed wages from a prostitute or that it should become public knowledge that he had lain with her remains an open question. He lets the matter lie, even though it bothers him that he did not get his pledge back. In what he says, his concern about his seal, cord, and staff are first in line.

11. "She is more just than I!"

The narrator brought Judah and Tamar together at the gate of Enaim, in the most intimate fashion, and then reported their individual procedures after the encounter. Now he brings them together again.

Whereas Tamar had learned through village gossip (נגד, vv. 13, 24) that her father-in-law was going to the sheep-shearing, now Judah hears in the same fashion, three months later, that his daughter-in-law is pregnant:

> Judah was told: "Tamar, your daughter-in-law, has played the whore! And see, she has even become pregnant from her whoring!" Then Judah answered: "Bring her out and burn her!" (Gen 38:24)

Without any investigation of the facts, the judgment and the punishment are declared. Tamar is still regarded by the general public as Judah's daughter-in-law, even though he has refused her the right of the sister-in-law to marry Shelah. The first and last word of the gossip is "whoring." The judgment has already been uttered. Judah imposes sentence without having spoken with the accused. Tamar is not to be stoned, as prescribed for adulteresses, but burned. This excessively horrible manner of death is

---

32. "Against his own will and without knowing it, Judah has achieved both his goals: offspring for his eldest son and protection for his youngest son" (Mieke Bal, Fokkelien van Dijk-Hemmes, and Grietje van Ginneken, *Und Sara lachte . . .* [Münster: Morgana-Frauenbuchverlag, 1988] 68).

threatened by Lev 21:9 as punishment for priests' daughters if they engage in premarital intercourse. We cannot determine from the OT texts whether the same punishment was prescribed for breaking a levirate marriage. At the moment when it becomes clear that Tamar did not intend to remain a widow all her life, Judah insists that he had not released her from the levirate obligation. Although he has no intention of bringing her into his house as his daughter-in-law and wife to his third son, he asserts the right of the head of the family.

> But as she was being brought out, she sent word to her father-in-law: "I am pregnant by the man to whom these things belong!" And she said: "See, now, whose these are, the seal, the cord, and the staff!" (Gen 38:25)

With a double accent achieved by two inversions, Tamar is set at the center of the actions. The first is done to her: she is led out. The second she does herself. Only when she is being brought to the place of judgment does Tamar break her silence. She sends the pledge to Judah and demands that he identify the seal, the cord, and the staff. Thus she does not release Judah from having to speak his judgment in full public view.[33] The supposed adulterer and father of her child is not unknown. It was not Tamar who sought publicity and scandal, but he himself, when he passed judgment on her.

The words Tamar sends along with the pledge are those that Judah once spoke, with his brothers, when he sent Joseph's blood-soaked robe to their father: "See, now!" (הכר־נא, 38:25; cf. 37:32).[34] There is only one difference, but it is a serious one: The woman has no crime to hide; instead, she is uncovering injustice! How wise Tamar had been to demand Judah's personal property as pledge, and how justified was his fear of being shamed, are now publicly apparent.

> And Judah acknowledged and said: "She is more just than I! For I did not give Shelah, my son, to her!" But he did not continue to know her. (Gen 38:26)

Judah recognizes the connections. Now he gives an entirely different judgment over the woman: She is more just than he, for he did not fulfill his promise of levirate marriage. Because he did not give her his son, she took the father. But Judah does not enter into a marriage with Tamar. It is explicitly emphasized that he did not again break the taboo against intercourse with a daughter-in-law.

---

33. This is pointed out by Helen Schüngel-Straumann, "Tamar," *BiKi* 39 (1984) 148–57, at 154.

34. This parallel was noted by John A. Emerton, "An Examination of a Recent Structuralist Interpretation of Genesis XXXVIII," *VT* 26 (1976) 79–98.

12. Tamar, the woman who founded the house of Judah

The last scene in the story corresponds to the first (vv. 27-30; vv. 3-5). The daughter of Shua had borne Judah three sons in the city of deception, Chezib. Two of the sons died. The twins whom Tamar bears, however, were begotten in Enaim, the dual fountain. They replace the two sons for whose deaths their father had accused his daughter-in-law.

> And when the time of her delivery came, see, there were twins in her womb. And it happened during the birth that one stretched forth its hand. And the midwife took it and tied something red around his hand and said: "This one came forth first!" And it happened that he drew his hand back and see, his brother came out. Then she said: "Why did you tear (פָרַצְתָ) a breach (פֶּרֶץ) for yourself?" And they called his name Perez (פֶּרֶץ). Afterward his brother came out, with the red thing on his hand. And they called his name Zerah. (Gen 38:27-30)

Like Rebecca, Tamar bears twins. This birth, like the other one, does not proceed smoothly. As with Jacob and Esau, the struggle for the advantage of being born first is reported as part of the birth process. The midwife takes care that the one who tries to force his way out first does not obtain the rights. The difficult birth injures the mother. The names given to the children are explained in terms of the birth process. It cannot be determined from the way the sentences are written whether it is the midwife or the mother who gives the reasons. The grammatically masculine forms of the naming (here, too, feminine versions are attested, cf. the Samaritan Pentateuch) should in any case be translated impersonally, since Judah is not present at the birth.

Judah is the only one of Jacob's sons whose genealogy is given in relation to the generations of the ancestors before him. There are notices of begetting and birth for the sons of Joseph and Asenath (41:50-52),[35] but they are not given a narrative framework. The house of Joseph is advantaged by the blessing of the tribal father Jacob (Genesis 48). But the genealogy of the house of Judah is linked, because of its narrative form, with the sequence of generations in the line of the promise. The births from the first marriage with the daughter of Shua are told in a way that alludes to Leah's bearing. But through the death of two sons Judah is in danger of being excluded from the line of promise. The woman who ultimately builds up his house is linked to him from the beginning of the story (v. 6), but he separates himself from her when, after the death of his second son, he sends her out of his house without provision and contrary to all justice (v. 11).

Tamar is depicted as a vital, determined woman who is not prepared to meekly accept the injustice Judah does to her. What her father-in-law

---

35. Here the sons are named by the father. The names interpret the course of Joseph's life.

refuses her through the last of his sons, she obtains directly from him. She sees marriage with a brother-in-law as an institution that provides for widows, and not as the continuation of male rights beyond death (cf. Deut 25:5-10). Tamar thus pursues unconventional paths, just as will Ruth, the maternal ancestor of the house of David.[36] Both women, through initiatives of female sexuality that are condemned in patriarchal society, endanger their reputations as "decent" women in order to reintroduce themselves into the genealogical flow of life out of which they, as childless widows, have been thrust by laws that are destructive of life.

The story of Tamar's giving birth is not accidentally formulated in reference to Rebecca's. Through his daughter-in-law Judah has been anchored at the point in the genealogy where the main line begins to divide into twelve equal strands. Through Tamar's story, Judah's line is established as the sole direct continuation of the family tree.

In the blessing of the tribes in Genesis 49, Judah's station, achieved through Tamar, is confirmed: He enters into the rights of the firstborn, after Reuben, Simeon, and Levi have excluded themselves by violent acts.[37] Again the stories of these brothers, the tribes of Israel, are written as the histories of women: It is through the stories of Bilhah, Dinah, and Tamar that the further history of Israel is determined. Their stories, too, are not private family tales. They write the history of peoples: Judah, the ancestral father of the Southern Kingdom, enters after them into the privileges of the firstborn; Joseph, the favored son of Jacob, achieves his outstanding position among the brothers, which at first was but a dream (Gen 37:5-11), by rescuing his people from famine. But Judah's story, like that of Joseph, is not a saintly legend from the outset; both have ragged corners and edges.

Just as the beginnings of the chronicle of the house of Judah were written by a woman, Tamar his daughter-in-law, so its continuation until the acquisition of the kingdom is again decisively determined by a woman: Ruth, the maternal ancestor of the royal house of Judah. In the blessing spoken over Ruth, Tamar is set alongside the women founders of the house of Israel, Rachel and Leah (Ruth 4:11-12). In the genealogy of Jesus Christ she is the only one of the mothers of Israel who is named. Neither Sarah nor Rebecca, neither Leah nor Rachel is mentioned. It is the unconventional women ancestors of the house of Judah, Tamar and Ruth, who are the mothers of the "son of David, son of Abraham" (Matt 1:1-17)!

36. Bal, van Dijk-Hemmes, and van Ginneken, *Und Sara lachte,* 73–74, recognize a parallel between the two Tamar narratives in Genesis 38 and 2 Samuel 13. They read Genesis 38 as a midrash on 2 Samuel 13.

37. The narratives in Genesis 34; 35:21b-22; Genesis 38, and the Joseph story are connected to the positions of the sons in the tribal blessing (on this see Blum, *Komposition,* 228–29). That this text group (except for the Joseph story) revolves around the fates of women is something that should not be overlooked.

Chapter Six

Subversive Women at the Beginnings of the People in Egypt

1. A little people becomes a "great nation" of the promise

The beginning of the book of Exodus presents a situation different from that in Genesis: Israel is no longer living in the promised land, in small social units, in family groups, but is eking out its existence in a foreign land as immigrant refugees from famine. The Joseph story functions as a bridge in the Pentateuch between the two great tradition complexes of the ancestral narratives and the Exodus. Joseph, the firstborn of Jacob's beloved Rachel, is sold by his jealous brothers (Genesis 37) and achieves high position in Egypt (Genesis 41). When famine breaks out in Canaan, he finally calls his family to join him in order to preserve their lives (Genesis 45–50).

The Book of Exodus[1] begins with a listing of the sons of Israel. In its form, this list imitates genealogies of names. But its introduction reveals it to be a list of immigrants: "These are the names of the sons of Israel who came to Egypt. They came with Jacob, each with his household" (Exod 1:1). The list includes only Jacob's *sons*. The families, the women and children, who belonged to them are simply subsumed under "each with his household." The female element in the genealogy is thus entirely lacking in Exod 1:1-5. This immigration list, despite its brevity, alludes to two other texts that did not neglect the female share in the genealogy:[2] The sequence of

---

1. For the structure and style of Exodus 1–2 see Gordon F. Davies, *Israel in Egypt.* JSOTSup 135 (Sheffield: JSOT Press, 1992); for Exod 1:8–2:10 see Cheryl J. Exum, "'You shall let every daughter live': A Study of Exodus 1:8–2:10," *Semeia* 28 (1988) 63–82.

2. For the position of women in genealogical texts cf. Irmtraud Fischer, *Die Erzeltern Israels.* BZAW 22 (Berlin: Walter de Gruyter, 1994) 8–72; for the lists of the names of the sons of Jacob see ibid., 48–56.

names follows the list in Gen 35:22b-26, arranged according to the progeny of the two principal wives, Leah and Rachel, and their two servant women, Bilhah and Zilpah. However, linguistic echoes and additional information point to the detailed immigration list of Jacob's extended family in Gen 46:5-27, which was partly extended into the generation of the great-grand-children. Genesis 46:8a begins with exactly the same words as Exod 1:1, אלה שמות בני־ישראל הבאים מצרימה, and ends with the same notice, that Joseph was already in Egypt and that the total of the immigrants was seventy[3] (Exod 1:5; Gen 46:27). Even though the list in itself has the character of a patrilineal genealogy, it is organized according to Jacob's *wives.* Ordinarily such lists count only the *male* offspring of a man from his wives. Here, however, the introduction itself deliberately emphasizes the *female* portion of those emigrating:

> Then Jacob set out from Beersheba, and the sons of Israel carried Jacob, their father, their *children,* and their *wives* in the wagons . . . and they came into Egypt, Jacob and all his offspring with him: his sons and his sons' sons with him, his *daughters,* and his sons' *daughters;* all his offspring he brought with him into Egypt. (Gen 46:5-7)

The wives, daughters, and granddaughters are emphasized in order to show that those who were coming into Egypt were already a little nation. In the body of the list, too, even though it is designed as a family tree of Jacob's *male* descendants, exemplary *women* are included: his daughter Dinah (v. 15), a daughter-in-law of Jacob in Simeon's list (v. 10b), Serah, one of Jacob's granddaughters from his son Asher (v. 17), and Asenath (v. 20), the Egyptian daughter-in-law who, as Joseph's wife, legitimates exogamous marriages. The fact that all the offspring listed are traced back through their mothers by means of the subsuming formula ("These are the sons of . . ." in 46:15, 18, 19, 22, 25) gives additional emphasis to the significance of women for the emigrating group.

Thus while Exod 1:1-5, in its brevity, appears to be a purely male list, the interweaving of the two lists from Genesis, both of them arranged according to mothers, makes it impossible to read it as a patriarchal narrowing of the family traditions. The observation of Jopie Siebert-Hommes[4] that twelve daughters in Exodus 1–2 rescue the twelve tribes of Israel can

---

3. Erich Zenger, *Das Buch Exodus.* GSL.AT 7 (3rd ed. Düsseldorf: Patmos, 1987) 30, refers to Noah's seventy descendants in Genesis 10, who there represent the whole of the population; here, with the number seventy, Israel is regarded as the "model of humanity."

4. Jopie Siebert-Hommes, "'But if she be a daughter . . . she may live!' 'Daughters' and 'Sons' in Exodus 1–2," in Athalya Brenner, ed., *A Feminist Companion to Exodus to Deuteronomy.* FCB 1/6 (Sheffield: Sheffield Academic Press, 1994) 62–74. The twelve "daughters" are the two midwives, the daughter of Levi, Moses' sister, the daughter of Pharaoh, and the seven priests' daughters.

also be applied to the initial list: The names of the twelve *sons* of Israel in the genealogy in the shape of a list of immigrants are then not only a link to Genesis, but a counterpoise to the twelve women who will rescue the community when it has grown into a great nation. Joseph's position in Exod 1:5 thus corresponds to that of Pharaoh's daughter. Both of them enable an integration into Egypt: Joseph for all Israel and the Egyptian princess for the one who will rescue Israel from Egypt.

2. Oppression

Israel's protectors in Egypt, Joseph and the Pharaoh who placed him in his high position, are long dead at the time narrated at the beginning of the book of Exodus (Exod 1:6, 8). But in the meantime Israel's extended family has developed into a powerful people. In the canonical reading of the two books of Genesis and Exodus this reads like a notice of fulfillment, both of the command to multiply in the creation account (Gen 1:28) and of the renewed blessing after the Flood (9:1), and also of the promises to the ancestors.[5]

What in Genesis was continually in view as a promise, that this would be a great nation, but seemed to develop only in a provisional way under constant threats of infertility and menace from without—this the ruler of the great empire on the Nile now confirms: in Egypt, Israel has become a people numerous and powerful (1:9), indeed, *too numerous* for the Egyptians. The prejudices directed at them are the same as those that fall on the poor, foreigners, and refugees today: they have too many children, they are lazy, and some day they may dilute our own people so much that they could take advantage of a national crisis and gain control.[6] All these stereotypes appear in a demagogic speech by Pharaoh to his people (1:9-10). The strategies that such tub-thumping speeches offer have also remained the same through the ages and are sold as visionary politics: "Come, let us deal shrewdly with it [the nation]!" (1:10a). However, Pharaoh himself does not undertake the concrete application of his "political goals"; instead, he leaves it to the people (v. 11: plural). The reduction in the number of births

5. "And God blessed them, and God said to them: Be fruitful (פרו) and multiply (ורבו), fill the land (ומלאו את־הארץ) . . ." (Gen 1:28). "And the children of Israel were fruitful (פרו) and prolific (וירבו), they multiplied and grew very strong and the land was filled with them (ותמלא הארץ אתם)" (Exod 1:7). Davies, *Israel in Egypt*, 182 brings together the parallel key words in Exod 1:1-7 and the corresponding passages in Genesis. However, the clearest echoes are Exod 1:7 with Gen 1:28; in this way the first two books of the Torah each possesses an initial note that points to promise and fulfillment.

6. Pharaoh's last fear is stated in deliberately ambiguous fashion. ועלה מן־הארץ in context means "rise up from the/over the land." However, עלה (escape from the land of Egypt) is the *terminus technicus* of the Exodus tradition (see Exum, "'You shall let every daughter,'" 68). Placing this fear in particular on the lips of Pharaoh prepares for the conflict in Exodus 5–12 over Pharaoh's refusal to let the Israelites leave.

is to be achieved through imposing the hardest and most demeaning work at inadequate wages barely adequate to sustain life. So that the oppressed may not revolt, brutal men are set over the Israelites as overseers. The nature of the forced labor is apparently intended to promote solidarity with the state: Israel's labor will be used for building royal cities (1:11).

Then, as now, such strategies have little success. The poor are always more fertile than the rich; the greater the oppression and impoverishment, the higher the birthrate (v. 12). When bitter toil does not reduce the number of births, the people are enslaved, stripped of all rights, and exploited; birth control through exhausting work is replaced by infanticide.

The narrative deals with the problem of oppression at several levels: The native Egyptians are contrasted with the foreign Israelites, the socially powerful against the socially weak, and in the next section men and women are contrasted.[7] However, the fundamental conflict is between the fascistic policies of Pharaoh and YHWH's fulfillment of the blessing of increase. The confrontation between YHWH and Pharaoh, which will reach its climax in the plagues, is already being prepared for in this chapter.

3. The midwives, Shiphrah and Puah

Pharaoh's second speech is addressed to the Hebrew midwives, Shiphrah and Puah (1:15-16). Two women whose profession is bringing life into the world are supposed to reverse their duty at the instruction of a despot, and destroy life instead! When brutal men have had no success against the Israelites, Hebrew women are brought in to carry out the next stage of the pogrom. For the Egyptians this is a clever solution, since it does not require them to get their own hands dirty.[8]

That only male children are to be killed is connected with patrilinear descent and the patrilocal form of marriage, which integrates the wife into the husband's family. A married woman has her identity through her husband; hence Israelite girls could marry into Egyptian families and be assimilated. In this form of society a nation that lacks men loses its identity—but slave women are always useful! It is true that in today's world we are better acquainted with the contrary situation: female fetuses are detected in the womb by amniocentesis and aborted. If a couple is not to have many children, then the one they have should at least be a son![9]

---

7. On this see Renita J. Weems, "The Hebrew Women are not Like the Egyptian Women: The Ideology of Race, Gender and Sexual Reproduction in Exodus 1," *Semeia* 59 (1992) 25–34, at 29–30.

8. Cf. Ina Willi-Plein, *Das Buch vom Auszug.* Kleine Biblische Bibliothek (Neukirchen-Vluyn: Neukirchener Verlag, 1988) 12–13.

9. For this practice, which occurs in Western societies in one-child families but is dominant in India and China because of state-ordered birth control, see Vibhuti Patel, "Amniozentese und

The midwives, however, reject this immoral rule for their service. They do not fear[10] the necrophilic Pharaoh, but God, the "lover of life" (cf. Wis 11:26), and they let the children live. The king's demanding of an explanation (v. 18) is equivalent to a disciplinary action: The two women must defend themselves because they do not kill! The midwives show no sign of fear or respect toward the mightiest man in the state: They do not deny that they have preserved life. To explain their innocence they toss an impertinent critique of Egyptian society in his face:[11] The Hebrew women are not as weakened as the Egyptian women; they are vigorous and give birth without midwives—which, of course, means that Israel is strong and vigorous, Egypt weak and necrophilic. That is all the midwives have to say in their own defense. Their words and deeds are framed by a reference to fear of God (1:17, 21).[12] God rewards their resistance to state power and increases the Israelites still more: God approves their disobedience and gives them families of their own (vv. 20-21).

In the New Testament at Matt 2:16-18 there is a counter-story in which the command to murder newborn boys is apparently given to soldiers ("he sent . . ."). They carry out the order without question. Whereas the women reflected critically on the command of the highest lawgiver and deliberately disobeyed it, for these men the unquestioned rule was: Orders are orders!

4. From intimidation to genocide

The Pharaoh cannot count on the women who help at birthings to carry out his orders for a "final solution." So he works on the lowest instincts of his people. His third speech (1:22) is again addressed to them. This time he does not just speak (1:9, 16); he *commands:* "Every son that is born you shall throw into the Nile, but you shall let every girl live!" (1:22). It is clear

---

Mord an weiblichen Föten," in *Frauen zwischen Auslese und Ausmerze.* beiträge zur feministischen theorie und praxis 14 (Köln, 1985) 50–54, at 51.

10. Siebert-Hommes, "'But if she be a daughter,'" 66, points to the word play in vv. 16 and 17: The Pharaoh gives an order about seeing (וראיתן) on the birthstool, but the midwives fear (ותיראן) God.

11. Helen Schüngel-Straumann, "Schifra und Pua," in Herlinde Pissarek-Hudelist and Luise Schottroff, eds., *Mit allen Sinnen glauben. FS Elisabeth Moltmann-Wendel.* GTBS 532 (Gütersloh: Gütersloher Verlagshaus Gerd Mohn, 1991) 45–50, at 47, interprets this justifying speech simply as a lie devised by female cunning. Weems, "Hebrew Women," 30, views the midwives' response more subtly: The Egyptians suppose that the Israelites are not like them; the midwives make use of their prejudice and the Pharaoh believes them because of his own ideology of inequality.

12. For the chiastic form of the midwife episode see Jopie Siebert-Hommes, "Die Geburtsgeschichte des Mose innerhalb des Erzählzusammenhangs von Exodus I und II," *VT* 42 (1992) 398–404, at 400–401.

from the context that only the offspring of the Israelites can be intended here. However, just as in v. 10, there is a deliberate ambiguity in the formulation. When Israel departs from the land, in truth the last plague will strike every son, this time of the Egyptians (12:29).[13] The whole people, each and every one of them, is now responsible for the extermination. Pharaoh "acts like a fascist dictator toward the Jews."[14] Older generations of Germans know what kind of surveillance and fear of denunciation provoke such compliance, remembering as they do the promulgation of the Nürnberg race laws!

5. Women with civil courage: mother, sister, king's daughter

Exodus 2 tells how people—again all women—deal with this sharpened command. An Israelite woman, a daughter of Levi,[15] becomes pregnant and bears a son. She is able to conceal the birth for three months. Of the child's father we learn only that he, too, is from the house of Levi. He apparently does nothing worth mentioning for his son's survival.

Three months after the birth, the danger of denunciation is becoming too great. The mother cannot hide her son any longer. So she builds a tiny, waterproof boat that is to save the child's life, as once the ark saved Noah.[16] Then she acts as Pharaoh had commanded—she takes the boy to the Nile. But she does not throw him into the stream; she places the ark in the quiet water among the reeds.[17] The woman thus turns the death-dealing command into a lifesaving act.

The narrative draws our attention back to the shore (2:4). There stands another woman who will take over the care of the little boy. The life-preserving deeds of the two women are placed alongside one another without links. It is not said that the mother has her older daughter as backup. This woman is not described as a daughter, but as "his sister." Therefore her act of rescue is to be seen independently of her mother and whatever orders she may have given. She does not act as a dependent of the family, but in family solidarity. She keeps watch and observes what happens with the child.

13. Exum, "'You shall let every daughter,'" 73, following Benno Jacob, points to this correspondence.

14. Zenger, *Exodus,* 31.

15. Calling the woman "a daughter of Levi" contrasts her with the "daughter of Pharaoh" (cf. Siebert-Hommes, "Geburtsgeschichte," 402).

16. תבה appears in the OT only here and in the narrative of the Flood. In a contextual reading of the Torah the lifesaving action of the daughter of Levi is thus paralleled with the action of YHWH in Genesis 6–8.

17. Siebert-Hommes, "'But if she be a daughter,'" 68–69, n. 14, sees a motif-correspondence to Exodus 13–14. The one who was in mortal danger and was rescued in the reeds (סוף) will later rescue Israel from mortal danger in the Sea of Reeds (ים־סוף).

To this very point on the Nile bank Pharaoh's daughter comes to bathe (2:5-6). She sees the little boat, has her maid bring it to her, and opens it—the tension is almost unbearable: The child is discovered by the daughter of the man who had given the command to kill it! The effect of the surprise on the princess is introduced with "and behold" (והנה), followed immediately by a description of what she found: "a crying baby boy!" And behold, the daughter of the unscrupulous man is overcome by pity. She knows what sort of child she has found here, and says so: "This is one of the Hebrews' newborn children!" (v. 6b). According to the command of her father and ruler she should throw the child into the Nile. But she resists it in her pity. The watching sister of the nursling, a "slave girl," dares to speak to this highborn woman, and even to make a clever suggestion, which she pretends, with diplomatic skill, is made out of servile zeal: "Shall I go and get you a nursing woman from among the Hebrews, so that she can nurse the child for you?" (v. 7). She will get a *Hebrew* wetnurse! She seizes the opportunity of the moment and interprets the situation for the concerned woman. In order to deny the Pharaoh's daughter any opportunity for doubt about her kindness, she doubly relates the child to her.[18] According to the sister's words it is now the princess who needs a wetnurse to nurse the child for her, not her crying brother. And the daughter of the man who planned the death of this child, overborne by this interpretation, actually accepts the suggestion. The real mother is brought, and—what irony!—Pharaoh's daughter says she will pay her to nurse her own child! In the princess' speech to the mother she does refer to the baby as "this child," but she accepts the sister's interpretation, that the child is to be nursed *for her.* So the baby is brought back, in good condition, to his own mother (2:9).[19]

When the child has grown he is brought to the daughter of Pharaoh, and he becomes her son. She adopts him by giving him the name Moses (משה). The explanation of the name, usual in such cases, in 2:10 interprets the Egyptian name Moses with a Hebrew etymology: "I drew him out of the water (משיתהו)."[20] As culmination of the twofold rejection of patriarchy, against the father and simultaneously against the "father" of the land, the

18. On this see Umberto Cassuto, *A Commentary on the Book of Exodus* (Jerusalem: Magnes, 1967) 20.

19. The section in 2:1-10 has a concentric structure; at its center is the discovery of the child by Pharaoh's daughter (vv. 5-6). The actions of the sister (vv. 4, 7-8) and the mother (vv. 2b-3, 9b) surround the core. The outer frame are the notice of the birth and the giving of the name (vv. 2a, 10). The actions of the physical mother and the adoptive mother correspond diametrically (seeing the child, taking, placing—bringing the boat, taking, seeing). On this see also Davies, *Israel in Egypt,* 99, 102.

20. Moses appears to be a short form of a common Egyptian name incorporating the verb *msj,* bear (cf. Thut-Mosis, Ramses). But Pharaoh's daughter derives the name from the Hebrew root משה, draw out. Ina Willi-Plein, "Ort und literarische Funktion der Geburtsgeschichte des Mose," *VT* 41 (1991) 110–18, at 117–18, concludes in view of the key word "bear" (ילד), whose Egyptian

king's daughter adopts the Hebrew boy as her son: A child for whom Pharaoh had commanded death because of his origins enters his own house and becomes his grandson! The common Egyptian name given to the child is, with its Hebrew interpretation, an enduring reminder for the daughter of her refusal of her father's command.

Moses is the only person in Exod 2:1-10 who has a name. It is true that Exodus 1 begins with a list of names, but Israel's massive fertility causes the sons of Jacob very quickly to become "the nation of the children of Israel" (1:9)—according to the promise, countless in number and hence impossible to name.[21] But the story of oppression and resistance is not about individual persons identifiable by name; it is about typical characters located according to their social position within the family: The daughter of Levi set alongside the daughter of Pharaoh,[22] so that the two together become the mothers of Moses; also the sister, representative of family solidarity in situations of crisis. It may be that the persons in the action (including the Pharaoh!) have no names because liberation from the house of slavery in Egypt belongs to the fundamentals of Israel's credo. Thus Deuteronomy repeatedly emphasizes the actualizing *we*. The Exodus event is not something that happened to a generation in the dim, distant past; it is the experience of the community of Israel even to the present day. The so-called "child's question" now asked at the Passover Seder makes this unmistakably clear:

> "In time to come, when your child asks you: 'What is the meaning of the decrees and the statutes and the ordinances that YHWH our God has commanded you?' then you shall say to your child: 'We were slaves for Pharaoh in Egypt. But YHWH brought us out of Egypt with a mighty hand.'" (Deut 6:20-21)

The namelessness of the victims and the resisters eases the identification of later generations with them: *We* were oppressed, and YHWH has delivered us. *We* today must also resist injustice and fear YHWH more than all the commands of the powerful!

Only the midwives, who feared God, have names. This may have to do with the literary-historical development of Exodus 1: Their story in vv. 15-21

---

equivalent is Moses, that the whole birth story in 1:15–2:10 is intended as an explanation of the name Moses.

21. So also Davies, *Israel in Egypt,* 100. Donald W. Wicke, "The Literary Structure of Exodus 1:2–2:10," *JSOT* 24 (1982) 99–107, at 100, advocates a contrary thesis: The namelessness in Exodus 1–2 is related to the oppression imposed on a nameless mass of slaves.

22. Exum, "'You shall let every daughter,'" 67, 74–75, points to the key word "daughter": Immediately after the command that the daughters are to be let live, the daughter of Levi appears and acts against it. The daughter of Pharaoh turns the command into its opposite by drawing the boy out of the Nile.

can be removed from the context without rupturing the thread of the narrative, but it has been carefully woven into the course of the story.

6. The infancy story of Moses—or the beginnings of liberation through women's resistance?

In terms of its literary genre, Exod 2:1-10 is usually counted among the infancy narratives. Such narratives trace the lives of important persons back to birth. In terms of tradition criticism that genre generally indicates a late stage. The older and more original genre is probably the announcement of an impending birth to the mother.[23] Such narratives emphasize the special, God-effected circumstances of the birth of a (male) child who will achieve eminence in later life. In Exodus 1–2, in fact, the announcement of the birth is missing. The "infancy narrative" is introduced by a simple account of marriage, pregnancy, and birth. The genres of birth announcement and infancy narrative already appear in the Hebrew Bible in conjunction with each other (cf. 1 Samuel 1–3); the best-known example of a homogeneous unit containing both is the infancy narrative of Jesus in Luke (Luke 1–2). The redacted motif of the miraculous preservation of the child through exposure and adoption is also found outside the Bible. The classic parallel is the infancy narrative of Sargon I of Akkadia.[24]

Can Exod 2:1-10 thus be called an infancy narrative of Moses? If we suppose an early point of origin and an originally independent unit of tradition,[25] this is possible. But the book of Exodus does not narrate a biography of the hero Moses; instead, it tells of the destiny of the oppressed and liberated people of Israel. The "infancy narrative" has been harmoniously woven into this web of tradition; it is inseparably linked at least to the last command of Pharaoh (1:22).[26] The embedding in the context makes Exod 2:1-10 an example story of resistance, applying the genre of the infancy narrative.

What is narrated here is the life-creating engagement of women in the widest variety of life-contexts: midwives and women giving birth, mother and daughter, slave woman and king's daughter. The women enter into relationship with each other across the barriers of generations and peoples

23. Cf. the passages in Genesis discussed above.

24. On this see Werner H. Schmidt, *Exodus*. BK II/1 (Neukirchen-Vluyn: Neukirchener Verlag, 1988) 53–58, and George W. Coats, *Moses: Heroic Man, Man of God*. JSOTSup 57 (Sheffield: JSOT Press, 1988) 43–48.

25. Thus, for example, Brevard S. Childs, *Exodus*. OTL (2nd ed. London: S.C.M., 1977) 11, who locates the infancy narrative temporally before the genocide tradition.

26. In 1:22 the motif of exposure in the Nile is prepared for by the king's command. The latter, in turn, is seamlessly linked at least with the first speech of Pharaoh and its effects (1:9-12). Only the story of the midwives in 1:15-21 could be separated without damage to the narrative thread. (On this see also Coats, *Moses*, 45). Exodus 1:13-14 is normally assigned to **P**.

as well as social boundaries, and they stick together to accomplish a goal: to maintain life against a death-dealing command!

The women presented here do not ask for the withdrawal of the despotic command. They ignore it. They act according to their own judgment, their own ethical norms. Shiphrah and Puah do it in their professional work. The daughter of Levi does it as a mother, her daughter in sibling solidarity, the daughter of Pharaoh out of compassion. None of the women is drawn into resistance by accident. They all decide, after consideration, for civil disobedience. They live it in a public context, where their engagement is demanded. Each gives, and each takes: The daughter of Pharaoh, who makes life possible, gives the child back to its birth mother to be nursed, and pays her for it. The mother in turn makes herself available as a wetnurse and ultimately surrenders her son to Pharaoh's daughter. The midwives preserve life; they do not threaten the women giving birth, but help them. They are not denounced for it; instead, they obtain the support of the God who is on the side of all these subversive women.

7. Women's learning communities and experiences in male society

God chooses this climate of resistance and the company of such self-determined women in which to have the man grow up whom God will ultimately send to free the people of Israel from the Egyptian house of slavery, resisting the power of the state. The narrative, beginning at 2:11, shifts its attention from the life-creating company of the women to the young adult man Moses within male society. One day[27] he goes out to his brothers and sees their enslavement. An Egyptian man strikes a Hebrew man. The word for "his brothers" is inserted twice in this verse, emphasizing the relationship to them of this young man who, in terms of the narrative context, is coming out of Pharaoh's palace. When the adoptive grandson of Pharaoh beholds the oppression of the Hebrews, his duty is clear to him. Moses has learned from the many women who preserved his life through their courage. He has absorbed their sense of injustice as well as the duty to fight against it.

When he has made sure that no one is nearby, he kills the Egyptian and buries him in the sand. The next morning he goes out again, and again he sees violence happening. Two Hebrew men are fighting. When he calls the guilty to account, asking why he is beating a member of his own people, he has to face the impudent counter-question: who has made him an "overseer's man," so that he can judge them? To the question about the legiti-

---

27. The introductory ויהי בימים ההם clearly formulates a new narrative beginning; there is a further correspondence in 2:23. For the embedding of these units in their context see Peter Weimar, *Die Berufung des Mose.* OBO 32 (Fribourg: Universitätsverlag, 1980) 19–21, n. 9.

macy of his judging them the man adds a more serious one: "Do you mean to kill me as you killed the Egyptian?" (2:14). The man lets him know that somebody was, after all, close by when Moses thought he was killing the Egyptian in secret. There is an undercurrent of threat that he will denounce him. Moses reacts with fear. He has to reckon with the possibility that the man has already betrayed him. And in fact, Pharaoh soon hears about the incident and seeks him in order to kill him (v. 15a).

The word-field of killing, striking, and fighting runs through this unit. The key word is אִישׁ, man. Moses has grown out of the life-protecting company of the women into the brutal society of men. In this oppressive society the women help each other. The men kill each other. While the external pressure on the women nurture in them the strength for boundary-breaking solidarity, among the men it breeds brutality. Even among fellow-sufferers in his own people, aggression breaks through, to say nothing of the lords and masters. Moses has a sense of justice, but he reacts just like the other men. He, too, has recourse to raw violence. His initiative against injustice makes him a murderer. Moses reacts as a man among men and is drawn into the spiral of violence. Now Pharaoh is seeking his life, too; indeed, he is seeking his life *again*. As a newborn he was kept alive by the resistance of the women. Now he has provoked persecution because he himself has killed. The man whom the women stole from the sphere of death through their cunning and courage has slid back into it because of his own first self-determined action—out of the sphere of the women, marked by the word-field "live." The midwives let the sons live and were accused because of it (Exod 1:1, 17-18). Exodus 2:1-10 is an example story for the preservation of life. And even Pharaoh's command allowed the daughters to live (Exod 1:16, 22). It almost seems as if the despot's command was unnecessary: the men are going to kill each other anyway. A command to kill female offspring would have been more effective in suppressing life,[28] because they all joined together on behalf of life.

Moses' (first) attempt to do as the women do and fight against violent power was a miserable failure. He was not guided by well-thought-out strategy, skillful diplomacy, or simple compassion, but by the male model of settling conflicts: brutal violence.[29] Whereas the first story of the women's resistance began with fear of God and saving of life (1:17-21), Moses' first

28. Exum, "'You shall let every daughter,'" 63, following the now-classic words of Phyllis Trible.

29. That this is not a cliché invented by feminists is demonstrated, even today, by the significantly higher crime rate among men, especially the statistics on violent assaults. Likewise, the violence of war (legitimated by custom) and its excesses are not simply social problems; they are problems of a *patriarchal* society. Despite all the outrage at the horrors of war, the misery of which falls especially hard on women, children, and old people, media reports scarcely ever make mention of the fact that violence is primarily a *male* problem.

story of resistance ends in fear of the despot and threat to life. Moses had learned only part of his lesson. All the while he was growing up, he had internalized the obligation to resist violent power. But he took his strategies for accomplishing that not from the women, but from the men. So Moses has to flee from the system he wanted to resist, and from its most powerful representative, the Pharaoh.

J. Cheryl Exum[30] has raised serious objections to the women's stories in Exodus 1–2: The women all appear in typically female roles and are restricted to the family circle and the care of children. Every action of the women is related to male offspring, especially the boy Moses. The story suggests that we should read the women as stabilizing the gender hierarchy and thus strengthening prescribed roles. The history of exegesis shows that such questions are justified. But if we read the entire prologue[31] to the Exodus event and thus also the stories that follow 2:10, a different picture emerges. The man Moses, around whom everything revolves, has to learn from the women what fear of God means, and has to follow a thorny path in working out their strategies for success. The stories in Exodus 1–2 stylize the threat to the male sex. But while the men of the oppressed group, such as Moses' father, remain passive or even turn against each other, the women find a means to act politically and in solidarity with each other. The women, in their engagement, do not remain in proper privacy. They move offensively against the representatives of oppression, the Pharaoh and his daughter. Their strategy of resistance is diplomatic but public confrontation. It is just this route that YHWH will order Moses to travel if he wants to lead his people out of Egypt.

8. The horizon of experience for the ancestors and their God

Moses flees toward the land of his ancestors and arrives in Midian. As with Jacob in Genesis 29, we find this refugee also at a well (2:15b). But the interest of the narrative is directed first to the priest of Midian, who has seven daughters. The seven women come to the well to water their father's flocks—just as Rachel did in Gen 29:9. But while Israel's ancestral mother was treated with respect, as everyone waited for her flock before joining her in drawing water, the seven daughters of the priest have to work alone. Even before they can water their flocks they are brutally shoved aside by the shepherds. The men in Midian are not much different from those in Egypt. Moses again takes the side of those who are suffering injustice. He

---

30. J. Cheryl Exum, "Second Thoughts about Secondary Characters: Women in Exodus 1.8–2.10," in *Feminist Companion to Exodus to Deuteronomy,* 75–87.

31. Cf. Charles Isbell, "Exodus 1–2 in the Context of Exodus 1–14: Story Lines and Key Words," in David J. A. Clines et al, eds., *Art and Meaning: Rhetoric in Biblical Literature.* JSOT-Sup 19 (Sheffield: University of Sheffield Press, 1982) 37–61.

helps the daughters[32] and waters their sheep as Jacob did for Rachel (Gen 29:10); he also avoids conflict with the shepherds.

When the daughters return to their father (2:18-19), his question about why they are back so soon gives us a glimpse of social relationships: Ordinarily the girls came later, because the shepherds pushed them aside every day when they drew water for their flocks. But this day a man stepped forward and took the part of the harried women. The fact that the girls identify their unknown helper as an Egyptian reflects his ambiguous status: the rowdy in 2:14 had already set him on the side of the oppressor people. However, the daughters' long speech and the father's response echo the key word in the last unit, איש (vv. 19, 20, 21) and convert its significance: The male society of Egypt was marked by brutality, and Moses let himself be drawn into it, but now, in his encounter with the young women, he enters into genuine solidarity, appropriate help against injustice—without the use of force. The priest of Midian invites such a man to join him for a meal, and Moses will settle down with this man. The two men join in common life.

As in the two comparable scenes in Genesis 24 and 29, the first contacts are made by women at the well. However, in a patriarchal society an invitation to a male guest cannot be uttered by a woman, and certainly not a marriage proposal. Both must come from the male head of the family. Since Moses, like Jacob, comes as a refugee and has no bride-price to offer, the woman's father must take the initiative for the marriage. Like Jacob before him, Moses enters into service with his father-in-law as a shepherd in order to pay off the bride-price (cf. 3:1).

Although the last unit in the narrative (2:11-15a) had no women in it, 2:15b-21 returns to the atmosphere of the beginning: The priest's daughters determine what will happen next. They encounter Moses at the well, and the longest speech is placed on their lips (v. 19), asserting the transformation of Moses from murderer to helper. It is they, also, who bring him to their father. One of the daughters, Zipporah, is given to Moses as his wife, and she bears him a son. However, according to the Masoretic text the naming of the son, contrary to the custom of the ancestors, is not done by the mother but by the father. Moses is thus placed in line with Joseph, who also named his children in exile, interpreting his life-context through the children's names (cf. Exod 2:22 with Gen 41:50-52).

The story in Midian places Moses within the horizon of experience and milieu of the patriarchs.[33] Like Jacob in his flight, he meets his future wife at a well, is invited into the father's house, and is accepted as a son-in-law.

---

32. Exum, "'You shall let every daughter,'" 81, points to the motif correspondence to 2:1-10: The man who was rescued by daughters now himself rescues daughters.

33. On this see Davies, *Israel in Egypt*, 148ff.

Unlike Jacob, however, he is not among relatives; like Joseph, he is in a foreign land. For a long time (v. 23a) he lives in the milieu of this family of shepherds, far from the inhuman empire of Egypt.

9. The call to liberate the people

The history of his people and the God of his ancestors begin to overtake Moses. Exodus 2:23 brings news of the death of the Pharaoh who was in power at 1:8 and who had oppressed the Israelites and ordered their deaths. The people groans in slavery and weeps the cry of the oppressed. The God who had supported and rewarded the midwives in their resistance to the unjust regime hears the cry of his people. He remembers his covenant with Abraham, Isaac, and Jacob, sees their offspring, and knows (2:25).[34]

But the oppressed children of Israel, according to Exodus 2, have lost their solidarity. What the women succeeded in doing, the men cannot manage. So, in order to liberate the people, God calls the man who, after an initial wrong turning, has followed the way of the women: Moses, with his sense of injustice and his engagement on behalf of the oppressed, who owes his life to subversive women and has found a new home through an encounter with women. The man who lives in the same life-context as the ancestors can also recognize their God and listen to him. The appearance of God in the burning bush, culminating in the revelation of the divine name, restores the continuity of the saving history of promise and support granted to the ancestors and their offspring. The life of enslavement will come to an end because YHWH will bring honor to his name and "is there." He hears, sees, and through Moses will free the offspring of the ancestors, whom he has made a great nation (Exod 3:7-10).

YHWH assesses correctly not only the situation of the oppressed, but also that of the oppressors: There will be resistance. The question of legitimacy will come from Moses' own people, yet again (2:14; 3:13-18), and freedom will be refused by the oppressors (3:19-22). Therefore the liberator God equips his emissary with the necessary tools for his negotiations. The strategies his God teaches him all have this in common with those of the women: they avoid direct violence. Only the *ultima ratio* will be the killing of the firstborn sons (4:23)—as Pharaoh's "self-fulfilling prophecy" (cf. 1:22) and a product of cause and effect.

Moses' departure to return to his own people is told with reference to Jacob's return (cf. Exod 4:19-20a and Gen 31:3-4). Like Jacob, Moses experiences a strange encounter with God in the night camp, at the point where he enters his homeland (cf. Gen 32:23-30 with Exod 4:24). Whereas

---

34. God's knowing in 2:25 (ידע) closes a parenthesis around the history of Israel's suffering that begins in 1:8 with the notice that the new Pharaoh no (longer) knew (לא־ידע) Joseph.

in 2:15 Pharaoh had sought Moses' life, but now all the people who had threatened him are dead (4:19), now YHWH himself is the threat.[35] But Moses does not escape through his own struggle; he overcomes by the alert assistance of his wife, the knowledgeable daughter of the priest. Zipporah circumcises her son and touches her husband's penis with the son's foreskin. Here interpretive words sound like the formula for an apotropaic ritual: "A bridegroom of blood you are for me!" (4:25b). As if the man's safety were determined by his relationship to his wife, she interprets the transferred act of circumcision not in terms of the threatening deity,[36] but toward herself. She accepts the Egyptian foreigner into the blood-kindred of her priestly clan and thus turns the threat aside. Moses has again been rescued from death by a woman![37]

The delivery of the people from the house of slavery, for which Moses has been called, is a long and difficult process. Moses does not, as in his early years, take the route of direct, violent confrontation. He seeks, as once the midwives and his sister had done, a direct but diplomatic confrontation with the powerful people responsible for the injustice, and he resists them. The learning he had done in the company of women bears fruit. In tedious negotiations with the Pharaoh he tries to obtain his people's freedom. The fact that he succeeds is due to the new foundation of his engagement, the one the women had modeled for him: He fears God. It was from fear of God that the midwives had drawn their strength for subversion. Now Moses draws from his fear of God the strength he needs for nonviolent resistance. Raw violence had brought him to fear other people. Fear of God makes him fearless, even before the Pharaoh who presents himself as God (cf. v. 2).

When, in Exodus' central saving action, the passage through the Sea of Reeds, a woman appears at Moses' side and, as leader of the people, gives the decisive interpretation of YHWH's rescue (15:20-21), the later genealogy proposes that this woman is Miriam, the sister of Moses (cf. Exod 15:20; Num 26:59; 1 Chr 5:29). In the canonical final text the rescuing sister of Exodus 2 is thus identified as Miriam. This woman has already shown

35. In each place we find the root בקשׁ. For this difficult narrative unit and interpretations that have been given it in the course of research cf. Schmidt, *Exodus,* 220–26.

36. This is also the interpretation of Alice L. Laffey, *An Introduction to the Old Testament. A Feminist Perspective* (Philadelphia: Fortress, 1988) 49.

37. This unit does not present an etiology of (infant) circumcision; v. 26b is probably a later addition that attempts to interpret the meaning of the ritual. Herbert Schmid's interpretation, "the pericope cannot be understood as a test of Moses, since then Zipporah would have been the one who passed the test" (*Mose.* BZAW 110 [Berlin: Walter de Gruyter, 1968] 31) comes closer to the point. Erich Zenger, *Exodus,* 65, refers to a correspondence with the Passover; there again the blood turns away the destroyer. The degree to which the unit was felt to be offensive, even in ancient times, is shown by the LXX, in which YHWH is replaced by an angel, and Zipporah does not touch the place "between his legs," but falls "at the feet" of the angel.

her courage and solidarity. Together with her, Moses leads the people out of Egypt (cf. Mic 6:4). And Miriam pours out this experience in hymnic theology: She, together with the liberated women, sings the first song of thanksgiving to YHWH, who has freed Israel from the house of slavery (Exod 15:21).

❧ Chapter Seven ❧

Naomi and Ruth:
The Unconventional Women Ancestors of the Royal House of David

1. Refugees from famine

The book of Ruth is *the* women's book in the First Testament. This is obvious not only from the name of the book, which commemorates a woman. In contrast to the other two "women's" books, Esther and Judith, the book of Ruth concentrates almost exclusively on women and their life stories.[1]

However, the book of Ruth—at least in its final canonical form—also relates the genealogical prehistory of the first king to rule over all Israel. Ruth is depicted within the succession of generations of the tribe of Judah as the great-grandmother of David (Ruth 4:18-22). Just as the whole people of Israel owed its survival in Egypt to courageous women (cf. Exodus 1–2), so the Judahite royal dynasty was founded on the initiative of two women on the fringes of society, on the brave actions of the widows Ruth and Naomi. That the book is primarily about women and not the legitimating story of a royal house is evident not only from the title, but especially from the structure of the actions. Although at the time the first edition of this book was written I was still convinced that the family tree in Ruth 4:18-22 had to be secondary for that reason, my more recent

---

1. For the women's relationships in the book of Ruth cf. Irmtraud Fischer, "Eine Schwiegertochter—mehr wert als sieben Söhne! (Rut 4,15)," in Herlinde Pissarek-Hudelist and Luise Schottroff, eds., *Mit allen Sinnen glauben. FS Elisabeth Moltmann-Wendel.* GTBS 532 (Gütersloh: Gütersloher Verlagshaus Gerd Mohn, 1991) 30–44. For feminist exegeses of the book of Ruth see Athalya Brenner, ed., *A Feminist Companion to Ruth.* FCB 1/3 (Sheffield: Sheffield Academic Press, 1993), and the bibliographical essay by Reinhold Bohlen, "Feministische Exegesen der Rutrolle," in Andreas Heinz, et al, eds., *Wege der Evangelisierung. FS Hans Feilzer* (Trier: Paulinus, 1992) 13–30.

researches,[2] following a gender-neutral approach with a feminist option, have concluded that the family tree must quite certainly have belonged to the original book: The book of Ruth continues the book of Genesis—from a woman's perspective. In this late stage the book consists of the narratives of the three generations of the ancestors, with their links to the general history of humanity (Genesis 1–11) and to the stories of Joseph and the Exodus (Genesis 37–40; Exodus). The passages in the text that link the different generations and places are made up of travel narratives and genealogies. Therefore if we are to appreciate the extension of Genesis in the book of Ruth as continuing the ancestral narratives we cannot do without the genealogy at the end. The women's book is quite rightly closed with a genealogy of men.

The first five verses present Elimelech of Bethlehem, a refugee from famine, together with his wife Naomi and his two sons. Elimelech dies in Moab, the land of refuge. The fact that his death notice in 1:3 describes him as "Naomi's husband" makes it clear that in what follows *she* will be the principal figure, since ordinarily in the First Testament wives are defined through their husbands, not the other way around. In v. 4 follows the notice of the marriages of the two sons. Mahlon and Chilion marry the Moabite women Ruth and Orpah. "Weak" (Mahlon) and "Fragile" (Chilion) die, giving full credit to their names,[3] and quickly, too. "There remained only the woman, without her two sons, without her husband" (1:5). The woman who narrates the book of Ruth thus makes it clear in the first five verses that the story to be told is about women.[4] The men leave the stage and die. Their women carry life forward—truly a programmatic exposition!

2. Naomi and her daughters-in-law

Without husband and without sons, in a foreign land: that is the low point in the life of the childless refugee widow Naomi. But it is also the starting point of a learning process for this woman—and for the readers of the book of Ruth. A woman without the company of men: that is the epitome of abandonment in patriarchal society. But that the company that re-

2. For these and more recent research see my publications: Irmtraud Fischer, "The Book of Ruth: A 'Feminist' Commentary to the Torah?" in Athalya Brenner, ed., *Ruth and Esther*. FCB 2/3 (Sheffield: Sheffield Academic Press, 1999) 24–49; eadem, "Der Männerstammbaum im Frauenbuch," in Rainer Kessler et al, eds., *"Ihr Völker alle, klatscht in die Hände!" FS Erhard S. Gerstenberger*. exuz 3 (Münster: Lit, 1997) 195–213; eadem, "Apropos 'Idylle' . . . ," *BiKi* 54 (1999) 107–12; and also my commentary on Ruth: Irmtraud Fischer, *Rut*. HThKAT (Freiburg: Herder, 2001).

3. In the book of Ruth there are almost no names that are not "expressive" (cf. Erich Zenger, *Das Buch Ruth*. ZBK 8 [Zürich: Theologischer Verlag, 1986] 33–36).

4. For more detail on the signals in the text that indicate a woman's point of view see Irmtraud Fischer, "Rut—*Das* Frauenbuch der Hebräischen Bibel," *rhs* 39 (1996) 1–6.

ally sustains life is to be found among women—that is developed, little by little, in the instructional narrative that is the book of Ruth.

While the exposition (1:1-5) reports one catastrophe after another—famine, refugee status, and the death of all near relatives—the next information indicates the beginning of an upturn. Naomi is not entirely alone; her daughters-in-law are with her. And YHWH has provided bread once again in her homeland, so that Bethlehem, the "house of bread," is once again worthy of its name. God's initiative allows Naomi, too, to act. She sets out to return home. Ruth and Orpah accompany her. In order to depict the life paths of the three women, the explanatory conversation that follows is not placed before the departure from Moab, but on the road, because only in that way can it show the alternatives: return to Judah or to Moab. Naomi's double command to her two daughters-in-law[5] does not indicate a deficient sense of community on the part of the mother-in-law, but rather her sense of responsibility: "Go back, each of you, to your mother's house" (1:8). Ordinarily a childless widow would return to her father's house (cf. Gen 38:11). But Naomi defines the home in terms of her own position, as the house of the mother.[6] She wants to see the two young women safe at home with their mothers. There, in the family circle, they will each find a new husband who will make a new home for them. Naomi's words stem from her wish that her daughters-in-laws' lives may not be like hers. They should not have to live as childless widows in foreign lands. With thanks for the love given to her and to the dead, she places both women under the blessing of her God, YHWH. Her parting speech and farewell kiss bring both daughters-in-law to tears. The loving community of the three women is to be broken on reasonable grounds! But

---

5. Danna Nolan Fewell and David Gunn, "'A son is born to Naomi!' Literary Allusions and Interpretation in the Book of Ruth," *JSOT* 40 (1988) 99–108, at 103–104, interpret this passage as Naomi's attempt to burn all the bridges between her and her Moabite past. Her desire to send her daughters-in-law back is said to be connected to her resentment toward the Moabite women against whom she nurtures (much like Judah with his daughter-in-law Tamar in Genesis 38) a subliminal and unspoken suspicion of being somehow responsible for the deaths of her sons. Ruth would prove to be a "millstone around the neck" for Naomi in her return home. This article has not remained unchallenged; cf. Peter W. Coxon, "Was Naomi a Scold? A Response to Fewell and Gunn," *JSOT* 45 (1989) 25–37, and their countering response: Danna Nolan Fewell and David Gunn, "Is Coxon a Scold? On Responding to the Book of Ruth," *JSOT* 45 (1989) 39–43. Fewell and Gunn are right to challenge the usual picture of Naomi, which represents her as an entirely selfless woman without interests of her own who acts solely for the good of her daughter-in-law.

6. Carol Meyers, "Returning Home: Ruth 1.8 and the Gendering of the Book of Ruth," in *Feminist Companion to Ruth,* 85–114, investigates female authorship and the presence of female experience in the book of Ruth. The "mother's house" offers a strong argument for this. We may add to Meyer's thesis that by mentioning the mother in his speech (2:11) Boaz, Ruth's husband, defines her origins not solely in terms of her father (cf. in contrast Gen 24:28: Abraham's servant does not follow this choice of words).

the daughters-in-law do not want to turn back; they want to go with Naomi, to her people.

Hence Naomi is forced to speak again, to persuade the two young women that they will be cutting themselves off from life if they go with her, an aging woman. She will have no more sons; even if they were begotten in this very night, it would be too late for these young women to wait for a levirate marriage,[7] something that could only be carried out by a physical brother of the two dead men. Naomi's first speech ended with a blessing; the second closes with a clear refusal. While the first was a statement of thanks and a wish at parting, the second is an attempt to persuade them that community with her means having no future. Naomi's bitterness comes to clear expression for the first time: "it has been far more bitter for me than for you, because the hand of YHWH has turned against me!" (1:13). And again the two young women lift up their voices and weep. This time it is not only because of the pain of parting, but also out of sorrow for their dead future with Naomi.

Orpah is reasonable. She does what her mother-in-law says, and turns back. Orpah is the rational woman who accepts the advice of an experienced woman. The parting kiss seals the community of the two women and their agreement. Ruth, however, is unreasonable. A third attempt at persuasion on the part of Naomi presents the departing Orpah as a model. Ruth ought to follow her sister-in-law; she should turn back and go home to her people and her God (1:15). Ruth, who up to this point was only weeping, now breaks her silence and presents her view of things. She urges her mother-in-law not to continue to press her with her urgent advice. Turning back means abandoning Naomi. Ruth, taking up Naomi's own words, presents her own view of life. The young woman will, for her mother-in-law's sake, leave her own people and land and follow the God of Israel, whom she has learned to know through Naomi ("your God"). This decision aligns Ruth with Abraham and Rebecca, who had also left land, people, and parental house to go to Judea (cf. Gen 12:1-4; 24:58; Ruth 2:11):

> Where you go, I will go; where you lodge, I will lodge; your people shall be my people, and your God my God. Where you die, I will die—there will I be buried!" (1:16-17)

With a self-cursing oath she swears fidelity unto death, and even beyond (1:17). This determined speech from Ruth silences Naomi's advice. The triple allusion to dying together with her mother-in-law causes every objection to fall away, and yet is a decision for life with a new family in the homeland. No further discussion between the women is related, but also no expression of joy over Ruth's faithfulness.

---

7. For the legal status of levirate marriage see Chapter Five, Part 9 above.

3. Naomi and the women of Bethlehem

The next scene, in 1:19-22, takes place in Naomi's home town, in Bethlehem. The entrance of the two women creates a sensation in the city. When the women there see her they recognize her and cry in astonishment: "Is this Naomi?" (1:19b). In this way they give her a chance to use her name to tell her fate: She will no longer be called Naomi, "pleasant," but Mara, "bitter." As in the second speech to her daughters-in-law, she laments that YHWH has brought bitterness upon her (1:13, 20). Four times over she traces the source of her misery—like a female Job-figure—to YHWH. Bitter, empty, and stricken by God's harsh dealing, she also acknowledges that *he* has brought her home (1:21). Naomi says nothing about being thankful that Ruth has accompanied her. It was her decision, and it did nothing to lighten her misery. However, the narrator does not forget the faithful Moabite: She explicitly emphasizes that Naomi has not returned alone to Bethlehem. Ruth, the Moabite, her daughter-in-law, came with her (1:22).

With the arrival in Bethlehem, Ruth's origins are explicitly addressed. Although according to 1:16-17 she has adopted Naomi's God and people, she remains "the Moabite woman" until her marriage to Boaz in 4:10. According to Deut 23:4-6, belonging to the people of Moab prevents anyone from being accepted into the community of Israel. In the post-exilic period the groups that polemicized against mixed marriages in the books of Ezra and Nehemiah (Ezra 9–10; Neh 13:23-31) appealed to this so-called Moabite paragraph, cited in Neh 13:1 as a command of Moses, explicitly referring to Moabite women. The book of Ruth represents an opposite[8] opinion and attempts to establish it as an equally valid interpretation of the Law: It tells a non-polemical counter-story to the texts that claimed the Moabite paragraph for their side and pointed to David's son Solomon as a negative example (cf. Neh 13:1-3, 23-31). In this way, in the very first chapter of Ruth, the ground was pulled out from under the argument of the groups that voted against the acceptance of foreigners into the community. For the prohibition on receiving Moabites was explained in Deut 23:5 on the ground that Moab did not provide the people of Israel with bread and water during their wilderness wandering. But now the Judahite refugees from famine find not only bread in Moab, but also a kind reception. And the Moabite woman who has left her people, her land, and her God to come to Bethlehem, in her YHWH-like kindness, provides bread for the Judahite woman even in her own homeland. The prohibition of the Law in

---

8. The exegetes who accept a late date of origin for the narrative frequently point to the unpolemic counter-position of the book of Ruth on the question of mixed marriages (cf., e.g., Amy-Jill Levine, "Ruth," in Carol A. Newsom and Sharon H. Ringe, eds., *The Women's Bible Commentary* [Louisville: Westminster John Knox, 1992] 78–84, at 79).

Deuteronomy is deprived of its basis by such a story, and so the command not to receive these foreigners is made obsolete.[9] The following chapters 2–4 will also successively demonstrate that the foreign woman will marry in Bethlehem according to all the rules of the Torah, and will be received as a Moabite woman even into the gallery of ancestral mothers of the nation and of the Davidic royal house.

When the two women return home at the beginning of the barley harvest, the arch between this point and the prehistory, which began with hunger (1:1), is closed; the scene is skillfully prepared for the events that will take place in Bethlehem during the harvest.

4. Bread from the daughter-in-law

The first thing one learns in ch. 2 is that Naomi is not entirely alone in Bethlehem; she still has family there. A relative, the landowner Boaz, is introduced immediately. Naomi's presentation of herself as returning completely empty and abandoned (1:20-21) is here again—as with the reference to Ruth in 1:22—corrected from the outset by the narrator.

When the two women arrive in Bethlehem it is not Naomi who takes the initiative, but Ruth. As a widow, she wants to claim the right to glean at the harvest (cf. Deut 24:17-22), and she consults with her mother-in-law. But unlike the readers, Ruth lacks information about the close relative. The brief, but loving encouragement: "Go, my daughter!" (2:2) shows that Naomi does not deliberately conceal this information. She seems to be frozen in her suffering; she is (as yet) incapable of any initiative. Thus it is "by accident" that Ruth gleans, of all places, in Boaz's field, where she immediately attracts his attention. He, too, addresses her cordially, but paternalistically, as "my daughter" (2:8), and explicitly invites her to remain in his field. With a realistic assessment of male misbehavior, he advises Ruth to join the women workers in the harvest, and he forbids the men to bother her.

This first dialogue between Boaz and Ruth (2:8-13) is marked by accommodation and respect for the woman who, like Abraham and Rebecca, has freely left her people and her parental house out of love for her mother-in-law. Although Boaz knows about the two widows, he, their relative, has not yet done anything for them. Apparently it is not family solidarity that impels this man to such accommodation, but the fascination of

9. On this see especially Jürgen Ebach, "Fremde in Moab—Fremde aus Moab," in idem and Richard Faber, eds., *Bibel und Literatur* (Munich: Fink, 1995) 277–304, and Georg Braulik, "Das Deuteronomium und die Bücher Ijob, Sprichwörter, Rut," in Erich Zenger, ed., *Die Tora als Kanon für Juden und Christen*. HBS 10 (Freiburg: Herder, 1996) 61–138, at 116. These two articles have substantially influenced the further development of my interpretation of Ruth represented by the second edition of this book.

Ruth.[10] The blessing he extends to Ruth wishes the woman protection, security, and a reward for her own blessed actions. Ruth's answer is marked by gratitude. She is aware of her insecure status as a foreign, childless widow. With a diplomatic choice of words she calls herself his "slave," but also says that he has "spoken to her heart," thereby expressing more than gratitude; she indicates that she has been comforted (2:13).

The man's attention then increases and becomes materially concrete: while in the morning he had permitted her to glean and to drink with his own workers, at midday he invites her to the meal (2:9, 14) and gives instructions that Ruth be allowed to glean from the whole field, and not only from the fallen remnants of the sheaves (2:15-16). In the evening Ruth returns home to Naomi with an abundant harvest, and also brings her the leftovers from her midday meal. Even before she can tell her mother-in-law which landowner's field she has gleaned in, Naomi blesses the generous man. Abraham's servant had praised YHWH in very similar words when, in his search for a bride, he encountered the young Rebecca (Gen 24:27; cf. Ruth 2:20).[11] The "providence" in the book of Ruth is thus interpreted in terms of what has gone before, in the time of the ancestors.

When Naomi hears the name of Boaz she remembers this relative as "one of our redeemers." This is the first time Naomi speaks of "us" in reference to Ruth and herself. The learning process in which Naomi is recognizing more and more clearly that the most important relationship in her life is not to a man, but to this faithful woman, is developing rapidly!

Now, for the first time, Ruth catches up with the knowledge that was already granted to the readers (cf. 2:1). But she herself, through her diligence (2:7) and the story of her life (2:11) has already built solid bridges to the man. She can tell her mother-in-law that the permission given her to glean is valid for the whole harvest. But that Boaz, according to what Naomi says, is *one* of the family "redeemers" prepares us for the appearance of the nameless redeemer (3:12; 4:1-8) who, by undertaking the levirate obligation, could still prevent Ruth and Boaz from becoming a couple.

Naomi approves her daughter-in-law's plan and is happy that Ruth means to stay with the women harvesters so she will not be bothered by the men. The mother-in-law apparently also knows about the "manners" prevalent in the harvest fields. Since both Boaz and Naomi speak of threats from men, the kind of approaches to be feared are clear: A single woman gleaning has to expect sexual harassment. It is now explicitly said that

10. Phyllis Trible, *God and the Rhetoric of Sexuality* (Philadelphia: Fortress, 1978) 178, points out that his passivity is not criticized, but in the rest of the action it subordinates him to the active women.

11. For the quotation-like allusions to Genesis in the book of Ruth see Irmtraud Fischer, "Das Buch Rut—eine 'feministische' Auslegung der Tora?" in Erhard S. Gerstenberger and Ulrich Schoenborn, eds., *Hermeneutik—sozialgeschichtlich.* exuz 1 (Münster: Lit, 1999) 39–58.

Ruth stays with the women workers through the whole harvest season, and lives with her mother-in-law (2:22-23; 3:2). The young woman keeps deliberately to the society of women and avoids the dangerous company of men. Readers are meant to keep this norm of Ruth's behavior in mind as the story moves on.

5. Ruth and Boaz

Now for the first time Naomi takes the initiative—not for herself, but for Ruth. For the same reason that she wanted to send her daughters-in-law back to their mothers' houses, she now makes a plan (1:9; 3:1): Ruth must find a place of rest, a place where she will be well off. Naomi wants to do something for her daughter-in-law, but she does not mean to "put her on the market." The beginning of her speech, with "shall I not seek some security for you . . . ?" poses a question for decision, leaving the choice to Ruth (3:1). However, starting with the loving address "my daughter," she suggests a daring plan: Ruth, who always stays with the women, should go during the night to a sleeping man, uncover his feet, and lay herself down! The mother-in-law's suggestion proposes that the young woman should hazard her reputation—which, in a patriarchal system of values, is women's most valuable possession. This time she is not to go to Boaz in her working clothes, but in a festival garment; she will be freshly bathed and perfumed. If he finds her there, Naomi thinks, Boaz will have to know what to do (3:3-4). The mother-in-law's intention is to initiate a marriage between Ruth and Boaz. But the purpose of the marriage is not, as in levirate marriage, to obtain a child for her dead son; rather, it is so that Ruth may be well taken care of. She sees marriage as the place of social security that will spare Ruth from worry about her daily bread. Thus Naomi's goal is an enduring security for Ruth,[12] not a potential son who could replace the one she has lost (cf. Deut 25:5-10).

As if Naomi had suggested the most natural thing in the world, Ruth agrees to this risky plan: "All that you tell me I will do." The subsequent scene at the threshing-floor crackles with erotic tension. Ruth finds Boaz sleeping between heaps of grain, uncovers his feet, and lies down. The narrative is here formulated in ambiguous language:[13] "feet" can also be a euphemistic expression for the sexual organs (cf. Exod 4:25; Deut 28:57). "Uncover" is often used to describe illicit sexual intercourse (cf. Lev 18:6-19). "To lie with someone" is also used to mean "to sleep with someone."

12. Only in the fourth chapter is female sexuality primarily directed toward offspring (cf. Athalya Brenner, "Naomi and Ruth: Further Reflections," in *Feminist Companion to Ruth*, 140–44).

13. On this see Ilona Rashkow, "Ruth: The Discourse of Power and the Power of Discourse," in *Feminist Companion to Ruth*, 26–41, at 37–39.

The encounter of the two by night is formulated by allusion to the action of Ruth's ancestor, the daughter of Lot, who lay with her father by night and then bore Moab (cf. Gen 19:30-38). Nevertheless, what actually happened between Ruth and Boaz that night at the threshing-floor is deliberately left in the dark. In any case, Ruth is the active person who causes the encounter to happen in this way.[14]

When Boaz awakens in shock and finds the woman lying at his feet, he asks her identity. Again, as at their first meeting, Ruth answers diplomatically: "I am Ruth, your servant" (3:9). But this time she chooses, from among the terms applying to underlings, not "slave," which in 2:13 had expressed her station among his menials, but "your (maid)servant," placing herself in relationship to Boaz.[15] Without waiting for him to tell her what she should do (3:4), she tells him what *he* should do: He is to take her under his protection, spread his cloak over her, because he is the "redeemer" (3:9). Simply put: this woman is asking the man to marry her!

6. Creative interpretation of the levirate obligation

What Ruth here suggests is a creative interpretation of the obligation to redeem, which regulates the reclamation of goods for relatives who have fallen into poverty (Lev 25:25-28, 47-55). The redeemer has an obligation to exercise solidarity in buying back the alienated property. Ruth suggests to Boaz a *halakha* to this legal institution by linking levirate marriage and the duty of redemption. The levirate obligation, which existed only between brothers, originally had nothing to do with the institution of *gᵉʾulla*, redemption, in the Pentateuch. It is true that both aim at the maintenance of the family and its share in the land given by YHWH. Ruth's combination of these two institutions of family obligation is a *halakha*, an interpretation of Torah, suited to her and Naomi's situation. Such an exegesis of the two laws already indicates that Ruth is pleading here not only for herself, but also for Naomi. She uses her mother-in-law's ties and the obligations of family relationship even though she herself has already established independent, adequate contacts to the man, and in doing so she leaves no doubt that she intends to remain true to the oath she has made to her mother-in-law (1:16-17). By linking the two laws she seeks an opportunity to permit Naomi to come with her into the house of her new husband.

---

14. Danna Nolan Fewell and David Gunn, *Compromising Redemption. Literary Currents in Biblical Interpretation* (Louisville: Westminster John Knox, 1990) 99–103, point out that while Ruth adopts her mother-in-law's plan, she quite independently carries out and is responsible for this encounter. Naomi is not mentioned at the threshing-floor.

15. The word slave (woman), שִׁפְחָה, indicates the station of a woman in the social unit of a family, while the term (maid)servant, אָמָה, emphasizes her relationship to the man (on this see Fischer, *Erzeltern*, 93–97).

Ruth, who has come adorned like a bride, openly asks Boaz for marriage. By the initiative of a woman who until this point has been described as extremely reserved toward men, the erotic tension has reached its climax. But it is abruptly broken by Ruth's appeal to the man's ethical behavior. Boaz answers with a blessing:

> "May you be blessed by YHWH, my daughter! This last instance of your loyalty is better than the first, for you have not gone after young men, whether poor or rich." (3:10)

This speech by Boaz is frequently interpreted to mean that the aging man is expressing his recognition of the fact that she is showing a preference for him and has not offered her love to younger men.[16] But from the course of the narrative it is clear that Boaz is acknowledging something that the narrator never tires of emphasizing: She has maintained her community with women.

In the form of a salvation oracle ("Do not be afraid . . .") he promises her that he will do as she wishes. His reason for this, however, is not his obligation as redeemer for Naomi, but his regard for her; he puts her on a level with himself (cf. 2:1): "for everyone of my people knows that you are a worthy woman!" (3:11b). It is true that he will choose his obligations as a relative as a strategy for bringing about the marriage, but his motivation is his attraction to Ruth.

The conversation in the night brings the success desired. Boaz is ready to do as Ruth wishes. But there is still a hurdle to be gotten over. Boaz is not the first redeemer (3:12-13; cf. 2:20). This discussion of legal complications thoroughly disrupts the erotic tension of the scene. When he asks her to remain with him through the night there is a link back to the mood at the beginning, but after this discussion it is more the beginning of the companionship of these two than an appeal to sexual union. Before it is yet day he urges her to leave the threshing-floor unnoticed. The woman's good name is to be preserved! But Boaz does not let Ruth go without a gift. What he can give her spontaneously, on the threshing-floor, is part of his harvest.[17] In parting he promises her that he will clarify the legal situation that very day. While Boaz is on his way to the city gate, Ruth returns to Naomi and tells her everything the man has done. She declares that the

16. With many commentators; it is pointed out, for example, by Mieke Bal in her publications on Ruth (cf. Mieke Bal, Fokkelien van Dijk-Hemmes, and Grietje van Ginneken, *Und Sara lachte . . .* [Münster: Morgana-Frauenbuchverlag, 1988] 77–99).

17. The Hebrew text has no measure for the "six barleys." Renate Jost, *Freundin in der Fremde* (Stuttgart: Quell, 1992) 56–57, interprets this as a symbolic gift of six barleycorns, meant to indicate fertility and the blessing of children (cf. the six sons of Leah). The number six expresses what is not yet perfected; the fulfillment of the promise is not yet accomplished.

gift is meant for Naomi. Thus the mother-in-law sees her plan affirmed: "for the man will not rest, but will settle the matter today!" (3:18b).

Naomi is right. Boaz waits at the gate for the still-closer relative who can claim the right of redemption before him. That this man has no name, but is only called "so and so," "XY," is again indicative of the significance of names. He does not want to marry Ruth, and thus he refuses to maintain the name of the deceased. His name is therefore rubbed out as fully as that of Mahlon. This redeemer only wants to buy the field from Naomi. Thus Mr. So-and-so cuts himself off from the *halakha* Ruth had given. But Boaz presents the matter as if only the two together were possible, the obligation of redemption irretrievably bound up with the levirate marriage (4:5), because he wants both. Before the elders at the gate (4:2-12; cf. Deut 25:7-10)[18] and the whole people, in conformity with the levirate laws, he accepts the obligation of redemption for Naomi and marriage to Ruth. As he had promised, the marriage is celebrated on the same day. When Boaz thus "acquires" (קָנָה: 4:5-10; cf. Jeremiah 32) the woman in marriage, the word does not refer to a marriage by purchase. The deliberate use of a technical term for redemption in the context of the levirate marriage links the two originally independent legal institutions into a single obligation of family solidarity.

7. A woman like Israel's ancestral women

The whole people and the elders, who witness at the acceptance of the obligation to levirate marriage and redemption, participate at the marriage of the strong man (אִישׁ חַיִל, 2:1) and the strong woman (אֵשֶׁת חַיִל, 3:11). The chorus of congratulations for the bridal couple then bestows on this unusual marriage a significance for the whole nation:

> "May YHWH make the woman
> who is coming into your house
> like Rachel and Leah,
> who together built up the house of Israel!
> May you be strong (חַיִל) in Ephrathah
> and call out a name in Bethlehem!
> May your house be like that of Perez,
> whom Tamar bore to Judah,
> through the seed that YHWH will give you
> from this young woman!" (4:11-12)

---

18. Georg Braulik, "Das Deuteronomium," 114–15, has since shown, with a synopsis, that Ruth 4 quotes the legal text from Deut 25:5-10.

While the congratulations are addressed to Boaz, Ruth is central; she is not, as usual in marriages, "taken" by her husband, but is presented as the active one, who comes into his house.[19] It is not the husband who is placed in line with the fathers of Israel; instead, the wife is written into the female genealogy of the nation to which she joined herself with her oath to her mother-in-law (1:16). The Moabite woman obtains a place in the ancestral gallery of the mothers of Israel! The two (שתיהם, 4:11) women, Rachel and Leah, who built up the house of Israel, are placed alongside the two (שתיהם, 1:19) women, Ruth and Naomi, who now together continue to build up the house of Judah.[20] The God whom Ruth came to know through her mother-in-law is to make these two like Leah and Rachel. As if it were a matter of course, the whole people says that these two women have built up Israel! Jacob receives not a word of mention; only the name bestowed on him echoes in "the house of Israel." This speech makes it plain that—contrary to what is found in Genesis, which almost exclusively lists patrilineal descent—there is also a tradition of descent from the mothers.[21] The congratulations thus transmit a piece of female historical writing and continue its tradition.

The second part of the congratulations is for Boaz, whose house is to become like that of Perez. But this house, too, goes back to the initiative of a woman. Tamar, like Ruth, had achieved levirate marriage by equally unorthodox means, and so had kept alive the house of Judah. The irregular use of "seed" (זרע) for a woman, included earlier in the wedding blessing for Rachel (cf. Gen 24:60), strengthens the impression that the following genealogy rests on the woman.

Ruth's marriage to Mahlon was childless for ten years (1:4-5). But now YHWH grants her fertility. After the elaborate, drawn-out narrative that precedes, here time is compressed. Adopting the literary genre of the ancestral narratives, the text sets notices of marriage, pregnancy, and birth one after another, without any mention of the father.[22]

The women of Bethlehem, who already participated in the tragic fate of these two women at the time of their arrival, now participate in their joy. They say what Naomi had learned during the harvest season in Bethlehem: A daughter-in-law like Ruth is worth more than seven sons! Thus she not

19. On this see Renate Jost, *Freundin,* 68.

20. The younger woman is always named first. Cf. Klara Butting, *Die Buchstaben werden sich noch wundern.* Alektor Hochschulschriften (Berlin: Alektor-Verlag, 1993) 34; for the interpretaton of the book of Ruth through the names of the mothers that are brought in here see Bal, van Dijk-Hemmes, and van Ginneken, *Und Sara Lachte,* 92–96.

21. For female genealogy see Irmtraud Fischer, "Affidamento in einer patriarchalen Gesellschaft. Frauenbeziehungen im Buch Rut," in Projektgruppe Interdisziplinäre Frauenstudien der Universität Graz, eds. (Paris, Milan, Graz, and Vienna, 1991) 123–25.

22. For these "genealogical" genres see Fischer, *Erzeltern,* 61–65.

only replaces Naomi's two dead children, she surpasses them (4:15). While Naomi had attributed her misery to YHWH, now the women assign to YHWH her happiness. The child Ruth has borne reintegrates Naomi into the flow of life. Through her daughter-in-law she has again acquired a child who revives the life-force. Here also the coloring of the ancestral narratives is resumed. The joyful reaction to the birth of a child, especially on the part of the women, is something we already encountered in the stories of Sarah (Gen 21:6) and Leah (Gen 30:13), and among the midwives with Rebecca, Rachel, and Tamar.

8. *A daughter-in-law: worth more than seven sons!*

Something unique is emphasized in 4:13, where there is no birth-notice for the father, but instead a bearing-for-Naomi (4:17a: יֻלַּד־בֵּן לְנָעֳמִי).[23] Something unique is brought to the fore here: Ruth does not bear for Boaz or for Mahlon. She bears for Naomi, to whom she has joined herself with an oath like a marriage promise. The child is the redeemer (4:14b) for Naomi, the one who brings back her life (v. 15a). Naomi came back to Bethlehem empty, without husband or either of her two sons (1:21), but now, through Ruth, she again has a son who will care for her (4:16). It is simply a matter of course that this son, whom these two women struggled to obtain, is named by the women. He does not receive a triumphalistic name: Obed is derived from עבד, serve.

It is true that the image of happiness at the end again shows the patriarchal ideal of a mother with her son—not her daughter—in her lap.[24] Ultimately it is only through male offspring that Naomi can be assured of reintegration into society and care in her old age, since daughters leave home when they marry and so can no longer care for their own parents, but only for those of their husband. But the women of Bethlehem give even this image a framework in female history: The son is the restorer-of-life for Naomi because Ruth, who loves her, has borne him (v. 15). Such an interpretation is the proper conclusion to the women's story of Naomi and Ruth. The mature woman who wanted to send her young daughters-in-law back to a normal life did not send them to the patriarchal houses of their fathers, but sent each to her mother's house (1:8). The woman who has modeled female community and solidarity is able, despite her bitter fate, to show Ruth her God and her people as the true place of safety and community. Through Naomi's influence, Ruth joins herself to her God, YHWH, and to her people, Israel.

---

23. This unusual feature has been clearly developed by Butting, *Buchstaben*, 38–45.

24. For Ruth as the epitome of a patriarchal image of women see Leila Leah Bronner, "A Thematic Approach to Ruth in Rabbinic Literature," in *Feminist Companion to Ruth*, 146–69.

The fate of the aging woman (chs. 1 and 4) surrounds that of the young Ruth (chs. 2 and 3). The two women support each other with what they have and are able to do. Naomi makes it possible for Ruth to be incorporated into the company of women in Bethlehem and opens for her the remaining family connections. Ruth supports Naomi, first through accompanying her, and then with her work, bringing her bread. But Ruth, whose steadfast love is like that of YHWH,[25] by her own initiative constructs secure relationships with a man who takes note of her and honors her, and who will support the two women beyond what is required for support of the poor. She asks this man, who has already shown his community spirit of loyalty to the two widows, not because of their family relationships but because of his fascination with Ruth, to marry her—contrary to every social convention. The social networks that sustain her, however, have from the very beginning been those of women. And even as the wife of a rich landowner she does not step outside that community. The book of Ruth is a book of women. Its narrative perspective allows us to conclude that it was written by a woman.[26]

9. King David's great-grandmother

The ending of the book in 4:18-22, which, as I have come to believe, issues quite deliberately in a purely male-oriented genealogy,[27] does nothing to alter this conclusion. At the end of the story a wholly agnatic family tree from Perez to David is added, in the genre of the *toledot* that is typical of passages in Genesis from the Priestly writing. The addition of this *toledot* presses for a reading of the Ruth narrative as a sequel to the ancestral narratives, already alluded to more than once in the course of the book of Ruth. The last *toledot* in Genesis was of Jacob (Gen 37:2). The sequence of generations after Judah, the first of which was told in Genesis 38 with the birth of Tamar's sons Perez and Zerah, is continued in the book of Ruth as the *toledot* of Perez. Corresponding to its function in the book of Genesis, these *toledot,* spanning great lengths of time, are written in tens (cf. Genesis 5; 11:10-32). If its seventh member is Boaz and its tenth is David, the concluding genealogy is the male variant of the female genealogy declared immediately before this: From Ruth, who replaces seven sons and therefore seven members of the ten-member family tree, stem the three further members, Obed, Jesse, and David. This great-grandson of Ruth will, like his great-grandmother, be better than the *seven* older sons of Jesse (Ruth 4:15; cf. 1 Sam 16:10-13). When David, in 1 Sam 22:3,

---

25. For the interpretation of the word "steadfast love" see Zenger, *Ruth,* 72.

26. For this see the collected volume, *A Feminist Companion to Ruth.*

27. My article, "Männerstammbaum," offers a thorough discussion of the literary-critical arguments against the originality of the concluding genealogy.

brings his parents to safety in Moab to escape Saul's persecution, this notice is probably the hook on which to hang the story of the Moabite Ruth,
created in the post-exilic period with the coloring and patterns of the ancestral narratives. The royal line of David and its history is traced back to
the initiative of a foreign woman who, because her steadfast love was like
that of God, was received into the community of the nation.

10. Interpretation of the book of Ruth through its different locations in the canon

The canonical position of the book of Ruth in the Hebrew Bible is different from its location in the Greek. The Hebrew canon places this book
among the Megillot, the so-called festival rolls. The book of Ruth is read
at Shavuot, the Feast of Weeks, which has seven well-established points of
contact in the book itself because the story takes place at the time of the
grain harvest. Naomi returns with her daughter-in-law to Bethlehem at the
beginning of the barley harvest (1:22). At the end of the harvest, Ruth marries Boaz (cf. 3:23). By its placement in the third part of the *Hebrew
canon,* among the *Kethubim,*[28] the book of Ruth is also read as a canonical interpretation of the immediately preceding text (in the usual, though
not the only attested traditional order), Prov 31:10-31. This closing passage of the book of Proverbs praises the אשת־חיל, the strong woman, concluding with the words:

> Many daughters have shown themselves strong,
> but you surpass them all!
> Charm is deceitful, and beauty is vain.
> A woman who fears YHWH—
> she shall be praised!
> Give her a share
> of the fruit of her hands,
> and let her works praise her in the city gates! (Prov 31:29-31)

These praises are appropriate for Ruth in every detail: She is the strong
woman (3:11) who surpasses not only the daughters, but even seven of
one's own sons (4:15). Her fame is founded not on her beauty, but on her
deeds, in which she makes YHWH's steadfast love a reality and gives the
fruit of her hands, in the form of bread, to her starving mother-in-law. And
the last chapter of the book of Ruth takes place at the city gate, in the public sphere, where Ruth is praised by all the people and set alongside the

---

28. This position points to a relatively late time of composition for the book of Ruth. For the
different traditions in arrangement of the festival rolls see Zenger, *Ruth,* 9–10; for its connection
with the book of Proverbs see Christian Frevel, *Das Buch Rut.* NSK AT 6 (Stuttgart: Katholisches Bibelwerk, 1992) 10, 114–15.

mothers of Israel. This canonical interpretation of Proverbs by the book of Ruth thus gives an example of how the story of such a strong woman can look. Ruth becomes the אשת־חיל (Ruth 3:11; Prov. 31:10-31) *par excellence*!

In the order of the *Septuagint canon,* which the churches have adopted,[29] the book of Ruth stands between Judges and 1 Samuel. This positioning, too, is not arbitrary; it has its basis in the book of Ruth itself. The opening statement in 1:1 about the time of the story dates the book to "the time of the judges"; 1 Samuel then tells the story of David, Ruth's descendant. Whereas the last chapters of the book of Judges clearly showed what kind of anarchic chaos can come to pass in the absence of a king (Judg 19:1; 21:25), and especially how a situation in which people are ignorant of any law affects women in an especially brutal way,[30] Ruth's YHWH-like engagement lays the foundation for the Davidic royal dynasty. In this canonical order the book of Ruth is placed at a point corresponding to its postulated historical location.[31]

The different positioning reveals a different emphasis in understanding: While the Hebrew Bible sees the book of Ruth as a paradigmatic woman's story, a "harvest tale," and also as an example of life-supporting *halakha* of the Sinai Torah, the Greek Bible interprets the book in terms of its concluding genealogy as a prehistory of the house of David. But by being placed immediately after the book of Judges, Ruth also becomes a contrast-story juxtaposed with the narrative about the sexual murder of the Levite's concubine (Judges 19–20), which also begins in Bethlehem and illustrates the social problematic of the relationship between the sexes. The Levite's concubine is a victim handed over by her unsolidary husband and their host and so, humiliated and degraded to the utmost, she becomes the victim of gang rape by an entire Israelite village. Finally, when the woman has been abused until she is unconscious, her husband cuts her into pieces because he has been dishonored. In contrast to the fate of this Bethlehem woman, the foreigner Ruth is shown in Bethlehem, protected by Boaz, avoiding the society of unbridled men, and secure in the home of her mother-in-law. In context, Boaz stands as a contrast to the Levite; he does not refuse his assistance to the woman. If the *male* village society in Judges 19 is the epitome of depravity and social disorga-

---

29. The extent of the canon used by the Reformed churches is that of the Hebrew Bible, but the order of the books follows the Septuagint canon.

30. For the association of the book of Ruth with the violent acts against women reported in Judges see Adrien J. Bledstein, "Female Companionships: If the Book of Ruth were Written by a Woman . . . ," in *Feminist Companion to Ruth,* 116–33, at 117.

31. David Jobling, "Ruth Finds a Home: Canon, Politics, Method," in J. Cheryl Exum and David J. A. Clines, eds., *The New Literary Criticism and the Hebrew Bible.* JSOTSup 143 (Sheffield: JSOT Press, 1993) 125–39, investigates the position of the book of Ruth in the Greek canon as well as the links of the resulting final text to the story of Hannah (1 Samuel 1–2).

nization, the *female* village society in the book of Ruth is the locus of social solidarity.

The canonical continuation in the story of Hannah (1 Samuel 1–2), like the book of Ruth, also echoes the ancestral narratives. Hannah, who is barren like the mothers of Israel (1 Sam 1:3), and like Rachel is a rival to her husband's fertile first wife, like Rebecca calls upon YHWH and names the son of her prayers Samuel, in the tradition of Israel's women ancestors (1:20). Ruth was worth more than seven sons to her mother-in-law (Ruth 4:15), but Hannah's husband Elkanah is not so for her (1 Sam 1:8).[32]

11. The book of Ruth in messianic perspective

From Bethlehem comes the first king over Israel. From this same place, Mic 5:2-4 hopes, will come the one who will rule over Israel, whose origins lie in the most distant past (5:2). The king of peace will be preceded by a new Ruth, who will bear him (5:3a). Like Boaz, he will stand fast in the strength of YHWH (cf. the wordplay with the proper name בֹּעַז and בְּעֹז, "in the strength of YHWH" in 5:4a). The one awaited in Bethlehem will be universal peace personified (a new Solomon?) because he will be revered to the ends of the earth.

The Gospel of Matthew adopts this promise of salvation from Mic 5:2-4 to elucidate the birth story of Jesus of Nazareth. When the Magi come to Herod and ask where the child is born, he inquires of the High Priests and all the scribes among the people (Matt 2:1-6). They quote Mic 5:2-4 in answer.

In "the genealogy of Jesus Christ, the son of David, the son of Abraham," Matthew quotes the short genealogy from Judah to David word for word from the book of Ruth, deviating only by inserting the three mothers, Tamar, Rahab, and Ruth (Matt 1:3-6a).[33] The pregnancy of Mary, the mother of Jesus, is not interpreted in terms of Mic 5:3, but from that of the woman in Isa 7:14, it is true, but, through the integration of the book of Ruth at the beginning, in Matt 1:2-6, and the location of the birth in Bethlehem, Mary is also depicted as a new Ruth. Mary, who is as courageous as Ruth in agreeing to follow a path that is unconventional for a young woman, like Ruth bears a redeemer, who for Christians is the redeemer of the whole world.

---

32. On this see Jobling, "Ruth," 133–34: he refers to the thesis of Mieke Bal in *Death and Dissymmetry: The Politics of Coherence in the Book of Judges* (Chicago: University of Chicago Press, 1988), seeing in the two verses a strengthening of the patrilocal (= virilocal) form of marriage.

33. Regrettably, the book of Ruth has also been used by Christian interpreters for anti-Jewish polemic (on this see Renate Jost, *Freundin,* 85–87).

🌸 Chapter Eight 🌸

Women Who Wrestled with God

A glass containing half its potential contents can be described as half full or half empty. Ancient Israel's society was patriarchal—like all the cultures in its environment, and like our present Western cultures to greater or lesser degree. For this reason alone it is not to be expected that women's cup would have been overflowing. It is therefore more appropriate to the texts and their *Sitz im Leben* to bring forward what is present under these conditions, even though it does not conform to the norms of an androcentric presentation. Hence it is all the more remarkable how many women are told about at Israel's beginnings, and how thoroughly they determine the course of family life, in terms of which, in fact, the history of the people is written.

The story of the beginnings of the people Israel has always been read by OT scholars as a *history of the patriarchs*. The majority of the texts they treated, however, should have made it clear that it can also be read as a *history of the women*. The biblical authors, female and male, wrote it as a history of the community with God, a people of both genders, and as such it should be interpreted in a gender-fair manner. These authors write with great sensitivity about female life contexts and experiences and present a God who takes the part of women, rescuing them from abandonment, oppression, and marginalization. From this point of view the stories of the rescue of women represent a critique of the patriarchal life context in which men are seen as entitled to surrender women to menace and violence for their own benefit.

Israel never wrote its "family chronicle," its national history, as a saga of heroes or a legend of saints. The fact that unlovely stories and crimes, betrayal of and violence against women are told—and not concealed— witnesses not only to a sober sense of reality, but also to human greatness. Not to conceal sin and failure in one's own history, but to deal with it in memory, is possible for Israel because it has always lived not only its present but also its past before the face of YHWH. The dark sides of the family chronicle hide neither physical and psychic nor socially legitimated violence against women, something that often leads Christians to assume an attitude of superior and defensive rejection of these texts. But if the cry of the victims is not transmitted, care is always in order: their experiences of suffering are all too easily marginalized and forgotten. There are oppressive words in the Hebrew Bible that may not be painted over with any kind of pretty colors. But when, as is repeatedly stressed in the stories about Israel's beginnings, YHWH takes the part of abandoned women pushed to the margins, these texts are to be read as "dangerous memories" that even today can give women assurance that their marginalization is not legitimate and is not to be justified, no matter how clever and voluminous the theories. YHWH's plan with Israel is often better represented by the actions of women than by those of men. Exodus 1–2 can stand as an example story for that, but in the stories of Rebecca and Ruth it is also evident that women do a better job of realizing YHWH's projects for a life in his company than the men in their surroundings.

The biblical authors apparently know that the society of men is only half of the whole, and reflects only a portion of God's history with humanity. They make the voices of women audible and illustrate Israel's national history with its God through persons of both genders. In doing so, they do not worship the idea of a "stronger gender." Even when the language suggests a narrowing focus only on the patriarchs, the narrated theology corrects this:

Abraham cannot bring the divine promise to fulfillment with just any woman. Sarah is the one from whom the promised son will be born. She is just as much the addressee and bearer of the promises as her husband. The twofold denial of Sarah as his wife through which Abraham abandons her is not accepted by YHWH. He rescues the woman from the "clever" plan of her husband and, in each instance, places her in her rightful position. But YHWH is not blindly partisan for the bearer of his promise. When she becomes the oppressor of her slave woman Hagar he stands against her and on the side of the weakest. Through his saving promises he makes Hagar, too, the bearer of a promise.

Abraham's genealogical line continues in his daughter-in-law Rebecca rather than primarily through his son Isaac. She is equal to her father-in-law in her unconditional choice to leave her land and family because she recognizes that the thing is from YHWH. Rebecca, not Isaac, receives the message from God that determines the future of her two sons. While the father chooses Esau as his favorite, Rebecca sees to it, in a not altogether honorable manner, that her favorite son, Jacob, who is God's choice, will carry on the line of the promise.

The struggles with God are carried on by both women and men. Leah and Rachel struggle with YHWH over the foundations of the house of Israel before Jacob has to survive his battle for blessing at the Jabbok. The women thereby fight *for* God, for God's attention and concern. The man fights *with*—or even against—God and means to conquer. The stories in Genesis 29–30, 32 are therefore not to be interpreted along gender lines as on the one hand trivial housewife literature and on the other hand sagas of heroes. The birth stories of the twelve sons are not example stories showing that women exist only to bear children. When God's people, Israel, writes its national history as family history, and not as military or royal or "papal" history, then in one generation twelve sons must be born to represent the construct of twelve equal tribes. The mothers, then, according to Genesis 29–30 are not little housewives; they are the founders of the nation.

Judah even has to make an explicit confession with regard to Tamar's way of living: "She is more just than I!" (Gen 38:26). This woman, who according to her father-in-law's ideas ought to remain a lifelong widow in spite of the promise of a levirate marriage, uses unconventional means to integrate herself into God's history with this people, as an ancestor of the house of Judah.

The beginning of the book of Exodus, so far as men and women are concerned, paints a sharp, black and white picture. The men are all trapped in the sphere of death. They communicate to those like them the horrible pressure created by the Pharaoh's command to kill. The women, on the other hand, are all faithful to life—and to YHWH. Their resistance brings them to solidarity across social and ethnic barriers. Even the daughter of Pharaoh acts as an exemplary righteous person from among the Gentiles, cooperating in the rescue of the rescuer of Israel. Moses, however, first enters into the company of the necrophilic men. It is only through a threat to his life that he learns, from women, the right path of nonviolent resistance. And only after this learning process in the milieu of his ancestors is he ready for the divine call.

The biblical woman author of the book of Ruth, the festival roll for the Feast of Weeks, celebrates the gift of the Torah on Sinai through her *halakha* of the institutions of levirate marriage and redemption, even for a woman from Moab, who according to Deut 23:4-9 must remain excluded from the assembly of YHWH. She does this far more appropriately than her male colleagues who wrote the books of Ezra and Nehemiah, who were zealous for an elite community of God. Ruth and Naomi make concrete, by example, YHWH's kindness and care for people and adopt Boaz into their learning community for life-sustaining actualization of the Torah. The applause of the women of Bethlehem, and indeed of the whole community of people in the town, assures both women that such a daughter-in-law is worth more than seven sons! In the agnatic family tree that extends from Perez to David, Ruth's son is the seventh in the sequence of generations after Tamar's son. The first and seventh members of the chain of generations owe their existence to the struggles of women for a place in the people of the promise.

The ancestral narratives do not have the same significance for Jews and Christians. For Jews, they tell the foundational story of their people. Their history of origins as a complex family story of women, men, and their children is a challenge to the Christian story of origins, founded on the twelve apostles, of whose wives and children nothing is said other than that they were abandoned. The "people of God of the new covenant" is not held together by family ties. If the history of this people of God made up of Jews and Gentiles is written exclusively as one of androcentric hierarchy, then the chalice is more than half empty. The history of the women of early Christianity who, for their faith, abandoned their fathers and mothers and even their husbands and children, is to the history of the church's origins what the history of the women in the ancestral narratives is—for the roots that Jewish women and men have through the mothers of Israel can be claimed by Christian women and men as their own insofar as they are the ingrafted twig in the mighty olive tree of YHWH (cf. Romans 11).

The church's preaching in our day would do well to join with the biblical authors and no longer regard the problems of the present day exclusively from a male perspective in the light of Sacred Scripture, especially since the Scriptures do not do so. The biblical authors themselves show us that fear of feminist challenges that might falsify the divine message is unfounded: The divine message *must* be actualized and the questions of the current time *must* be addressed if they are to be newly proclaimed to people in every age and touch their hearts. The "woman question," which is always at the same time a social question, especially since women in patriarchal societies are not allotted either equal rights to shape culture or a corresponding share in resources, is, alongside the ecological question, among the most urgent problems of our time. Not to take these challenges seriously, and to suppress them or to give yesterday's answers to today's questions does not solve the problems!

The Sacred Scriptures are not overburdened, by this kind of gender-fair inquiry, with questions that are foreign to them; rather, they are more authentically interpreted because these questions take seriously that God acts with and in and for women as well as men. The narratives show us that women sometimes have a better sense for interpreting and actualizing the divine word and bringing to fulfillment the divine plan.

To those who seriously pursue justice and seek YHWH in their days, Deutero-Isaiah recommends (cf. Isa 51:2): Look to Abraham *and* Sarah, not only to the fathers, for women have wrestled with their God for the founding and endurance of their people!